Self-Concept, Self-Esteem, and the Curriculum

James A. Beane
St. Bonaventure University

Richard P. Lipka
Pittsburg State University

Allyn and Bacon, Inc.
Boston   London   Sydney   Toronto

Library of Congress Cataloging in Publication Data

Beane, James A., 1944-
  Self-concept, self-esteem, and the curriculum.

  Bibliography: p. 243
  Includes index.
  1. Curriculum planning. 2. Students—Psychology.
3. Self-perception. 4. Self-respect. I. Lipka,
Richard P. II. Title.
LB1570.B382 1983   375'.001   83-8780
ISBN 0-205-08042-1

Printed in the United States of America

10 9 8 7 6 5 4 3 2 1   88 87 86 85 84 83

To Jim, Jason, and John Beane
and
Jennifer and David Lipka

Contents

Preface   ix

Acknowledgments   xiii

1   Understanding Self-Perceptions   1

The Study of Self-Perceptions: Past and Present   2
Defining Self-Concept and Self-Esteem   5
What It Means to Enhance Self-Perceptions   7
Levels of Self-Perceiving   10
The Self as Multidimensional   11
Influences on the Self   13
The Process of Self-Perceiving   15
The Developing Self   17
The Childhood Self   18
The Transescent Self   20
The Adolescent Self   23
The Adult Self   26
Summary   28

CONTENTS

2   Institutional Features and Student Self-Perceptions   29

Climate: From Custodial to Humanistic   30

Grouping: Labels and Expectations   37

Decision-Making and Control   41

The Peer Group and the Self in School   45

Enhancing Perceptions of Self as a Growing Person   52

Self-Perceptions and School Achievement   54

Working with Parents   57

Dropping Out and Staying In   61

Teacher Self-Esteem   66

Summary   70

3   Curriculum Planning to Enhance Self-Perceptions   73

Part I Curriculum Planning and Self-Perceptions   74

Self-Perceptions and the Good Life   77

Society and Self-Perceptions   78

Human Needs and Self-Perceptions   81

Goals that Support Self-Perceptions   83

Self-Perception Characteristics of Learners   85

Self-Perceptions and Constructs of Learning   91

General Resources to Support Self-Perception Enhancement   94

Self-Perceptions and Curricular Approaches   95

Part II Curriculum Planning for Specific Teaching-Learning Situations   103

Organizing Centers   108

Objectives   114

Content   117

Activities   119

Resources   122

Measuring Devices   125

Summary   135

4   Illustrative Curriculum Plans   137

A Format for Curriculum Plans   **137**

Sample 1: The Family   **139**

Sample 2: The Self and Contemporary Media
(Transescence, Adolescence)   **159**

Sample 3: Living In Our School (Elementary)   **164**

Summary   **169**

5   State of the Art and Hope for the Future   171

Part I State of the Art   171

Self-Perceptions as an Educational Issue   **176**

A View of the Self-Enhancing School   **179**

Part II The Future and the Self-Enhancing School   188

The Person-Centered Society   **189**

The Shifting Population Age   **190**

Technology   **193**

Getting from Here to There   **195**

Stewardship for Young People: Where Did It Go?   **205**

**Appendix A   When Young People Tell about Themselves
   in School   209**

Appendix B   Sample Self-Perception Interviews   229

References   243

Index   257

Preface

In the domain of feeling there is a Promethean fire which
burns alike through all ages and generations of man—
Arthur Jersild, *In Search of Self* (1952, pp. 31-32)

Several years ago we were having a discussion about how school values seem to influence the values of young people. At one point, the discussion focused on a hypothetical incident. Suppose a young boy is overly aggressive toward his peers, even to the point of gaining a reputation as a bully. He comes to school and goes to a physical education class with a teacher who wants to help young people and thus likes to give them positive feedback. On this particular day, the class plays a game of dodgeball. The young boy, being physically aggressive, plays a hard game, flinging the ball with tremendous velocity at his classmates, hitting one after another. Finally he is the last player left and the teacher hurries over to congratulate him, saying loud enough for all to hear, "You're the winner, good for you!" The teacher, meaning well, further praises the boy, making sure that he knows he has won and deserves to be held in high esteem by the class. But what has the boy learned? Our feeling was that even though the teacher meant well, the boy had learned that being aggressive and physically overpowering was good. In short, the teacher had reinforced anti-social behavior and further suggested that the boy should feel good about himself as a bully. From this example we began to construct others similar to it and thus began to see numerous illustrations of how the school reinforces other values as well as self-perceptions (such as those held by the young bully).

As this line of thinking unfolded, we were led more and more into the area of self-concept and self-esteem. It was evident that a great deal of work had been done in this field. Educational psychology had contributed hundreds of empirical studies, while the curriculum field was represented by numerous books, articles, and speeches presenting a philosophical/moral case for affective education. However, it was clear that little had been done on an interdisciplinary basis to bring together the research of the former with the theory of the latter, even though this would seem to offer a more compelling case for the place and power of self-perceptions in the school.

This book represents an attempt to blend educational psychology and curriculum planning with a focus on self-concept and self-esteem. In doing so, we tried to look at how psychological research supports affective curriculum planning and how curriculum planning might serve as a means to implement that research. Hence, this book is both an extension of more specialized volumes and a departure from them.

Educators are charged with the task of helping young people experience healthy growth and development. Today we know that this means much more than just intellectual and physical growth. If we are to help, we must also define ways of nurturing personal and social growth. At the core of these are the perceptions young people have of themselves. In other words, an educational program without an emphasis on enhancing self-perceptions is an incomplete program. If such an emphasis is to emerge in schools, we believe educators must become familiar with theory and research on self-perceptions, as well as the kinds of curriculum plans and instructional procedures that might serve to implement them. Thus the book begins with a look at theory and research, and proceeds through subsequent consideration of how institutional features affect self-perceptions, how curriculum planning might be used to enhance self-perceptions, sample unit plans for that purpose, and, finally, what might be done to promote self-perceptions as an educational issue.

While many concrete examples are given of educational practices that enhance self-concept and self-esteem, this is not a "cookbook" of techniques. For the most part, the book may serve as a source of ideas and guidelines for developing what ultimately might be called a self-enhancing school. We believe that professional educators are not looking to be told what to do and how to do it, but rather are open to suggestions that might make their work more worthwhile for young people. Furthermore, professional educators recognize that knowing what and how to do something is only part of their responsibility. To be truly effective, they must also know why they are doing it.

Finally, we have purposely kept the book relatively short in length. Hopefully, this will make it more accessible and readable for teachers whose time is already pressed to the limit with their many other professional responsibilities.

J. A. B.
R. P. L.

Acknowledgments

Those who undertake preparation of a book receive the support and assistance of many people throughout the project. We are no exception. The late Louis E. Raths inspired many of our ideas, serving as a reminder that understanding the school requires trying to see it through the eyes of children and youth. Our colleagues, Philip Eberl and Karle Wicker, were and are a constant source of support, both personally and professionally. Maureen Kirby and Ann Slavin, graduate assistants, helped develop many of the ideas in Chapter 1. Joan W. Ludewig, also a graduate assistant, was a mainstay in the research reported in Appendix A and also helped edit initial drafts. Professors Robert S. Harnack and Conrad F. Toepfer, Jr., reviewed sections of the manuscript and suggested many ideas for its improvement. Patricia McNeil and Shirley Ausman demonstrated enormous patience in typing and editing the final manuscript. Finally, we are indebted to our friends at Allyn and Bacon: Margaret Quinlan and Jeff Johnston for encouraging us to pursue the project, and Hiram Howard and Sue Canavan for seeing it through to completion.

1

Understanding
Self-Perceptions

In November of 1974 a group of educators participated in a visit to an innovative high school. One program that was of particular interest involved a large group of students in community service projects. To explain the program, arrangements were made for a half dozen students to make short presentations about their projects to the visiting group. One student, a young man, explained that since September he had spent two or three afternoons during the week and most of Sunday visiting an eighty-year-old man who was confined to a nursing home. During the course of the visits the man had spent many hours relating his extensive knowledge of the Civil War to the young student and had also taught him how to play chess. The two had long conversations about personal interests and the like. When he had finished speaking, one of the educators asked the young man if he planned to pursue a career in gerontology, nursing, or some area related to his community service project. The young student proceeded to say that he planned to drop out of school in January, having committed himself the previous July to joining a branch of the military. There was a pause and then he said that he had not done well in school in previous years, knowing for some time that he would quit as soon as he was old enough to join the military. However, he added, if he had had the experience with this elderly man sooner, he would not have quit school. Finally, the young man said he knew that the visitors were teachers and thought he should tell them about his situation.

Here was a case of a young person who, in a short time, had developed a new and different view of himself as a result of a particular kind of educative experience. Where his self-concept had previously lacked clarity, it suddenly took on clearer meaning. Where he had felt that his choices for the future were limited, he now saw a field of opportunities open to him. He had found a sense of belonging and participation.

One wonders how many other students there are in our schools who, like that young man, find themselves with unclear self-concepts and values. Surely there are many; perhaps thousands. Our concern in this book is with how educators can help young people clarify their self-concepts and improve their self-esteem; in short, how to enhance self-perceptions of students. The task is not an easy one. It involves working with parents, sharpening teaching skills, rethinking many institutional features of the school, and committing our intelligence to more thoughtful and comprehensive curriculum planning. To do this we need to understand both the theory of self-perceptions and the kind of practices that offer the most promise for their enhancement. Thus we will turn first to theoretical considerations of how and why self-perceptions function in human development.

The Study of Self-Perceptions: Past and Present

The idea of seriously trying to know and understand oneself can be traced back many centuries in the history of art, music, literature, and other areas of the humanities. Many of these works are still studied today, as they represent the artist's, composer's, or author's means of self-expression and the revelation of personal feelings, values, world views, and the like through their work.

In recent years interest in self-perceptions has increased dramatically; however, this new movement is somewhat less concerned with the humanities. Instead, more emphasis has been placed on attempts to scientifically analyze the causes and effects of self-perceptions in terms of behavior, attitudes toward others, achievement, and other variables. As a result, several thousand research studies and numerous journal publications and books have gradually begun to provide a clearer and more comprehensive understanding of the place and power of self-perceptions in human growth and development.

The current interest in self-perceptions evolves largely from the work of William James (1890), who developed a theory of self through personal introspection and observation of others' behavior and attitudes. James suggested that the self is both a "knower" and an object of knowledge. In other words, the self may act as a thinker and perceiver, as well as an object to be thought about. Thus an individual may think and know about many things, including himself or herself. James also theorized that individuals have three selves: a material self including, for example, one's body and personal possessions; a social self involving a sense of human relations and status; and a spiritual self centered in desires, inclinations, and emotions. All of these, according to James, act in a dynamic way as we seek self-preservation and self-enhancement.

Cooley (1902) speculated that the self is actually a "looking-glass self," and thus the process of knowing about oneself is actually one in which we come to view ourselves as we believe others view us. This notion can be interpreted simply in the sense that self-perceptions are a function of feedback from others. Mead (1934) further developed this idea in suggesting that self-perceptions actually develop in a context of social interaction and are largely influenced by the feedback an individual gets from others. Mead also contributed the idea that self-perceptions are *multidimensional*, consisting of perceptions of various roles one plays, and *hierarchical* in that some of these dimensions are more important to us than others.

A more refined theory of the function of feedback from others was developed by Sullivan (1953). He noted that individuals placed more importance on, or were more influenced by, feedback from some persons than from others. Those with the most influence he designated as "significant others," and even among these, Sullivan assigned the term "most significant others" to those of the highest importance to the individual. Rosenberg (1979) offered a more "precise" interpretation of significant others in reporting his research which showed that children, for example, rank their mothers as most significant, followed by fathers, siblings, teachers, friends, and general age-mates.

The work of Snygg and Combs (1949) and Rogers (1951) has come to be of critical importance to the understanding of self-perceptions. Snygg and Combs outlined a theory of the phenomenal self based on the idea that the world of the individual consists of what one *perceives* the world to be, which may be more or less different from what the world really is. In other words, what is true for the individual is what he or she perceives to be true, regardless of whether the perceived truth has any basis in fact. For Snygg and Combs, then, self-concept is defined as "those parts of the phenomenal (perceived) field which the individual has differentiated as definite and fairly stable and which are perceived as true." For example, a person might view himself as overweight, even though his weight may be well within medically recommended limits. Rogers, as well as Lecky (1945) and Allport (1955), recognized the power of these kinds of perceptions in assigning self-perceptions a central position in personality where they act as a source of unity and maintenance for the individual. However, all of these theorists also suggested that self-perceptions are in need of enhancement, aiming at what Maslow (1956) termed "self-actualization"; the idea that the individual views himself or herself as healthy and capable of functioning adequately in the world. It should be noted, however, that Rogers placed much more emphasis on the individual as an initiating source of self-perceptions than did Mead, Sullivan, and others who saw self-perceptions as more dependent on environmental influence.

The contributions of others such as Wylie (1961, 1979), Kelley (1962), Coopersmith (1967), Gergen (1971), Jourard (1971), and Epstein (1973) have added valuable insight into the evolving theory of self-perceptions and their place in human growth and development. While disagreement persists over some issues and needed study continues, nearly a century of theory and research offers some fairly consistent ideas about self-perceptions. These include the following:

The concept of self has a central place in personality, acting as a source of unity and as a guide to behavior.

Self-perceptions are multidimensional and hierarchical, although at one level they tend to blend into a general sense of self.

Self-perceptions tend to seek stability, consistency, and enhancement.

Self-perceptions may be based on roles played by the individual, as well as attributes one believes he or she possesses.

While the self may be an "initiator," self-perceptions arise mainly in a social context, influenced largely by feedback from "significant others."

4

As efforts to clarify the meaning and power of self-perceptions have evolved, increased attention has been paid to how they function in young people. Since self-perceptions are learned from experiences and are critical in the process of constructive growth, it is generally agreed that they ought to be of particular concern to those persons, including educators, who have the responsibility of nurturing development of children and adolescents. Hence, growing emphasis has been placed on the function and development of self-perceptions in schools. Before proceeding to that specific issue, however, we will first look at several aspects of self-perceiving that appear to be of special importance for educators.

Defining Self-Concept and Self-Esteem

One of the difficulties faced by those who wish to work seriously with self-perceptions is the lack of agreement about how various terms ought to be defined. This disagreement has led to confusion not only in research, but in practice as well. One important example of this dilemma is confusion over the terms *self-concept* and *self-esteem*. While the two have been used interchangeably for many years (Shavelson, Hubner, and Stanton, 1976), they actually represent two distinct dimensions of self-perceptions (Beane and Lipka, 1980).

Self-concept is defined here as the description an individual attaches to himself or herself. The self-concept is based on the roles one plays and the attributes one believes he or she possesses. For example, in answer to the question, "Tell me about yourself," a person might say that he or she is "tall (or short)," "fat (or thin)," "honest (or dishonest)," "an eighth grader," "a native American," "a tennis player," and so on. Each of these items is descriptive, and whether or not an item is actually true or false, it is perceived to be true by the individual and therefore is part of the personal self-concept.

In short, self-concept is defined as the description of self in terms of roles and attributes. When we refer to the self-concept of others, we thus might say that it is accurate or inaccurate, realistic or unrealistic, clear or confused, or use other terms to specify the quality of the self-description. Note that self-concept is not referred to as positive or negative since it is only a description of the perceived self and does not involve a value judgment of that description by the individual.

5

Self-esteem, on the other hand, refers to the evaluation one makes of the self-concept description and, more specifically, to the degree to which one is satisfied or dissatisfied with it, in whole or in part. For example, an individual might describe herself as tall (self-concept) and then go on to say that she is happy or unhappy about being tall. This latter judgment is an indicator of self-esteem since it indicates how the individual feels about the description. In other words, self-esteem involves the individual's sense of self-worth or self-regard manifested in such feelings as "I am happy with myself" or "I don't like myself." Thus when we refer to the self-esteem of others, we may say that it is positive, neutral, or negative, or use other terms that denote the quality of the self-esteem or the intensity of the individual's feelings.

Self-esteem judgments are based on values or value indicators such as attitudes, beliefs, or interests. For example, an adolescent might describe himself as a good student (self-concept), but may wish to change that (self-esteem) because he wants to be accepted by peers who devalue school success (value indicator). Understanding the place of values in the formation of self-perceptions is of particular importance since it highlights the fact that self-judgment is personal, and that inferring self-esteem from an individual's self-concept is a risky venture. For example, a teacher working with the adolescent just described may have difficulty understanding why the student may begin to show a decline in school achievement. The teacher, not knowing the value-base of the student, may further complicate the situation by praising the student's work in front of the peers who devalue school success, in an attempt to bolster self-esteem. The point of understanding the place of values in self-perceptions is that an individual may not have the same self-esteem judgments others would have under similar circumstances.

The leader of a street gang devoted to aggressiveness may thoroughly describe himself as tough, violent, ruthless, and uncaring, and go on to express happiness with that self-concept even though such behavior violates basic social customs. The oldest child in a several-sibling, closely knit family might state a personal preference for playing with younger children and be quite happy about doing so, despite the generally held adult belief that this attitude represents immaturity and can be inferred to mean negative self-esteem. As adults, we may learn to accept the latter child as we come to understand that being accepted by one's exact age-mates is not necessarily a prime value for all youth. On the other hand, as we work with the gang leader we learn that simply by telling him he ought to feel good about himself we may reinforce anti-social values. Thus if we are to help in reconstructing the self-concept, the first area of consideration must be that of values. To clarify this point, Table 1.1 shows some possible self-concept descriptions and how these might be considered with regard to self-esteem depending on an individual's value-base.

In sum, then, we see self-concept and self-esteem as distinct dimensions of the broader area of self-perceptions, the former being descriptive and the latter being evaluative. Furthermore, self-esteem judgments are personal and based on values or value-indicators. The adult who wishes to enhance the self-perceptions of individual learners must first identify which component needs attention, always being sensitive to the dangers of inferring self-esteem on the basis of values held by anyone other than the learner.

Throughout the remainder of the book, we most frequently use the generic term *self-perceptions*. In light of the definitions just given, when we refer to "enhancing self-perceptions," we refer to both clarifying self-concept *and* improving self-esteem. In some cases, however, either self-concept or self-esteem is specifically mentioned. When this is done, we are referring to one or the other particularly, rather than using the terms interchangeably.

What It Means to Enhance Self-Perceptions

Throughout this book, we use the word *enhance* in relation to various aspects of self-perceptions. Given the difference between self-concept and self-esteem, as well as the inclusion of values as part of self-perceptions, the word actually has several meanings.

Self-concept has been defined as the description an individual attaches to himself or herself. To *enhance* self-concept therefore means to do one or more of the following:

1. Help clarify or sharpen the content of the description.
2. Help individuals develop an accurate self-description.
3. Suggest new dimensions that might be added to the description.
4. Encourage self-descriptions that are based on reality.
5. Encourage individuals to think in-depth about their self-concept.

Table 1.1

Illustrative Self-Concept Attributes and Consequent Inferred and Actual Self-Esteem

A Actual and/or Inferred Self-Concept Attributes	B Inferred Self-Esteem (Conventional Assumptions)	C Actual Self-Esteem		
		Positive	Neutral	Negative
Success at School Tasks	Positive (since children are assumed to value school success)	Member of a peer group which values school success	Member of a peer group which is indifferent to school success and values social success instead	Member of a peer group of which others do not have success in school and, in fact, devalue school success
Preference for Younger-Aged Playmates	Negative (since children who prefer younger playmates are assumed to lack confidence with actual age-mates	Oldest child in a several-sibling, closely knit family	Success as playmate with some age-mates and older children	Consistently rejected as playmate by actual age-mates
Lack of Skill at a Physical Game	Negative (since children assumed to value skill at physical game playing)	Member of a family group which strongly de-values physical game playing and strongly values academic success	Indifference to physical games with personal values placed on other kinds of activities	Member of family which emphasizes and values physical game skills

Reprinted with permission of *Child Study Journal*, vol. 10, no. 1 (1980).

6. Help individuals see themselves as others see them.

7. Encourage individuals to continually reflect upon their self-description in terms of clarity, accuracy, breadth, and depth.

8. Help individuals discover the sources of and influences upon the self-concept.

Self-esteem has been defined as the relative value one attaches to the self-concept or the degree to which one is satisfied with it. Thus *enhancing* self-esteem means to do one or more of the following:

1. Improve self-evaluation skills as a basis for evaluating the self-concept.

2. Encourage individuals to develop a sense of their own personal worth.

3. Help individuals reflect on their self-esteem and the values on which it is based.

4. Encourage individuals to think of themselves in positive terms.

5. Help discover reasons why the individual is unhappy with any dimension(s) of the self-concept.

6. Help find ways to improve dimensions of self-concept with which the individuals are unhappy.

7. Help individuals examine sources of and influences on self-esteem.

The formulation of self-esteem is based on values or value-indicators, such as beliefs, aspirations, interests, and the like. Thus when we speak of enhancing self-esteem, we mean also the enhancing of values or value-indicators. Here we refer to doing the following:

1. Help clarify values or value-indicators.

2. Encourage the development of values.

3. Promote the process of valuing (Raths, Harmin, and Simon, 1978) through encouraging consideration of alternatives and consequences of choices, promote analysis of lifestyles to determine if values are being carried out, and offer opportunities to act on the basis of values held.

4. Help individuals examine the sources of and influences on personal values or value-indicators.

5. Encourage individuals to "think" and improve thinking skills.

Finally, the phrase "enhancing self-perceptions" is used as a generic term to refer to all three of the previous processes simultaneously—enhancing self-concept, enhancing self-esteem, and enhancing values. When the school is a place where all of this is done through institutional features and curriculum plans, it may properly be referred to as a "self-enhancing school."

Levels of Self-Perceiving

One of the characteristics of self-perceptions is that they seem to function at three different levels: specific situation, categorical, and general. First, each of us in our daily lives engages in *specific situations* through which we exercise and develop our knowledges, skills, attitudes, beliefs, and the like. These may include physical activities, discussions with others, and so on. As a consequence of these activities, we receive feedback about ourselves. This feedback may come from others or it may be formulated personally on the basis of some standards we set for ourselves. Internalized, the feedback thus becomes part of our self-perceptions.

The second level at which self-perceptions function is the *categorical level*. Here, as a result of specific situations, we formulate ideas about ourselves with regard to roles we play or attributes we believe we possess. For example, a child might have *role self-perceptions* as a son or daughter, as a brother or sister, as a peer, as a learner, and so on. In addition, the child might have *attribute self-perceptions* regarding physical features or development, personal intelligence, and the like. It is important to note that while attribute self-perceptions may be influenced by others, they are personal and perceptual. This means, for example, that the adolescent who believes he or she is overweight holds that perception as true even though others may say otherwise. A specific example of this is anorexia nervosa, a disease that involves an obsession with weight and physical appearance, a distaste for food, and, consequently, extreme malnutrition and possibly death. Even when extremely thin, these individuals are obsessed with the idea that they need to lose weight.

A third level of self-perception functioning is the *general sense of self*. At the general level, we may find ourselves saying something like, "All things considered, I am a pretty good (or a pretty bad) person." The general sense of self is probably based on the outcome of many specific situations and weighted in favor of those roles and attributes we value most. Because parents are so highly valued by children, for example, a particular child may have a positive sense of self at the general level so long as positive feedback is received from parents, even if that from others is much less positive.

For those concerned with enhancing the self-perceptions of others, understanding the three-level concept is important, particularly when it is recognized that as self-perceptions move from the specific toward the general they are increasingly resistant to change. For the person who feels generally negative about self, this judgment is based on the weight of the evidence from many specific situations that function as perceptual screens through which new situations are processed. Thus a single incident on which positive feedback is received cannot be expected to influence the general sense of self, nor can very generalized statements such as, "You're a good person, you shouldn't feel negative about yourself." In fact, after long-term negative feedback, the individual may reject such a suggestion or view its source as dishonest. What seems to be needed, on the other hand, is a continuous series of specific situations in which positive feedback is received or, in the event previous situations were misinterpreted, a guided review of past experiences with help directed at reconstructing the individual's interpretation of feedback received. Suppose, for example, a high school student has for many years been told that she is not good at science. The concerned teacher might discuss these past experiences with the student and look for cases where skill was shown by the student, or perhaps, if warranted, help the student see how such judgments were inaccurate or poorly made. Then the teacher might plan with the student a series of science activities in which success is probable and, once attained, help the student internalize the feelings of success and develop expectations for the same in the future. More about this specific issue will be said in Chapter 3. For the time being, however, it is important to recognize that self-concept and self-esteem function at three levels, and those who work with young people must be aware of this in identifying the nature of self-perceptions and determining ways of helping to enhance them.

The Self as Multidimensional

As noted previously, self-perceptions are based largely on roles we play and attributes we believe we possess. The range of roles and attributes one might attach to oneself is almost limitless, and perceptions may be held for each one. Young persons, for example, may have self-perceptions across or within a wide variety of dimensions. These may include some of the following, as well as others:

Self as Member of a Family
as son or daughter
as brother or sister
as grandchild
as niece or nephew
as older or younger sibling
as parent
as aunt or uncle

Self as Peer
as playmate
as member of a clique or club
as best friend

Self as Person with Attributes
height
weight
hair, eye color
skin color
physical development

Self as Student
as learner
as participant in school activities
as academic achiever

Clarity and accuracy of the self-concept may vary from one dimension to another, as may the sense of self-esteem, depending upon values held. Thus the young person may focus on one or another area as self-perceptions develop.

Another feature of the multidimensional self is the tendency to emphasize personally distinctive aspects (McGuire and Padawer-Singer, 1976.) For example, a person who reports self-concept in a situation in which he or she is in a racial minority is more likely to mention race than one who is in the majority. Also, children in homes in which the father is absent are more likely to mention fathers than those from two-parent homes.

The implications of the multidimensional self for those concerned with enhancing self-perceptions are similar to those involved with recognizing the place of the general sense of self. Specifically, when we sense that a young person is having self-perception problems, we must determine the particular dimension(s) involved. Our efforts may then be directed toward the specific area of difficulty. As such, they are likely to be more successful than if we merely speak to some general and less well-defined sense of self.

Influences on the Self

Those concerned with enhancing self-perceptions must, of necessity, be concerned with what influences their formulation—the environment with which the self interacts and the individual's own self-reflection.

Kelley (1962) and Mead (1934) suggested that the self develops almost entirely as a result of interaction with others. This thinking implies that while both the environment and the individual play a role, the environment is more powerful. The environmental theory is further refined by the idea that we screen our environment by paying attention to those persons whom we consider to be "significant others." As we play out our roles in specific situations, we receive feedback from others and use it to modify our self-perceptions. The revised or refined sense of self is then tested in new situations as we search for new and hopefully validating feedback from the environment.

On the other hand, we recognize the fact that the self uses a variety of processes to screen experiences and feedback. These may include screening of information, selection of acceptable feedback, scanning of memory, and others (Gergen, 1971; Hamachek, 1978). In this sense, the individual may play a larger role in self-perception formation since environmental feedback is selected, screened, and interpreted. However, these screening procedures are based on concepts that were probably environmentally influenced in previous experiences. There seem also to be cases where the individual transcends the environmental cues. On the positive side of the ledger, we have individuals like Martin Luther King, Jr., or Albert Einstein, whose behavior suggested that their self-esteem transcended the less than approving environment by which they were surrounded. Historically such individuals have been few enough that they appeared atypical. At any rate, it appears that the individual's self-reflection does play a role in self-perceptions even though it may be of uneven influence. On the negative side of the ledger would be the adolescent with anorexia nervosa who, as previously described, also transcends environmental cues.

We would suggest that for most persons the environment looms larger than individual reflection in self-perceptions, recognizing that society desires such a relationship and structures its institutions, including the school, toward that end. Three particular instances add weight to this argument. The first has to do with locus of control or the sense one has of one's power in life experiences (Lefcourt, 1976). We may have external locus of control (depending on others for direction) or internal locus of control (the belief that we can control our own life). Research has shown that locus of control may be influenced by various kinds of environments. For example, internal locus of control is more typical of persons who are in environments that allow for and require self-direction and independence, while external locus of control is more characteristic of highly controlled situations.

The second example involves what is known as "learned helplessness" (Ames, 1978). In this case, some individuals come to believe that they cannot do anything on their own, and in the event they do, they tend to explain their success in terms of some nonpersonal reasons. Persons who have learned to be helpless evidently do so as a consequence of long-term feedback that suggests they are incapable of succeeding on their own. It is worth noting that these persons also have more negative self-esteem than do those of whom learned helplessness is not a characteristic.

The third example that seems to support the power of the environment is found in the work of Lewin, Lippitt, and White (1939). In this study, behavior of individuals was observed in three different kinds of settings: democratic, authoritarian, and laissez faire. In each case, the behavior of the group was consistent with the characteristics of the environment. Individuals in the democratic setting tended to interact and cooperate, while those in both the authoritarian and laissez faire settings tended to become frustrated, aggressive, and confused. To the extent that behavior is influenced by self-perceptions, this work suggests that various environments can encourage various kinds of self-concepts.

In sum, then, both the individual self and the environment play a role in forming self-perceptions. However, the environment, particularly those persons who are perceived as "most significant," evidently has a more powerful role. Those concerned with enhancing self-perceptions must thus be sensitive to the environment they construct and the degree of significance they have in the lives of others.

The Process of Self-Perceiving

As pointed out earlier, most theorists agree that the self is dynamic rather than static. In other words, the self, in seeking stability, consistency, and enhancement, is in constant interaction with the environment and is subject to change modification or refinement. Further, the concept of self may be only momentary since new feedback is continuously received. We have noted elsewhere that self-perceptions have a structure consisting of a hierarchical order of role and attribute dimensions. By the same token, the self has at its disposal a number of devices or procedures to process new experiences. At times these may act in defense of the current structure, while at other times they may support dissonant information, aiming toward self-growth. Gergen (1971), Hamachek (1978), Rosenberg (1979), and others have delineated numerous processes, among which are the following:

1. The self may *organize* new information or experiences, adding to the number of self-concept dimensions or to those already present, thus enhancing the quality or quantity of its structure.

2. The self may *scan* its structure or memory to determine whether new information or experiences are similar to those in the past or to the present structure of self-concept.

3. The self may *screen* new information or experiences to determine whether they will enhance or threaten the current structure.

4. The self may *alter* or bias new information in an attempt to make it fit the present structure and thus contribute to stability.

15

5. The self may *choose* to engage in or avoid new experiences depending on whether they are perceived to be potentially helpful or debilitating to the present structure.

6. The self may *reflect* on new information or experiences to determine why and how they might enhance its quality. This reflection may also include consideration of the consequences of assuming new identities or dimensions.

7. The self may act as a *motivating* force in the search for new experiences that will either support the present structure or create the kind of conflict out of which growth may take place.

8. The self may *judge* the structure itself on the basis of experiences and values in an attempt to determine a sense of self-worth or self-esteem.

These devices suggest that the self is a kind of scientist in the sense that it uses various process by which it tests, adapts, refines, and evaluates its structure (Epstein, 1973). Unlike the true scientist, however, the self makes no claim to objectivity, but rather is perceptual and thus subjective by definition. As Jersild (1952) pointed out, "Our findings indicate that the normal person comes to terms with himself and views himself more on an emotional basis than on an intellectual basis. The self feeds, as it were, more on feeling than on thought" (pp. 54-55). In other words, the self, in seeking stability, consistency, and enhancement, may choose to simply avoid threatening situations, to select certain sources of information and exclude others, to alter undesirable feedback, or to simply ignore it. To turn the coin over, we might suggest that it is exactly this nonscientific nature of the self that makes the task of studying and even describing the self so difficult. To suggest, for instance, the precise conditions under which a particular individual might change his or her self-concept is most difficult since outside influence will always be subject to the process devices just described. For this reason also, attempts to change someone else's self-perceptions often fail.

The process of self-perceiving is by no means linear and thus cannot be reduced to a simple diagram or formula. In reality, the interaction between the individual, the environment, the self-concept structure, and the process devices is constant and may involve one or more self-dimensions and devices simultaneously. At a simplistic level, however, we might describe the process as one in which the individual with a self-concept structure interacts with the environment, and as new experiences or information are encountered, they are processed by devices in such a way that the self-concept structure is strengthened, refined, or unchanged. (See Figure 1.1.)

The Developing Self

While self-perceptions develop largely in a social context, their nature and content also depend partly on the developmental characteristics of particular stages of growth. For example, the lack of physical power in early childhood makes individuals at that stage dependent on the environment for basic survival. Thus young children may not only recognize their need for adults, but also conduct themselves in ways that assure their support. Adolescents, on the other hand, may believe themselves to be capable of independence and thus want little to do with adults, relying instead on peers or personal introspection. The purpose of this section is to describe the relationship between developmental stages and self-perceptions. It is important to note that while the stages are somewhat age-related, they actually represent physical, cognitive, and social characteristics which may emerge at different ages for different individuals.

Figure 1.1
The Process of Self-Perceiving

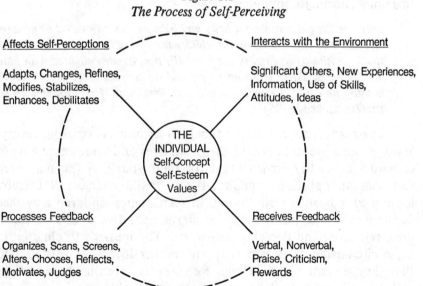

Affects Self-Perceptions

Adapts, Changes, Refines,
Modifies, Stabilizes,
Enhances, Debilitates

Interacts with the Environment

Significant Others, New Experiences,
Information, Use of Skills,
Attitudes, Ideas

THE
INDIVIDUAL
Self-Concept
Self-Esteem
Values

Processes Feedback

Organizes, Scans, Screens,
Alters, Chooses, Reflects,
Motivates, Judges

Receives Feedback

Verbal, Nonverbal,
Praise, Criticism,
Rewards

The Childhood Self

Educators who work with young children are well aware that when children first come to school they already have feelings and beliefs about themselves in terms of adequacy and competency. This recognition makes a good deal of sense, given the idea that self-perceptions arise out of interaction with and experiences in the environment. In other words, from the very first experiences in life, young children begin to develop a sense of themselves.

For young children, self-perceptions are largely a function of feedback from parents or guardians since these are the most significant others. Certainly older brothers and sisters and other adults may play some role in the formulation of self-perceptions, but interaction with parents or guardians is most critical. Furthermore, it is becoming increasingly apparent in child study that the development of clear and positive self-images in children depends on the kind of home environment or climate provided by parents (e.g., Hymes, 1963; Briggs, 1970; Purkey, 1970). Feelings of personal adequacy may be described as related to feelings of trust, love, belonging, and acceptance. Thus the home environment in which the parents demonstrate that they trust and love children and that children have a welcome place is the kind of environment from which healthy self-concept and self-esteem might be expected to evolve. Hymes (1963) made this point succinctly in saying:

> Lucky is the child to whom body and hands speak an overriding message of pride and joy. Lucky is the child whose experiences with mothering speak to him of unconditional love! His parents are delighted with him, just as he is. There is nothing he could do to earn more love; there is nothing he could do which would take love away. He is loved with no strings attached (p. 25).

For many young children this kind of home is far from reality. Many parents are unhappy in their own lives or do not know how to construct a healthy environment for their young. A few may even feel that an oppressed childhood will "build character," thereby leading to a healthier adulthood. In such homes, children may face constant physical punishment or abuse, tentative and conditional love, rejection, and denial of self-worth. The message to children in these circumstances is that they are neither loved nor trusted, and that they do not really belong. Remarkably, even in these settings children still strive for love and affection since this emotional need is so strong and because parents are so significant. To secure a place, though, the children may have to surrender their self-worth and accept a degraded role. A life such as this is one of desperation, and self-perceptions are initiated in a precarious way. That such homes exist is demonstrated by the increase in child abuse in our society, as well as the more subtle trend among adults to center their lives around their own gratification to the exclusion of their children.

For their more fortunate cohorts, however, early childhood is a good start toward healthy self-perceptions. Parent-infant bonding (Fraiberg, 1977) is strong, and constant encouragement supports efforts to learn to walk, to talk, to take care of themselves physically, to manipulate objects, and to "get the feel of the world." Coopersmith (1967) has characterized this kind of home as one in which children experience parental warmth, respectful treatment, and clearly defined limits. His research suggests that the home in which this is the case produces children who tend to have positive self-esteem.

In middle childhood, children begin to experience a wider world of adults and peers, yet parents continue as "most significant others." Learned skills like communicating and manipulating are tried out in new settings, particularly the school. Though the home is still readily available, hopefully for support, the self-perceptions are opened to feedback from teachers, classmates, and others. Self-thinking at this point is centered in self-competence (How well do I do at games, at school projects?) and acceptance outside the home (Do other children like me? Is my teacher nice to me?).

When children talk about themselves in school they tend to focus on those aspects of their life to date (Lipka, Beane, and Ludewig, 1980). Play and adult guidance have previously been dominant themes. Thus children in their early school years describe themselves most positively in a context of school activities that seem like play (e.g., learning games), under the guidance of "nice" teachers.

In later childhood, the peer group begins to emerge in the category of "significant others," as may teachers or other adults who provide positive feedback in areas that the child prizes. With the earlier onset of pubescence, many of the self-concept related ideas historically reserved for emerging adolescence are normally occurring in what has traditionally been viewed as later childhood. For example, boy-girl relationships and concern for physical appearance are presently becoming preoccupying motives with eight- and nine-year-olds. In cases where individual children clearly exhibit such tendencies, the enlightened educator might well study ideas of self related to the next higher age group.

In sum, though, it might best be said that the kind of school environment that enhances self-perceptions of children is the one most like the home that does so. A sense of inadequacy or incompetence developed in the earlier years is difficult, though not impossible, to overcome. The whole matter of growing and developing would be much easier if the beginning stages were happily experienced. Under the guidance of trusting teachers who help build constructive peer relations and who develop confidence in learning, the child may quickly gain a sense that he or she is capable of living effectively in the larger world outside the home. This heightened sense of self-worth is of real value as the onset of transescence, the more stressful next stage of development, begins.

The Transescent Self

There is probably no more dramatic age period in the human lifespan than transescence or emerging adolescence. This period of development is marked by the onset and achievement of puberty, the emergence of the peer group as "significant others," and the onset of formal cognitive operations or the ability to deal with conceptual, abstract relationships.

The age of achieving puberty has been dropping steadily for the past century (Forbes, 1968). Today most young people undergo this process between the ages of ten and fourteen (Bromberg, Commins, and Friedman, 1980). During the course of this period there is considerable change in not only internal functionings, but in external physical aspects such as height, weight, secondary sex characteristics, and so on. The adolescent who emerges from transescence is most often very different from the child who originally began the period. Such dramatic changes are a substantial topic for self-perceptions, since they mean that the individual must reconstruct the physical sense of self in terms of a new and changing physique. Concern about physical development is further complicated by the tendency of individuals to compare their development to that of others. Procedures such as "gang showers" after gym class make such comparison an obvious and on-going event. Many of us remember the hours spent in front of the mirror checking to see if anything was happening, feeling inferior if our development was slower than that of others and self-conscious if it was faster. One commonly finds in the transescent group a desire to be taller, stronger, and more attractive—a sign that many of these young people strongly desire some change in themselves (Lipka, Beane, and Ludewig, 1980).

The physical changes involved in transescence also bring about the capacity for sexual activity and with it the need to redefine oneself in terms of sexuality and relationships with others. For a growing number of transescents, sexual capacity leads to intense and complicated sexual experiences with others, but for many the desire for such activity is limited to the fantasies of masturbation. In either case, the self as a sexual person is open to reconsideration and is a powerful factor in transescent self-perceptions. For those whose sexual experiences lead to veneral disease, pregnancy, or other outcomes, the sexual dimension of self may become even more problematic.

Simultaneously, the transescent also feels new and heightened concern about the peer group. While parents may continue to be "significant others," the peer group takes on greater significance, particularly in such areas as dress, behavior, and values. Certainly approval and acceptance by peers is a preoccupying motive for transescents (Lipsitz, 1980). This need is manifested in the emergence of tightly constructed cliques or groups, each one concerned about who may or may not be accepted, and consisting of individuals who are happy to be in and willing to do generally whatever is required to retain membership. Often, however, the values of the peer group conflict with those of parents, and thus many transescents are confronted with continuing conflict over rules and regulations, interests, activities, and so on. Hence, the transescent typically experiences uncomfortable dissonance between the self-perceived need to be an accepted member of the peer group and to retain the security of family membership.

The same kind of conflict may arise in relation to teachers and other adult authority figures where the peer group devalues school achievement, school and community rules, and other institutional features. It is possible, though, that this latter conflict may be of less concern to transescents than family conflict since parents tend to be more significant in their lives than teachers and other adults (Rosenberg, 1979). On the other hand, when the transescent perceives parents and other adults at odds with the peer group, conflict may be highly intense and the self-concept may be permeated by a feeling that "no one understands me." Such feelings are undoubtedly one factor in the increasing rates of suicide, drug and alcohol use, and adolescent pregnancy. In any event, self-perceptions during transescence are constantly influenced by the emerging peer group and the continuing adult environment. The struggle for independence that arises in adolescence may begin in the earlier stage, but for most transescents, self-perceptions are largely influenced by peers and adults, and the need to be accepted and understood by others is a powerful issue.

The other development that occurs in transescence is the onset of formal cognitive operations (Piaget and Inhelder, 1958). While the child has been limited to thinking about concrete relationships between concepts and ideas, the transescent begins to develop a capacity for abstract or conceptual thought. It may be that this occurrence accounts as much as the peer group for conflict with parents and other adults, since formal operations would allow for questioning of values and ideas. It is important to note, however, that there is a difference between the onset of formal operations and their maturity or qualitative use (Elkind, 1980). Most transescents do not develop the latter during this period in a general way, a fact which may possibly be attributed to the apparent brain growth plateau identified during ages twelve and fourteen (Epstein and Toepfer, 1978). For this reason, many transescents may be observed applying a personal sense of logic to problems they face. Many young people experience initial school achievement problems during transescence; while there are many reasons for this, one is probably that schools at this level often emphasize tasks that require mature formal operations (Toepfer, 1980). The sense of self as learner may thus experience feelings of inadequacy as the curriculum plans of the school overshoot the transescent's cognitive capacity.

Nevertheless, self-perceptions during transescence become the subject of continuous introspection as young people attempt to think more deeply about themselves. Self-perceptions may thus be more complex and the need to try out new roles stronger. Whether or not such introspection is reasonable and logical is certainly a concern, but the fact that it is taking place and that it marks the onset of the adolescent "identity crisis" makes transescence a critical period in the development of self-perceptions.

Finally, consideration of self-perceptions in transescence would not be complete without noting the role that the school itself may play in their formulation. Most children experience school through the framework of the self-contained classroom in which a single teacher may get to know them well and view them holistically and humanistically (Willower, Eidell, and Hoy, 1967). The immediate peer group may be limited to a particular group with which the vast majority of time is spent. The transition to the junior high or middle school presents a much more complex situation. The transescent is most often forced to deal with a larger and less familiar peer group, several teachers, and a more competitive reward system. Teachers often have less opportunity to get to know learners and are frequently oriented to custodial views of teaching and learning. The sense of self as learner and as peer may thus be subject to confusion or dissonance, and this may be further complicated by the relatively impersonal climate of the junior high or middle school as compared to the elementary school. The point is that school itself may interact with the other factors cited to compound the self-perception problems faced by many transescents.

Since transescence is virtually unique in the dramatic changes that characterize it, the period might also be considered as one of acute vulnerability. Changes in physical status, social relations, and cognitive level require a veritable rethinking of self-perceptions in virtually all dimensions. The development of reasonably clear self-concept and generally positive self-esteem offers the chance for a smooth transition to adolescence. Unresolved self-perception issues, however, may be carried over into adolescence and create new problems in that period.

The Adolescent Self

Adolescence is often differentiated from other age periods by its characteristic "identity crisis" (Erickson, 1968). At this time, youth are often concerned with the attempt to answer questions like "Who am I?" "What will I do with my life?" and other self-concerns. This internal questioning is manifested in the trying out of new roles, the identification of occupational/career preferences, and especially in the struggle to develop the independence from parents and other adults, which is associated with adulthood.

The definition of adolescence in our society still suffers from ambiguity. Some theorists equate the term with age and thus suggest that adolescence occurs roughly between the ages of eleven and any-where from eighteen to twenty. Others define adolescence as the span of years from the onset of puberty to the adoption of adult roles and responsibilities. This conflict between age and role defini-tion is a source of confusion in the adolescent self-identity search. For example, the sixteen-year-old who is a mother and who holds a part-time job qualifies for adolescence in terms of age, but with re-gard to her roles and responsibilities, she is an adult. On the other hand, the frame of reference appears to be reversed in the case of the twenty-two-year-old college senior whose top priority is fraternity parties and who depends on others for economic and emotional support. Given this ambiguity, one might look nostalgically at Mead's (1950) description of the rites of passage in primitive society by which a young person was quickly brought to adulthood by some ritual or ceremony.

As Mead pointed out, however, the period of adolescence as we know it is peculiar to Western and westernized civilization. Our "holding pattern" of adolescence appears to grow out of two reasons. One has to do with maintaining a degree of stability in the market place by keeping adolescents out of the work force. The other seems to involve a belief that youth should be given a period of protection as they clarify their self-identity and make plans for the future. For adolescents, however, the ambiguous "holding pattern" in which they are expected to act like adults, but in which adult privileges are withheld, may lead to lack of clarity in self-concept in terms of roles and responsibilities.

For adolescents, the development of social connections is a powerful factor in self-perceptions. Rosenberg (1965) documented the idea that adolescents are highly concerned with what others think of them. His data also suggested, however, that high self-esteem adolescents were less likely to be bothered by poor opinions of them than were low self-esteem adolescents. In adolescence, this priority placed on social relations is particularly focused on those of the opposite sex. Of interest here is the idea that role self-perceptions in adolescence are based in traditional sex-role stereotypes (Wylie, 1979). Wylie's review of several studies on this topic suggests that adolescent males and females identify ideal roles for themselves and each other based on the male as competent and aggressive and the female as warm, expressive, and preoccupied with social affiliation. Such a conservative view of sex roles may grow out of apprehension about conflict in self-perceptions involved in crossing stereotype lines. This does not mean that these adolescent views will necessarily carry over into adulthood. Rather, it means that as we observe the self-perceptions of adolescents in relationship to members of the opposite sex, we ought to be aware that those perceptions tend to be rooted in sex-role stereotypes.

Another aspect of adolescence that is receiving attention with regard to self-perceptions is the increasing incidence of adolescent pregnancies. Approximately one million adolescent women become pregnant each year (Polley, 1979; Wexler, 1979). Of these, 600,000 give birth, and 85 to 90 percent keep their babies rather than give them up for adoption or foster homes. Historically, adolescent pregnancies have been viewed as unfortunate mistakes. More recently, however, many adolescent women have chosen to become pregnant in the belief that a baby will provide the kind of unconditional love and acceptance that they perceive society does not. This particular type of adolescent pregnancy may thus be viewed as growing out of a gap in self-perceptions; namely, a feeling of being rejected. Research on adolescent mothers indicates that compared to nonmothers of the same age, the former have more self-concept confusion, lower self-regard, and less satisfaction with family and social relationships (Polley, 1979; Wexler, 1979). Following the birth of a child, most adolescent mothers also experience feelings of economic inadequacy and social isolation. Thus, problems with self-perceptions may not only contribute to adolescent pregnancies, but become complicated by them. Perhaps the same might be said about other situations adolescents face, including use of drugs and alcohol, crime, and so on.

In the fall of 1979 we conducted a follow-up study of persons who had graduated from high school in the years from 1946-1950. One of the questions asked was, "What is your most vivid recollection of high school?" Answers included selected teachers, activities, and anecdotes. One response, though, was particularly interesting.

> *My answer may be a bit of a shock to you. It was the very first thought that came to mind and I've weighed it very carefully the past two days before writing it on paper.* They were the unhappiest years of my life.

No doubt many individuals experience unhappiness during adolescence, but most probably tend to forget such feelings as new experiences unfold in adulthood. Nevertheless, some individuals evidently still recall, even after thirty-five years, the quality of their adolescent self-perceptions.

In sum, adolescent self-perceptions probably have a good deal to do with adolescent behavior and attitudes. The frustration experienced in trying to develop a clear and positive sense of self in this period is certainly difficult in the face of cultural ambiguity regarding adolescence. The dual standard that expects adult responsibility but withholds adult privileges must often be a source of confusion.

The Adult Self

In adulthood, self-perceptions are characterized by seeking stability; that is, the individual views himself or herself and is seen by others as consistent in expected situations. The stability we envision comes from two related sources. The first of these is a progression through social roles and social states. That is to say, adults have milestones as do children; however, adult milestones are largely socially induced (Neugarten, 1969). For example, in young adulthood the issues are marriage, parenthood, entering the world of work, and investing oneself into the lives of a few significant others (e.g., spouse, children). In middle age, self-perceptions are tied to new family roles such as the mother-in-law, the grandparent, or the child of aging parents. In old age, the issues are again different. Here, self-perception will be formed by such social states as retirement and roles such as widow or widower.

Second, the self-perceptions stimulated by these social roles and states will be constructed, changed, and/or evaluated as the result of the accumulation of experiences. Neugarten's (1969) metaphor makes this most meaningful:

> The mental filing system not only grows larger, but it is reorganized over time, with infinitely more cross-references. This is merely one way of saying that not only do the middle aged differ from the young because they are subject to different formative experiences, but because of the unavoidable effects of having lived longer and having therefore a greater apperceptive mass or store of past experience (p. 123).

The confounding variable in all this is that these social roles, states, and accumulated experiences originate in an age-status system whereby a society allocates the rights, duties, and privileges to individuals differentially on the basis of age (for example, being eighteen to vote or thirty-five in order to run for president). In fact, the strong normative properties of the age-status system tend to act as "brakes" or "prods" on the movement in or out of social roles (Neugarten, Moore, and Lowe, 1965). The individual may begin to use age to deny a role and role self-perception. At one point, a twenty-five-year-old male may indicate, "I am a new father"; while at a later time, say age fifty-five, the same individual may feel that "I am too old to be a new father."

The age-norming process may also manifest itself in the way a person is viewed by other people in terms of age expectations. For example, having people surrender their seats on a bus might serve to disconfirm an individual's self-perception of being young and robust.

Further, there is always the chance of discontinuity in these evolving social roles and states. The sudden death of a spouse, forced retirement, or being physically abused by a young person can force dramatic changes in self-perceptions. One can well imagine the self-esteem cost of a forced retirement that has the individual perceive himself or herself economically as a second-class citizen, when previously the person was in the economic mainstream.

In adulthood, the normative properties of our age-status system permeate the self-perception process; that is, to perceive oneself as "on" or "off" time with regard to one's life span causes the individual to examine and reevaluate the generalized self-concept that he or she has established. To view oneself as "on" time makes for a sense of a predictable life cycle.

Unfortunately, many individuals come to believe that they are "off" time and have fallen short of their goals and aspirations with the resultant decay of self-esteem. Individuals in this instance may misperceive, distort, or avoid any new situation in order to reduce the introduction of any new complexity into their lives. In some instances, this process may prompt severe feelings of inadequacy and anxiety—behaviors which are being popularized as "burn-out."

In sum, while adult self-perceptions are seeking stability, this stability is taking place at a time when the individual reaches his or her maximum number and range of environmental interactions. Flexibility and healthy self-perceptions will develop in environments that make use of or build from the accumulation of experiences of the individual and that pay attention to the age-status system in which the individual resides.

Summary

In this chapter we have focused on the general concept of self-perceptions. The concern of human beings with knowing about and understanding themselves can be traced back several centuries through literature, art, and other forms of self-expression. In the twentieth century the study of self-perceptions has become a growing topic for scientific theory and research. The present status of this work suggests that self-perceptions include self-concept and self-esteem, are largely influenced by the environment, are hierarchical and multi-dimensional, and are subject to several processing devices as they search for consistency, maintenance, and enhancement.

Further, the content and process of self-perceptions are, to some extent, age-related. Those in childhood are largely dependent on the family and home environment even as they extend into school experiences. In transescence, self-perceptions are subject to virtual reconstruction as the physical self changes, the peer group emerges, and formal operations begin to emerge. Adolescent self-perceptions are highly related to the so-called "identity crisis," which is compounded by growing awareness of the social environment and development of more intense relationships with members of the same or opposite sex.

In the several thousand studies of self-perceptions that have been done, those involving school suggest a persistent relationship between self-perceptions and a variety of school-related variables (Wiley, 1961, 1979; Purkey, 1970; Rosenburg, 1979). Among those are academic achievement, participation in class and other activities, completion of school, pro-social behavior, perceptions of peers and teachers of the individual, and self-direction in learning. The same body of research suggests that the school can and does contribute to the self-perceptions of learners.

For these reasons, an understanding of self-concept and self-esteem in general, how these function in youth, and how the school might enhance or hinder these must be major concerns of those responsible for curriculum planning and implementation.

2

Institutional Features and Student Self-Perceptions

When young people come to school they bring along images of themselves. As they experience everyday life in school these images may change or new ones may be developed. In each school experience there is potential for stabilizing or changing self-perceptions and, depending on the consistency and continuity of situations, the possibility for affecting even the general sense of self (Kifer, 1978; Kash and Borich, 1978; Purkey, 1978).

In some cases, school personnel engage in careful planning to develop an environment in which self-perceptions are most likely to be enhanced. In others, self-concept and self-esteem receive little attention; however, the lack of attention does not mean that self-perceptions are not affected in school. Self-perceptions are formulated as a result of the experiences found in the school situation, whether they are planned or not. The problem with not paying attention to self-perceptions through careful planning is that the consequences may be largely unpredictable. In other words, school programs and features that are *not* planned so as to enhance self-perceptions may have one of three consequences. First, they may actually be enhancing; second, they may have no real effects; or third, they may hinder development of self-perceptions or even act in a debilitating way. Since self-perceptions are so important in human development and since most schools include enhancement of self-worth among their goals, the first outcome is too risky and the second and third are simply not acceptable. The only way to assure the enhancement of self-concept and self-esteem is to give careful attention to how the school affects them.

The school is maintained by society as an institution for dealing with young people. As such, it has many *institutional features* (Beane and Lipka, 1977) including climate, rules and regulations, methods of grouping and grading, professional behavior, and so on. Through these and other institutional features, the school makes a persistent effort to become a "significant other" for learners, suggesting behavior standards, interaction patterns, self-concept dimensions, and the like. Studies of institutional features have indicated that they define the "hidden" curriculum of the school and that the self and social lessons that emerge from them are at least as powerful, and perhaps more so, than the academic (Snyder, 1973; Overly, 1970; Macdonald and Zaret, 1975; Apple and King, 1977). The content and application of institutional features is an expression of the school's values, and the suggested learnings are clear. Is it possible that where competition, physical punishment, humiliation, and conformity are emphasized that many students take these seriously enough to internalize the values they imply? Can the same be said for situations that prize cooperation, creativity, and careful thinking? We think so!

Within this framework, then, this chapter will involve an analysis of various features of the school as an institution and how they tend to affect learner self-perceptions.

Climate: From Custodial to Humanistic

"I like this school—my teachers like me"—Male, Age 11

The climate of schools and classrooms has been a topic of considerable attention in educational thinking over the past two decades (Fox, Luszki, and Schmuck, 1966; Jackson, 1969; Walberg, 1974; Macdonald and Zaret, 1975; Aspy and Roebuck, 1977; Apple, 1979). The term *climate* refers to the atmosphere or milieu that permeates or underlies all of the transactions and interactions that take place in the school setting. In one sense, the school and class climate serve as the backdrop for everyday living in those settings and thus is a major determinant in the quality of life for learners.

Generally two types of climate are described: custodial and

humanistic (Willower, Eidell, and Hoy, 1967). *Custodial climate* is characterized by concern for maintenance of order, teacher preference for autocratic procedures, student stereotyping or labeling, punitive sanctions, moralizing by authorities, impersonalness, and emphasis on obedience. In contrast, *humanistic climate* is characterized by preference for democratic procedures, high degrees of interaction, personalness, respect for individual dignity, emphasis on self-discipline, flexibility, and participatory decision-making.

Willower and Jones (1963) conducted a comprehensive analysis of a junior high school, including interviews with staff and observational records of faculty meetings, classes, the cafeteria, and assemblies. They concluded that "while many other matters influenced the tone of the school, pupil control was a dominant motif." In the particular school studied, they noted the following characteristics:

1. Older teachers communicated the need for pupil control to younger teachers.
2. The faculty lounge conversations often tended to "tough talk," including ridiculing students.
3. In hiring a new principal, the faculty priority was on tough discipline.
4. Teachers held "collusion meetings" with guidance and administrative personnel in order to promote solidarity in grading of students, particularly those who were to fail.

In contrast to the Willower and Jones study, Howard (1978) described efforts by a high school staff to build a humanistic climate in place of a custodial one. In that particular setting, personnel took specific steps to improve climate. Among those noted were:

1. Workshops were developed to improve communications skills and to learn how to share in decision making.
2. Clear goals were established that committed the school to enhancing self-esteem.
3. Projects were implemented to improve the physical attractiveness of the school.
4. Mini-courses were aimed at improving self and social skills.
5. Failing grades were eliminated—only work done was recorded.
6. Participatory decision making was established through representative committees.

Howard also described indicators of school improvement that grew out of the project, including fewer drop-outs and requests for transfer, less violence, increased personal freedom for students, and community recognition.

These single case reports not only serve as practical examples of the two different types of climate, but they also indicate the difference in the quality of life for learners (and faculty) in each. Within this context, a humanistic climate also appears to offer benefits for learners in the area of self-perceptions.

Deibert and Hoy (1977) studied the relationship between type of climate and self-actualization of students in forty high schools. Data collected in the study suggest a statistically significant relationship between the two variables. Specifically, the more custodial the high school, the less self-actualized students tended to be. On the other hand, students in more humanistic high schools demonstrated greater degrees of self-actualization.

Like the Lewin, Lippitt, and White (1939) study cited in Chapter 1, the work of Deibert and Hoy suggests that students acquire a great deal from the climate in which learning is to take place. In the situations reported, it was evident that in climates that emphasize external control, young people learn to depend on others for direction, whereas in climates that put a premium on self-control, individuals tend to learn to be self-directed. Since locus of control is closely related to self-actualization, these and similar studies of school climate demonstrate the need to carefully consider ways to develop humanistic climates in schools.

This concept is also associated with the classic notion of "negative affect," in which it is held that when students feel threatened in school, they tend to feel less positive about themselves and experience less success than when they are in a supportive setting. We have met some educators who seem to feel that a threatening and custodial climate is somehow "good" for young people; that such an atmosphere helps prepare them for the "real" world of adulthood. At the same time, however, some of these educators are also quick to point out the need for improved working conditions, such as more decision making in the curriculum and budget process. The point here is that internal locus of control is an educational goal not only for professionals, but for students as well. Further, the fact that some learners lack self-direction skills does not justify their placement in settings that continually rely on custodial procedures. Like other skills, those

———————————————————— Case 2.1 ————————————————————

The Jefferson County Open High School Program*

The Jefferson County Open High School, which is an option available to any student in Jefferson County, was established in the fall of 1975. The initiative to create such a program came from community members, students, parents, and staff of the Open Living Schools in Jefferson County. There are 180 students who were accepted on a first-come, first-served basis from those who applied with their parents' approval. Transportation to the school is provided by the school district.

The program is ungraded, individualized, and self-paced. It requires a high degree of self-discipline and responsibility on the part of the learner. To help develop these traits, each student chooses a staff member as an advisor, with whom the student will plan and evaluate a personal learning program. This program may be pursued in a variety of ways, including classes within the school, classes at other Jefferson County schools or local colleges, guided independent study, group projects, educational trips, or apprenticeship in the community.

It is the student's responsibility, with the help of the advisor, to document all learning experiences and to obtain supporting statements from people with whom the student has worked. This documentation is used to determine whether Jefferson County graduation requirements have been satisfied, as the transcript for college applications, or as the high school record for prospective employers.

Students and parents are also involved in the governance of the school, in making policy decisions within the school, and in hiring and evaluating the staff.

———

*Courtesy of Arnold Langberg, Jefferson County Open High School, Evergreen, Colorado.

involved in self-direction must be nurtured by responsible educators who systematically help learners move toward the less structured learning activities that appear to enhance internal locus of control. To do less would be like refusing to teach a student to read because he or she did not know how upon entering school. Such an attitude would be deemed irresponsible in the case of reading, and it ought to be regarded in the same light in the case of locus of control.

Locus of control, participatory decision-making, interaction, and other topics related to humanistic climates will be discussed in succeeding sections. However, before leaving the topic of climate, two issues are worth noting. The first issue concerns the reward system used in the school.

Reward System

Reward systems typically are based on two types of structures: competitive and individual. In the competitive structure, learners are rewarded for doing better than their peers. Only a relatively few receive high awards or grades, while the rest are led to believe that they are not as capable or are outright inferior. For example, Yarborough and Johnson (1980) compared students from an elementary school that used traditional marking systems with students from a school in which marks or grades were not given. They found that high ability students from "grading" schools demonstrated better total adjustment (e.g., positive attitudes toward school, peers, and adults) than high ability students in "nongrading" schools. However, lower ability students in

--------------------------------- Case 2.2 ---------------------------------

Student Team Learning*

The most extensively researched and widely used cooperative learning methods were developed by David DeVries, Keith Edwards, Robert Slavin, and their colleagues at Johns Hopkins University (Slavin, 1980). These methods include Student Teams-Achievement Divisions (STAD), Teams-Games-Tournament (TGT), and Jigsaw II, in addition to many modifications and special purpose cooperative methods. In STAD, the teacher first presents a lesson. The students take individual quizzes on the material. The scores the students contribute to their teams are based on the degree to which they represent an improvement over the student's own past average. The teams with the highest scores are recognized in a weekly class newsletter. In TGT students represent their teams in academic games. Students compete with others of similar past performance so that, as in STAD, any student who prepares well can be successful. Jigsaw II is a modification of Aronson's (1978) Jigsaw method.

Jigsaw. In Jigsaw, each student in a five- to six-member group is given a unique piece of information on a topic the whole group is studying. After they have read their sections, the students meet in "expert groups" with their counterparts from other groups to discuss their information. Then the students return to their groups and teach their groupmates what they have learned. The entire class may then take a test for individual grades.

Jigsaw II (Slavin, 1980) is a modification of Jigsaw designed to integrate this method with the other student team learning methods and to simplify the teacher preparation required to use the method. In Jigsaw II, students are assigned to four- or five-member teams. They read narrative materials, such as social studies chapters, short stories, or biographies, and each team member is given a special topic on which to become an expert. The students discuss their topics in "expert groups," and then return to teach their teammates what they have learned. Finally, the students take a quiz on the material, and the quiz scores are used as in STAD to form individual and team scores.

Learning Together. The cooperative learning method closest to pure cooperation is that designed by Johnson and Johnson (1975). Students work in small groups to complete a single worksheet, for which the group receives praise and recognition.

Group-Investigation. The Group-Investigation model (Sharan and Sharan, 1976) is the most complex of the cooperative learning methods. Students in small groups take substantial responsibility for deciding what they will learn, how they will organize themselves to learn it, and how they will communicate what they have learned to their classmates.

Cooperative learning methods vary considerably, but their differences are primarily alternative ways to deal with the same problems inherent in cooperation. For example, most of the methods make it impossible for one student to do most of the group's work. In STAD and Jigsaw II, students take individual quizzes without the help of their teammates to add points to their team scores; each student must know the material. In TGT, students play academic games with members of other teams to add points to their team scores; again, each student must know the material in order to contribute a high score. The Jigsaw, Jigsaw II, and Group-Investigation methods make it impossible for the group's work to be unevenly distributed by having each student become an expert on some part of the group task.

References

Aronson, E. *The Jigsaw Classroom.* Beverly Hills, Calif.: Sage Publications, 1978.

Johnson, D. W., and Johnson, R. T. *Learning Together and Alone.* Englewood Cliffs, N.J.: Prentice-Hall, Inc., 1975.

Sharan, S., and Sharan, Y. *Small-Group Teaching.* Englewood Cliffs, N.J.: Prentice-Hall, Inc., 1976.

Slavin, R. E. *Using Student Team Learning* (revised edition). Baltimore: Center for Social Organization of Schools, The John Hopkins University, 1980.

*Robert E. Slavin, "Synthesis of Research on Cooperative Learning," *Educational Leadership* 38: (May 1981): 655-659. Reprinted with permission of the Association for Supervision and Curriculum Development and Robert E. Slavin. Copyright © 1981 by the Association for Supervision and Curriculum Development. All rights reserved.

"nongrading" schools showed better adjustment than their counterparts in "grading" schools. Furthermore, when age, sex, race, socioeconomic status, and ability were controlled, there was no difference in academic achievement measured by standardized tests. Since competitive rewards (e.g., grades) have no academic motivation, their use for this purpose is unjustified.

In the end, this procedure serves only as a direct attempt to suggest to learners what their self-concepts ought to be. In other words, those schools and classrooms in which competitive reward systems are used seem to have the intention of having large numbers of learners view themselves as incapable. Such an intention is simply indefensible when we know that self-concept as a capable person or successful learner is critical in achieving success. Individual reward systems that place learners in personal competition with themselves also present difficulties since they tend to have an isolating effect, separating individuals from their peers. The fact is that self-perceptions in youth are largely dependent on social connectedness—the feeling that one is accepted as part of the group. For this reason, those educators who wish to enhance self-perceptions need to make efforts to replace competitive and individual reward systems with cooperative reward structures that emphasize group work.

Slavin (1981) has described several techniques for cooperative learning in the classroom based on the use of learning teams or groups. He points out that cooperative learning offers advantages to students over competitive and individual systems in a variety of areas, including both academic and social outcomes. In particular, self-esteem is enhanced in these team settings because they promote acceptance by the group and because students experience academic success.

Punishment System

The second issue that needs attention here is the punishment system used in the school. Many schools deal with anti-social behavior through procedures that have the intention of humiliating or degrading students (Brenan, 1972). The most ludicrous form of these is corporal or physical punishment (Hyman, 1979). Such procedures create only temporary changes in behavior, do little to improve values or attitudes, and seem to satisfy only the most custodial of adult attitudes. Furthermore, the degraded feelings that are part of the immediate punishment tend to evolve into generalized negative feelings about the self and the school as a whole. Pro-social behavior is clearly related to clear and positive perceptions of the self as a capable, competent, and accepted person. Anti-social behavior is most often a function of negative or confused self-feelings. Thus, the way to help students overcome such behavior is to enhance their self-perceptions.

Teachers and other educators need to spend less time inventing ways to control students and more time asking questions like the following: "Do I make students feel welcome in school? Do I accept them regardless of home backgrounds and previous school experiences? Do students have a say in what happens here? Are my curriculum plans interesting and related to the real concerns of learners?" When these and similar questions are answered in the positive, learners are likely to act in pro-social ways. Throughout this book, we describe numerous methods for enhancing self-perceptions. We suggest that these also be considered as ways to develop a more constructive and pro-social community in the school.

In sum, it is clear that theory and research on school climate and its relationship to self-concept and esteem support those climate dimensions defined as humanistic. The existence of custodial climate in schools should be an urgent matter of concern to educators. To the degree that clear and positive feelings about self are desirable as antecedents and outcomes of schooling, the development of humanistic climates should be a continuing goal for those concerned with enhancing self-perceptions in school.

Grouping: Labels and Expectations

"I am in the highest honors class—I want to change that because people think I'm stuck up"—Female, Age 15

Much of the time students spend in school is spent in groups. Typically, two major types of grouping patterns are used: heterogeneous and homogeneous. The former refers to group settings in which students are brought together on a random basis or in which a broad spectrum of characteristics is purposefully represented. The latter involves the construction of groups on the basis of some characteristic the group of students presumably holds in common. These might include such factors as intelligence, aptitude, interest, talent, achievement, or others. Homogeneous grouping is often extended into tracking systems whereby a particular student remains with the same group for all or most of the school activities.

Homogeneous grouping often acts as a form of labeling, as students are informed either explicitly or implicitly that they are similar to others in the particular group in ways other than the variable used for grouping. Perhaps the most noteworthy effect of this labeling process is the principle called *teacher expectations* (Rosenthal, 1970; Good and Dembo, 1973). Good and Brophy (1973) have detailed the steps of this process as follows:

1. The teacher expects specific behavior and achievement from particular students.

2. Because of these expectations, the teacher behaves differently toward different students.

3. This treatment by the teacher tells each student what behavior and achievement the teacher expects from him or her and affects his or her self-concept, achievement motivation, and level of aspiration.

4. If this teacher treatment is consistent over time, and if the student does not actively resist or change it in some way, it will shape his or her achievement and behavior. High-expectation students will be led to achieve at high levels, but the achievement of low-expectation students will decline.

5. With time, the student's achievement and behavior will conform more and more closely to that originally expected from him or her (page 75).

The most common example of this process is that of homogeneous grouping based on ability as derived from an intelligence/achievement test score. The expectations related to ability take root in at least three ways.

First, individuals within the group may be perceived as having characteristics beyond the homogeneous variable. For example, the teacher may believe that "bright students are cheerful" and "slow learners cannot engage in discussion."

Second, teachers often tend to treat students differently depending on their perceptions of the label. Students perceived as "bright" are provided with more "wait time" to answer questions, are praised more frequently, called on more frequently, and given more nonverbal attention by their teachers.

In addition to the forementioned variables, students perceived as "slow" have marginal or inaccurate answers praised, have less demanded of them, and are given less public feedback to their responses (Good and Brophy, 1973; Rubovits and Maehr, 1973; Brophy and Good, 1974). A revealing illustration of such a differentiation is that teachers tend to wait 2 seconds for students whom they perceive as bright to answer questions, while those they perceive as not bright are typically allowed only 0.9 second. Interestingly enough, on the average, teachers tend to wait about 1 second for student answers, while if they increase the wait time by just 2 seconds, to a total of 3 seconds, they are rewarded with longer and more complete responses from the students (Rowe, 1974). In other words, teacher perceptions as manifested in "wait time" often hinder student accomplishment— a problem particularly affecting those students perceived as "slow."

Third, teacher expectations are used to support and solidify ability tracking the the school, a process which tends to act as a de facto definition of status within the social system of the school (Wilson, 1971; Rosenbaum, 1976). The value of ability as it becomes attached to a particular group implies the worth the individual ought to have among peers, and the persistence of the single group in the particular track discourages interaction across groups. In this case, students themselves may come to stereotype perceptions of individuals in other groups since there is limited opportunity to interact enough to get to know the "others."

While the use of ability produces expectations, it produces little else of importance to educators. Fifty years of research reviewed by Esposito (1973) suggests that ability simply does not have the advantages some think it does. In the area of academic achievement, ability grouping offers an advantage to a few, but not all, high ability students while operating to the disadvantage of the average and below average ability students. In areas such as interpersonal regard, it is disadvantageous to all groups of students. The idea that ability grouping fosters affective and cognitive development simply does not make sense when one looks at research on the topic.

Foshay (1980) offers a compelling view of teacher expectations in his "Metaphors about Children" (see Table 2.1). Be it ability or the metaphors offered by Foshay, grouping by a singular dimension places the school in a direct attempt to intervene in student self-perception by suggesting the dimension by which the self should be described. While this may reinforce the self-perception already held by the students, it is equally possible to create dissonance and lack of clarity within the students, who then place themselves in conflict with the institution.

Table 2.1
Foshay's "Metaphors about Children"*

1. *The Child as Flower:* the child as natural learner, inclined toward wisdom and needing little adult guidance in learning.

2. *The Child as Nigger:* the child as stereotyped property, without rights, incapable of learning without teacher direction and severe punishment.

3. *The Child as Enemy:* the child as an object of efficient strategies, children as "target" populations, subjected to the latent meanings of recent military-like educational jargon.

4. *The Child as Cog:* the child as a part of a smoothly running, machine-like school and as a functionary in the educational bureaucracy.

5. *The Child as Machine:* the child as an object of manipulation by educators, devoid of a personal self with motives, aspirations and so on.

6. *The Child as Chameleon:* the child as simply a victim of circumstances who will react predictably to his/her surroundings.

7. *The Child as Miniature Adult:* the child as non-child, aiming toward adult behavior and rewarded when actions are adult-like.

8. *The Freudian Child:* the child as a victim of unconscious and mysterious forces beyond his/her control as well as ours and thus beyond the guidance of educators.

9. *The Child as Gentleman:* the child in the process of becoming part of the elite in terms of social standing and good manners.

10. *The Child as Reasoner:* the child as emphatically cognitive, to be educated in terms of cognition with de-emphasis on other aspects of humanness.

*Arthur W. Foshay, ed., "Curriculum Talk," *Considered Action for Curriculum Improvement,* 1980 Yearbook (Alexandria, Va.: Association for Supervision and Curriculum Development, 1980), pp. 83-88. Reprinted with permission of the Association for Supervision and Curriculum Development and Arthur W. Foshay. Copyright © 1980 by the Association for Supervision and Curriculum Development. All rights reserved.

The development of appropriate grouping procedures might sensibly start with the idea that the self is multidimensional, a fact that suggests students recognize they have a variety of personal characteristics. Furthermore, the fact that students with a similar self-concept characteristic may regard any particular item differently indicates that it may or may not be important to them and that others may be more or less skilled in an area than they are. In other words, students recognize variety in themselves and others.

This discussion, however, should not imply that self-concept and/or self-esteem ought to be used as a grouping variable. Like others, these can become institutionalized in a rigid and singular way which is antithetical to the idea of the multidimensional and evolving self (Lipka and Beane, 1978).

For these reasons, schools ought to strive for multidimensional grouping patterns. In some situations an objective might be enhanced by bringing together students with a variety of self-concepts, self-esteems, and values so that they may explore, analyze, and learn about themselves and others. In this case, heterogeneous grouping appears highly appropriate.

In other cases, groups may be formed on the basis of some particular homogeneous variable. Groups of this type might be formed around interests, past achievement in some skill area, physical maturity, or the like. At no time, however, should students be led to believe that the variable has any meaning beyond its relation to the objective at hand. Rather, teachers should be open in explaining to students why they have been brought together in a particular way. In this way we may assure learners that we are aware of their multidimensional selves and that we accept diversity while avoiding generalizations.

Decision-Making and Control

"I do what my teacher says—I don't like doing what she says"—Male, Age 8

One of the key issues in developing a positive sense of self-worth is the degree to which an individual perceives personal control over his or her life. Locus of control, the term used to describe this perception, typically tends in one of two directions (Dweck, 1975; DeCharms, 1976; Lefcourt, 1976). The first, *external* locus of control, describes the perception that one's life is controlled by others. *Internal* locus of control, on the other hand, refers to the belief that one is in control of one's own life.

Many schools, especially those with a custodial climate, place a premium on the maintenance of order and, furthermore, act as if order can only come in the presence of highly structured rules determined by the institution and perpetuated from year to year. The common use of such procedures led Carlson (1964) to suggest that

41

schools as institutions in our society might aptly be compared to prisons and mental institutions since attendance at all three is legislated and, once there, individuals tend to have no say in governance. Such a comparison may seem cruel and odious, but the fact remains that this is essentially true in many places (Haney and Zimbardo, 1975).

Schools that express the value of external locus of control through institutional regulations introduce highly questionable content suggestions to learner self-concepts. Elaborate and traditional rules imply to students that they are irresponsible, potentially evil, and helpless in governing their own lives. Those students who learn well from this semi-hidden curriculum may be vulnerable to the extreme case of locus of control—"learned helplessness." In such cases, learners come to believe that they are literally helpless in terms of developing skills. Ames (1978) studied 192 fifth graders with high and low "self-concepts" as learners in competitive classroom settings. She concluded that high self-concept children tended to perceive that success was due to their own ability, while low self-concept (learned helplessness) students did not make this connection and further did not appear to accept positive feedback on a successfully completed task as referring to self-competence.

This point is not meant to imply that all students in schools that have well established institutional rules will learn to be helpless. However, some curriculum analysts have indicated that such behavior on the part of school authorities is intentional as the schools appear to value conformity and dependence (Macdonald and Zaret, 1975).

If we are to promote internal locus of control as a dimension in learner self-concept, we must begin to move away from institutionally imposed rules and toward decision making that emphasizes cooperation and independence.

Case 2.3

The Town Meeting

The town meeting is a process whereby the intermediate students interact to formulate the policies and procedures by which the school community is to function. The main purpose is to help children develop from an egocentric or self-centered stage of development to an ethnocentric stage whereby they develop social awareness and responsibility to the school community. The student's self-identity is still very important and must be fostered; however, each individual must contribute to make the school democratic process work, as we must do in our everyday life.

Specific objectives to be met by the town meeting are:

1. Development of values and morals.
2. Development of rational thinking.
3. Developing an awareness of one's own feelings, opinions, and desires.
4. Learning how to become an active participant in the democratic process.
5. Learning appropriate and inappropriate behavior.
6. Learning the process of conducting a public meeting.
7. Development of leadership roles and skills.
8. Development of listening skills.
9. Development of oral communication.
10. Developing awareness of student responsibility.
11. Learning how to formulate rules and regulations.
12. Learning how to implement rules and regulations.
13. Planning and implementing special projects (parties, field trips, after-school activities, special events, etc.).

Procedures

1. The town meeting is conducted by a student leader who is also responsible for formulating the agenda.
2. Students and staff must contact the student leader to be put on the agenda.
3. Since meetings are scheduled for Tuesday, the agenda is to be posted on Monday and presented in homerooms on Monday or Tuesday.
4. The jobs of student leader and secretary will be rotated every three weeks so that as many students as possible have a chance to assume these roles.
5. Any business not covered in the previous week's meeting will be discussed first under "old business."
6. The person who places an item on the agenda is responsible for introducing the item to the group.
7. Discussion on any item should be no longer than ten minutes. A speaker may express his or her opinion on an item only once.
8. After discussion, a motion must be made as to what action is to be taken on an item. A vote is then taken by a show of hands.
9. Student leaders and secretaries (for each three-week period) are chosen by a written-ballot election by students.

*Courtesy of Robert Smith and George Hess, The Children's School, Northern Potter School District, Ulysses, Pa.

One way of approaching this need is through the use of teacher-student planning, a procedure that encourages the participation of students in the determination of curriculum plans (Waskin and Parrish, 1967). Teaching-learning situations consist of topics, themes or problems and related objectives, subject matter, activities, resources, and measuring devices. Each of these components represents an opportunity for students to be involved in curriculum planning. Whether certain objectives will be pursued by the whole group or particular individuals, whether to use certain materials and not others, whether to use paper-pencil tests or analyze student logs are all examples of curriculum decisions usually made by teachers alone, but which can be made by teachers and students together or, at times, by students alone. Furthermore, these kinds of decisions are powerful in the everyday lives of learners as they govern classroom life. As we begin to develop this method, our effort ought to aim toward higher degrees of student planning as evidence of internal locus of control. This technique will be discussed further in Chapter 4.

A second strategy for enhancing internal locus of control is to involve students in the wider governance of life in the school, such as the determination of rules that apply to all students (House, 1970). This might typically be done through the use of town meetings in which all students participate. On a bi-weekly or monthly basis, for example, students, teachers, and administrators may come together as a group to discuss and debate issues that affect life in the school. As a result of discussions, decisions may be made about the need for rules and regulations. Assuming that such meetings begin early in the year, the group may construct its own set of rules and, as time passes, revise them or delete those that are no longer necessary. Town meetings of this type may also take place in classrooms or in team-teaching situations. In addition to promoting a sense of self-governance, town meetings have the added advantage of enhancing development of moral reasoning (Reimer, 1981). Kohlberg (1975) and his associates use this as one aspect of their "just community" concept and have found that students in these settings evidence increasingly higher levels of moral reasoning.

In the case of both teacher-student planning and town meetings, the issues with which the students deal must be real and their roles legitimate. In this way, these approaches differ from others, such as the student council in which select groups of students often simply serve as an agreeable arm of school authorities. Real student involvement may be less expedient than authoritarian methods, but the potential for enhancing the sense of self-worth and internal locus of control is a compelling reason for its persistent use as a method of decision-making.

The Peer Group and the Self in School

"I don't like high school cliques—they are detrimental to individuality"—Female, Age 15

In many cases young people develop self-perceptions as a result of expectations of and interaction with peers. With young children, when peer feedback is unrealistic or negative, parents and other adults can help overcome it. As the child becomes an adolescent, however, the peer group or particular individuals within it can assume the "significant other" role. This phenomenon seems particularly likely if parent-adolescent conflict already exists. As a result, the values and self-perceptions of the individual may derive from constructive or destructive, pro- or anti-social sources. Thus the peer group context, particularly in transescence and adolescence, becomes a critical concern in the self-perception framework.

The relationship between the self and the peer group reaches special status in school since this institution represents the daily gathering place of youth. Pressure to perform adequately in the intellectual, social, and physical dimensions of schooling, and to do so in full view of peers, is a persistent and permeating feature of the school (Asch, 1956). Concerns about what to wear, with whom to associate, and how to "act" academically are brought to full force in the school. This context is further complicated by institutional behavior of some educators who insist upon competition among students in formal and informal situations. Statements such as, "Why can't you be like other students?" and "You wouldn't be accepted by the group" are certainly not unusual in adult-adolescent interaction. In addition, young people may be faced with peer pressure in areas of sexual behavior and use of alcohol and other drugs. All of this adds up to potential difficulty for the individual and how he or she perceives self. In light of the relationship among self-perception and other areas of growth and development, the interaction between the individual and the peer group is one that ought to receive careful attention from educators (Bradley and Newhouse, 1975; Zeichner, 1978).

The influences of the peer group on self-perceptions may take on special dimensions in particular circumstances. For example, Rosenberg (1979) points out that white children and black children both may have self-concepts of numerous dimensions of which race is only one. To the degree that the peer group influences the sense of self, however, it is possible that interaction between some white and black youth, or those of other racial and minority ethnic groups, might cause some individual difficulty. Learned racial and ethnic bias and stereotyping, when communicated to the minority individual or group, may result in questioning of self-concept and self-esteem (Proshansky and Newton, 1968). In his articulation of the needs theory, Raths (1972) pointed out that prejudiced, biased youth may well be so as an outgrowth of their own unmet self-concept needs. The connection between these two ideas illustrates how the self-perception problems of one group or individual may be related to those of another. This issue clearly reflects the need to study and enhance not only the self-perceptions of youth, but also the related interaction.

―――――――――――――――― Case 2.4 ――――――――――――――――

A School Exchange Program*

One way of offering students opportunities to expand their self-concepts is to promote interaction with peers who have different backgrounds and experiences. Realizing this, personnel at the rural Andover, New York, schools organized a student exchange program which brought students from the Harry S. Truman High School in New York City to Andover. The purpose of the exchange was to have two sets of students who live in very different locales compare their values through an interactive experience.

During the planning stages the rural students developed a questionnaire which elicited responses to political, social, economic, environmental and other issues. The questionnaire was completed by students, educators, and citizens in both communities. During the actual visit small groups were formed in which each group predicted the results and then discussed how the actual results compared to those predicted.

A second activity involved in the exchange was the writing and presentation of a play by students from each school depicting what they believed life was like in the other community. In both cases adults took a "hands off" stance. Because of the "vivid" portrayal of characters like prostitutes, muggers, dope peddlers and others, parents and other citizens were told that if they attended the plays they must remain afterward for discussion sessions on stereotyping of other people. The latter were carried out as serious discussions and the adults were surprised to see how capable the young people were of analyzing and interpreting the topic.

Other activities included presentations of slide shows by each group of its school and community, a dance, a picnic, and various local tours. Perhaps the most interesting part of the exchange, however, was that involved in the hosting of individual students from the city by their rural peers. A variety of issues emerged such as fear of impoverished youngsters to have guests see their home and reluctance to house students from racial and ethnic minorities. In the end these fears were overcome when the two groups had a chance to meet each other and see the fallacies of stereotyping.

This program had tremendous benefits for the students involved, as well as the community as a whole. Those from the city had a chance to experience first-hand life in a rural community and to meet people from that setting. Those from the rural community had a chance to meet urban students and to think about their own community as well as their ideas about other people. The establishment of friendships, correspondence and vacation visits serve as evidence that individuals from both groups underwent some degree of reorganization of their ideas, opinions and values. Perhaps the most telling incident from the visit occurred when one parent refused to have a student from a racial minority stay in his house. Upon hearing this a local couple in their 70s volunteered to house both the local host and the visitor. What better way could there be for adults to help young people to see the dangers of stereotyping and the value of accepting others as human beings regardless of who or what they are?

---

*Courtesy of Elmo Barden, Principal, Andover High School, Andover, New York.

One perspective on dealing with the issues of peer interaction and self-perceptions is that taken by Raths (1954, 1969) in his work on status systems in groups. Borrowing from the work of Lasswell (1948), Raths suggested that there are eight qualities that seem to be used by groups to grant status to individuals.

1. **Well-Being** (physical strength and endurance, capacity for work and play, contentment, etc.)

2. **Skills** (abilities and proficiencies that are valued by the group)

3. **Knowledge or Enlightenment** (being well-informed in areas about which the group is concerned)

4. **Influence** (being able to influence others and participate vigorously in decision-making)

5. Wealth (having resources that can be helpful to the group)
6. Rectitude (virtue and conscience; having clear values and morals)
7. Respect (having standing, being held in high regard by others)
8. Affection (acceptance, regard; being liked by others, being friends with others)

Since these dimensions represent characteristics upon which social acceptance is based, they may also be viewed as possible dimensions of self-concept. In other words, as the group prizes one or more dimensions and assigns status, individuals may also develop a sense of where they stand on any dimension (self-concept) and a sense of satisfaction or dissatisfaction (self-esteem).

The actual status systems may have been identified through the use of sociograms, direct status listings by students on each dimension, or by observations of how individuals are treated by the group. Once done, the teacher may plan a course of action, keeping in mind that the group itself establishes its own status system and only the group can change it. A teacher cannot actively intervene for a student. For example, telling students that "they ought not to treat Johnny that way" may have the group perceive the teacher as ignorant or not "with it." Rather, the teacher must construct environments in which all students have a chance to earn status. There are many ways in which this might be done by the teacher, including the following:

1. Provide a rich variety of experiences such as broad-based, multidisciplinary group projects that will be enhanced by the skills or resources that individual students may contribute.
2. Design special assignments that will allow out-of-school skills and hobbies to be demonstrated by individual students.
3. Encourage students to participate as peer tutors for other students in the school setting.

This matter of status is of obvious concern to those who wish to enhance self-perceptions. In addition, the place of status in the classroom has implications for effective teaching. The research already noted suggests that teachers who recognize the student status system and work with it tend to have higher morale in their groups than those teachers who are unaware of or violate the system.

Another method of helping young people clarify social self-concepts and enhance self-esteem decisions is to help them understand their peer group as a social system. Typically, the analysis of social systems is reserved for graduate study in the behavioral sciences; however, there seems to be no logical reason why this is so. One illustration of this method might be a unit in which a group undertakes a study of the school as a social system. Topics might include an analysis of student cliques, a study of socio-economic status as it relates to variables like school attitudes and behavior, or an analysis of the personality characteristics of student leaders. Through such study, young people might be helped to understand the context of peer behavior, the logic or illogic of social status, and their personal relationship to the social structure of their peers.

A third method involves the direct teaching of interpersonal skills. These may include the use and effect of various conversational responses such as freeing and binding responses, the nature and power of nonverbal communications, and methods of conflict resolution (Johnson, 1981). Students might then be given opportunities to exercise these skills in small-group work as leaders and nonleaders and to examine the nature of peer interaction both in and out of school. Further, these methods might also be used by teachers as models in carrying out various class discussions and decision-making situations. The power in this third technique is that it is based on the idea, noted in Chapter 1, that self-perceptions are influenced by others, particularly "significant others." We will suggest later that parents, as significant others, ought to learn constructive patterns of interaction to use with children. Here, however, recognition is given to the increasing significance of peers in the formulation of self-perceptions. Thus, rather than trying to intervene directly in self-perceptions, teachers and other adults need to work through the more "significant" peer group by enhancing the nature and quality of interaction among young people themselves.

Each of these methods, as well as others like them, is an attempt to enhance the quality of peer interactions and the peer-related perceptions young people have of themselves. They require, however, that teachers be interested in these issues and be willing to use small-group work through which actual interaction may be tried and analyzed. In addition, teachers must learn and teach methods of interpersonal communications, such as clarifying responses and group dynamics techniques. Perhaps as learner self-perceptions gain attention as a goal of educators, renewed efforts will be made to pursue these related teaching attitudes and skills.

_____ **Case 2.5** _____

Direct Teaching for Self-Image Improvement*

The concept of teaching leadership and coping skills is an integral part of the success of Greenacres Junior High School. Since 1974 this philosophy has determined the direction of positive image building in the classroom and interpersonal relationships.

The program that was developed in 1974 was aimed at improving the leadership skills of those involved in the student council. This involved a two-day leadership conference held at a local camp. Participants attended sessions on parliamentary procedure, communications skills and problem solving. They also developed action plans with time lines.

Interested staff members were also involved in the planning, supervision and implementation of the plans. Upon evaluation of the leadership conference, it was decided that not only the leaders of the school could benefit from this but also students, staff and classified personnel. It had become increasingly evident that how people feel about themselves determines their effectiveness and leadership at school or on the job. Therefore, this added a new challenge and dimension to the overall program.

The next year the conference was moved to a local motel near the Greenacres Junior High School. All of the class representatives as well as the student council members attended. The program consisted of one day of the same leadership skills taught during the previous leadership conference and one day of activities to improve self-image. The latter was part of the new dimension being added to the conference. With the conference closer to the school it was also easier to involve a greater number of staff, so they too could become aware of the concepts.

In 1976 the Self-Image Concept was developed further. The Junior High School Principal, Assistant Principal and a consultant, with the school district's approval, worked together to develop an Image Conference that would include every student in the school, all certified staff and all classified staff. The program itself was also expanded and specialized for each grade level with each day's conference lasting from 8:30 A.M.-7:30 P.M.

The seventh-grade program consisted of the self-image concept and within this framework the following topics were addressed:

1. Developing a trust level
2. Positive image building
3. Responsibility and accountability
4. Perceptions

The eighth-grade program focused on communication skills, but they also received a review of the image concepts. Some of the communication skills that were explored were:

1. One way-two way communication
2. Listening exercises
3. "I" messages
4. Discovering feelings

The ninth-grade program reviewed the image concepts, but expanded into stress management. This was a new area but well received. Some of the major points covered in this session were:

1. What it is
2. How you can identify stress in your life
3. How it affects people
4. What you can do to prevent or cope with stress

Each school staff member attended one day of the conference to take part in the discussions. The benefits of this were twofold; everyone became aware of the concepts being taught, thus giving the students and teachers some common ground, and communication lines between the students and teachers were opened.

After the sessions were completed the students went back to Greenacres Junior High School where they were fed dinner. Following this was a series of rap sessions in which parents and students had the opportunity to share their frustrations and concerns. The final part of the evening included a dance for the students and a meeting of the parents with the consultant. In this meeting parents were given much of the same information given the students during their session. This also opened up communication lines between the students and parents through a common point of reference.

The benefits from the conferences seem to be very significant. It has opened up communication lines from student to student, student to staff, staff to parents and staff to staff. The fact that everyone experienced the conference and had the same reference point has been beneficial to all. Another factor that cannot be measured but is very important is the pride within the school. The students and staff are very proud of the programs and this pride carries over into school pride and self-pride. This becomes vital to the development of our positive school climate. This pride has also aided in the discipline procedures throughout our building. Two direct results of the conferences have been the development of a self-image class being offered as an elective to the ninth-grade class and a student council which now functions as an active council and carries the responsibility of teaching leadership skills.

---

*Courtesy of Glenna Smith, Greenacres Junior High School, Greenacres, Washington.

Enhancing Perceptions of Self as a Growing Person

"It would be boring to be eleven all your life"—Female,
Age 11

One common feature of schools is that young people attending them
are isolated from other age groups. Not only are they separated from
youth of other ages, they are also isolated from older persons, with
the exception of educators who are not necessarily representative of
the adult society-at-large.

The age graded, age-isolation of the schools is inappropriate in
light of the fact that one dimension of self-concept, the self as a growing developing person, is tied to perceptions about self at previous
and future ages. Inasmuch as this dimension seems common (Lipka,
Beane, and Ludewig, 1980), the age of isolation of youth may interfere with the clarifying possibilities that arise when one can observe
other people of different ages. The isolation of older from younger
youth seems to be based on the idea that different age groups, having
different characteristics, are not compatible and may even need to be
protected from each other. We believe that this is an unfair view of
older youth; the latter seem often to have highly altruistic views of
younger children, sensing a need to help, protect, and encourage
them. The view that such isolation flows naturally from the increasing
sophistication and sequence of curriculum plans seems equally unjustified when one considers the many nonacademic activities, and
the potential for more, in which such variables as interest supersede
age as a grouping variable.

The isolation of youth from adults other than educators arises
perhaps out of ideas that knowledge worth knowing is the exclusive
property of educators and that educators are necessarily "most"
qualified (by training) to work with young people. Both views are
highly questionable. In the first place, no teacher or group of teachers
could possibly be familiar with the breadth of developing knowledge
which youth may find of value in their lives. Second, many parents
and professionals from other youth-oriented agencies are experienced
and skilled in techniques for helping young people to learn and grow.

To overcome the disadvantages of age-isolation, those concerned
with enhancing this aspect of self-perceptions might well consider a
number of arrangements (e.g., Way, 1980). In the area of working
with "youngers," one classic idea is that of the multi-age tutorial

setting (Lippitt and Lippitt, 1968, 1970; Ehly and Larsen, 1980). Research on cross-age tutoring indicates that it is a highly effective way to help young people both academically and interpersonally, often in cases where teachers have not succeeded. Furthermore, this technique appears to offer these benefits to both tutor and tutee.

Another possible strategy is school sponsorship of a big-brother/sister program in which older youth take responsibility for working with an individual younger child in terms of academic, social, and physical skill development. Still another is use of direct child-study activities in the curriculum. These may include studying the growth and development of young children, conducting experiments with children such as those designed by Piaget, and undertaking theory-based systematic observations which can be done with children while baby-sitting. In all of these, teachers have the opportunity to help individuals analyze their own background through the use of discussions, family scrapbooks, personal time-lines, and genealogical studies. These activities may lead to broader questions about the contribution of past experiences to present self-perceptions, attitudes, and values. Perhaps if these kinds of activities were used, we might begin to understand Dewey's (1916) definition of education as "the reconstruction or reorganization of past experience which adds to the meaning of experience, and which increases ability to direct the course of subsequent experience."

Bringing together youth and elder persons is an idea that has received a good deal of attention recently as we have begun to understand the unfortunate stereotypes of old persons, which have characterized traditional thinking. One of the most promising methods for helping youth to enhance their self-perceptions as potential adults is to involve elders in the everyday life of the school. (Tice, 1979). This means that elders are encouraged to come to school to participate in learning activities, share hobbies with youth, converse over multi-age lunch tables, or simply discuss issues of mutual concern. By the same token, schools might encourage young people to participate in continuing education activities which a spectrum of adults may also attend. Like the direct activities with younger children, these might also be supplemented with curricular experiences through which youth study the process of aging, perceptions of aging, and the persistent needs, problems, interests, and concerns of adults. By these means, young people might be helped to clarify and enhance the perceptions they have of themselves as potential adults.

In addition to the understanding of self as a developing person, the activities described here for working with "olders" and "youngers" also offer another advantage to self-perceptions. Kelley (1962) points out that one characteristic of a self-actualized person is that "he sees his stake in others." Unfortunately, one of the emerging dimensions of our society is the emphasis placed on self-gratification, sometimes at the expense of others. By working with persons of other ages, young people may begin to see the importance of human interdependence and the need to be concerned with the social welfare. That people of different ages can work with each other in the area of self-perceptions is pointedly noted by Jersild (1952): "The little child knows what it is to have his feelings hurt, to be sad, to be disappointed, to feel the disapproval of others, and to feel disapproval of self, with much the same basic psychological meanings as are experienced by the postgraduate student." The sense of belonging and participation that may evolve from younger-older relationships is critical to the development of positive self-esteem; and to the extent that schools promote these through interaction with other age groups, they are thus making an important contribution to the self-perceptions of youth.

Self-Perceptions and School Achievement

"I don't feel good about myself when my grades are low"—Female, Age 15

Presumably the curriculum plans and day-to-day activities of the school are directed toward helping learners achieve various goals and objectives in all three domains of learning. The degree to which self-perceptions enter into school achievement has been the subject of a great deal of research in recent years. The weight of this evidence suggests that there is a persistent interaction between the two variables; self-perceptions influence school achievement and school achievement influences self-perceptions (Purkey, 1970). In other words, learners who have confidence in their ability to achieve tend to do better in school than those who lack confidence; likewise, learners who experience success in school tend to have more confidence in their ability to succeed than those who have not had success. Within the framework of this concept, however, it should be noted that positive self-perceptions as learner appear to be generally necessary, but not sufficient for school achievement (Purkey, 1970), since, regardless of self-perceptions, learners will probably not succeed if the objective, activity, or resources are far beyond their readiness level.

As noted earlier, young people describe their self-concept in school along a variety of dimensions, including self as engaged learner and self as academic achiever (Lipka, Beane, and Ludewig, 1980). Within these dimensions, learners further describe themselves in relation to specific situations such as class activities, subject or skill areas, and the like. Thus the multidimensional concept of self as different from the general sense of self occurs within the student role just as that role is one of many others (e.g., self as peer) in which self-perceptions are formulated (Brookover, Thomas, and Paterson, 1964).

The interaction between self-perceptions and achievement is illustrated in numerous studies. For example, Ludwig and Maehr (1967) constructed an experimental situation in which sixty-five male students, aged twelve to fourteen, were divided into three random groups. Each group was given either positive, negative, or no feedback about their performance on physical tasks from supposed "experts." As might be expected, those receiving positive feedback evidenced gains in physical self-concept and increased preference for physical activities, while the opposite was the case for those receiving negative feedback. In addition, the self-concept changes carried over into related areas, such as general physical fitness and skill, and persisted for up to three weeks. For those students for whom negative feedback was incongruent with their original self-concept as evidenced by pre-test scores, there was a quick recovery to the former self-concept later, but for those with originally poor self-concept scores who received positive feedback, the gain in self-concept persisted and even generalized to related areas.

In the research previously mentioned, Brookover, Thomas, and Paterson (1965) studied the relationship between self-concept of ability (in school) and academic achievement for 1,050 seventh graders. They found that there was a significant correlation between the two variables, even when IQ was controlled. While this pattern appears to hold up at all grade levels (Purkey, 1970), there appears to be a change in the pattern of self-perceptions across grades. For example, Morse (1964) found in one study that 84 percent of third graders reported that they were proud of their work in school, as opposed to only 53 percent of eleventh graders. Furthermore, Anderson (1978) found that the academic self-concept shifted between sixth and eighth grade from personal (criterion-referenced) evaluations to perceptions based on peer comparisons (normative).

Harris (1971) studied the development of academic self-concept in 110 seventh graders and 109 eleventh graders. Information gathered from the two groups indicated that academic self-concept involved three factors: how certain the individual is of his or her ability, how accurate the self-ability is perceived to be, and how optimistic or pessimistic the individual is toward his or her ability. In addition to finding that each of these was related to actual achievement, Harris also concluded that, with age, adolescents may learn to assimilate feedback such as success or lack of it on actual tasks, but do not learn to cope with factors such as teacher expectations or grouping patterns which make them feel unsure of themselves.

Recently the work of Bloom (1968, 1980) and others concerned with mastery learning has shown that as academic achievement is ensured and experienced, self-concept as learner improves. This work is consistent with other studies (e.g., Bailiffe, 1978), which have demonstrated the general principle that academic success leads to academic self-confidence. The idea that successful achievement enhances self-perceptions (while the lack of success has a negative influence) has tremendous implications for the sequence of school experiences. For those who have continuous success, the overall school experience offers an opportunity for persistent enhancement of self-perception as learner. For those who have continuous lack of success, the cumulative experience offers a debilitating series of events that may lead to serious skepticism about one's ability to succeed.

The obvious implication of the interaction between self-perceptions and school success is that educators must develop ways to move from expectation and acceptance of failure toward the development of techniques that ensure success. Achievement in school is tied to a variety of factors, such as teacher expectations, climate, parent support, and social acceptance, and the techniques suggested elsewhere in this chapter may enhance achievement as much as self-perceptions.

We would be remiss if we did not address the issue of class size here. For many years, research on the relationship between class size and various student outcomes has been judged inconclusive. With the recent introduction of summary statistical techniques, however, educators may now be fairly certain that movement to smaller classes is advantageous to students. Specifically, as class size decreases below twenty, one can expect increases in academic achievement and, more importantly, improvement in students' attitudes toward teachers, motivation, attitudes toward life, interest and enthusiasm for class-work, and peer group linkage (Glass and Smith, 1978: Smith and Glass, 1979).

That schools are still a long way from the transition to humanis-tic climate with regard to academic achievement is evidenced by the current trend toward retaining students in grades they "fail." How-ever, Jackson (1976) reviewed forty-four studies on the effects of promotion and retention of low-achieving students and concluded that there is no valid empirical basis to support retaining children who have academic or adjustment difficulties. We can only surmise that retention of students serves as a convenience to educators who are unwilling to accept individual differences among students and the individualized curriculum planning and teaching required to meet those differences.

In sum, self-perceptions and academic achievement seem to have a persistent relationship, and the former appear to be differentiated by activities, subjects, skills, and other school situations. To ignore the power of that relationship is to risk offering students a continually debilitating experience. To recognize and build on the relationship offers the opportunity to enhance not only self-perceptions, but school achievement as well.

Working with Parents

"My family does a lot of things together"—Female, Age 6

A popular belief among many educators is that the difficulties young people have in school are due to problems caused by parents and that those problems cannot be overcome. At one level, this assumption is unjust since schools often have features which themselves deter learn-ing. At another level, the assumption may be partly based in fact.

Parents have ideas regarding the value of schooling as well as ex-pectations about what and how their children will do in school. The fact is that parents tend to be the "most significant others" for children and, to some degree, for adolescents (Brookover, 1965; Rosenberg, 1979). Thus the feedback young people get from their parents about the nature and quality of their school work is a powerful influence in student self-perceptions. The extent of this power is illustrated by an experimental study by Brookover (1965) with forty-nine ninth-grade students who had achievement problems in school. For a period of nine months these students were divided into three groups. The first group worked with a counselor who played a positive and supportive role in evaluating the ongoing work of the group. The second group received continuous positive feedback from an outside "expert" (working with the study) about their work. The third group was given supportive feedback through their parents who, working with the researcher, developed improved expectations and feedback techniques for interacting with their children about school. The strength of parental influence was demonstrated by the finding that the first two groups had about the same level of improvement, while the third showed considerably more growth in their self-concepts as learners and in school achievement.

It is clear that if educators are truly concerned with enhancing the self-perceptions of young people, they must develop improved means for enhancing the expectations parents have for their children and the quality of parent-child interaction. One increasingly popular means of doing this is through so-called "parenting" workshops in which the school sponsors a series of meetings aimed at improving parent skills. Unfortunately some of these discussions focus only on helping children with schoolwork, concentrating on the parents' role in punctual homework, observance of rules, and other institutional expediencies. More attention ought to be paid to topics and skills such as interpersonal communciation, family field trips, unusual games or crafts that can be done cooperatively, and, of course, direct discussion of the kinds of parent expectations and feedback that help rather than hinder self-perceptions.

Another variation is to provide guided observation programs (Guttman, 1978) in which educators cooperate with parents in observing and analyzing the child's behavior in school. A third possibility involves the formation of child study groups consisting of parents with children of similar ages, who meet to discuss common problems, successful parenting techniques, and other mutual concerns. Such groups might be sponsored by the school, through a parent-teacher group, but ought to meet in homes, be led by parents, use available community resources on child development, and frequently involve interaction with children.

A second general strategy evolves through improved use of individual parent conferences. While this technique has been used for many years, especially in elementary schools, it has often presented problems. One concern is that the teachers' comments may reflect only academic work and often in comparison to how others are doing. Another problem is that the teachers may not take the time to find out what the parents' expectations are and thus the teacher may inadvertently provide information that reinforces negative parent evaluations. For example, the teacher says to the parents, "Your child is doing all right in reading, but is doing very well in social relations." This comment may be interpreted through parent expectations to actually be saying, "Your child is not doing as well as she can in school because she spends too much time socializing with other students."

To overcome these problems, such conferences ought to involve the parents, the teacher, and the student, focus on what the learner has done in terms of his or her own development, and concentrate on clear and accurate descriptions of actual work or behavior. In this way the teacher can be sure that both the parents and child get the same interpretation of the conference, and may then further discuss with both their expectations for school. Where problems are encountered, the teacher may help plan responsibilities that all three parties will undertake in helping to overcome them.

A third general strategy builds on the twofold idea that success enhances self-perceptions and that parents can be powerful advocates in school learning. A good deal of evidence suggests that school achievement is greatly enhanced for children from "teaching homes," homes in which the parents make an attempt to actually supplement the teaching of the school by asking questions and providing clear explanations (e.g., Hess and Shipman, 1965, 1968). That so many educators direct parents not to help their children with homework or other assignments seems rather strange in light of the "teaching home" concept. A more sensible course of action would appear to involve attempts by the school to get parents involved in teaching their children. Cooperative planning sessions, for example, could initiate instances of "homework" or home projects which call for parents and children to work together to solve problems, find information, or discuss issues. Specific examples might include developing "family trees," developing a neighborhood map based on metric measurement, recording home energy use, conducting home fire drills, and the like.

While these and similar methods may enhance student self-perceptions and learning, the contemporary school faces a more particular issue with some learners. As the rates of separation, divorce, and subsequent single-parent homes increase in our society, some children may face unusual problems in self-concept and esteem. The loss of a parent for whatever reason may cause youngsters to have feelings of deprivation, guilt, or rejection (Rosenberg, 1965). Others may face rejection by peers whose parents cannot accept newer patterns of family structure. Still others may feel confused by school topics, activities, and materials such as those focusing on Mother's or Father's Day, the nuclear conventional family, and other aspects of traditional family living. This problem may be further compounded by teacher bias toward youngsters from nontraditional homes. For example, Santrock and Tracey (1978) showed thirty teachers a video-tape of an eight-year-old child interacting with peers. Prior to viewing, half the teachers were told he was from an intact, two-parent home, while the other half of the teachers were told he was from a divorced home. When asked to rate the child on a behavior checklist after the viewing, those who were told he was from a divorced home rated him more negatively in terms of happiness, emotional adjustment, and ability to cope with stress.

To avoid becoming a debilitating factor in the self-perceptions of young people from nonconventional families, educators need to become more sensitive to learners' individual needs and feelings. Curriculum plans, including materials, activities, and home assignments, need to be carefully examined to be sure that they recognize diverse family patterns and that school personnel are not a secondary source of confused or negative feelings about self.

With the increasing emphasis on parent's roles and responsibilities in learning, growth, and development, educators will undoubtedly discover many new and exciting ways to work with them. What we as educators must keep in mind is that we do not shed our use of instructional/teaching techniques when we leave the classroom. Working with and teaching parents requires the same careful, thorough planning we devote to the teaching of their offspring. The basic enhancing strategies discussed throughout this book must be kept in focus when we interact with parents. The power parents have in developing their children's self-perceptions suggests that those concerned with the latter ought to pay careful attention to the emerging ideas in this field.

Dropping Out and Staying In

"I don't like school—I've been in school too long"—Female, Age 16

Most states require attendance in school up to age sixteen or seventeen. This means that up to that age the formal education of young people is ultimately the prerogative of their teachers since the students cannot leave school even if they want to. However, once the compulsory age is reached, many adolescents choose to physically drop out of school. Of those who remain, many continue to attend school even though they have mentally dropped out (Kelley, 1963). One can only wonder how many young people would physically leave school before the compulsory attendance age if they were allowed to and how many remain beyond the age simply because they feel that, having gone that far, they might as well stay on until graduation. These two patterns of behavior are consistent with the symptoms of frustration inasmuch as one represents withdrawal while the other represents submission. In other words, both kinds of dropouts appear to be indicating that school is, in their perception, not a personally worthwhile experience.

Figure 2.1 illustrates a matrix that might be used to think about the relationship between self-concept and school attendance where the latter is a choice. By using the matrix, one can describe four different cases involving that relationship. In each case, the critical factor is the self-concept as it relates to the issues of self-fulfillment in adolescence (described in Chapter 1 and this chapter). For example, self-concept dimensions might revolve around relationship with peers,

Figure 2.1
Self-Concept and School Attendance by Choice

	Stay-In	Drop-Out
Clear Self-Concept	Case 1	Case 3
Unclear Self-Concept	Case 2	Case 4

immediate and long-range personal plans, perceived personal strengths and weaknesses, interests, values, and so on.

Case 1

Many adolescents have developed a clear and realistic self-concept. They have a sense of clearly defined interests and values and have made plans for themselves for the future. Furthermore, they may feel that the school supports both their present self-concept and their future plans. These young people view the school as a valuable experience that offers an opportunity to maintain self-perceptions and to get them where they want to go. For example, an individual of this type might consistently experience success in school, enjoy the kind of learning the school promotes, and see learning and success as steps toward higher education. For this person, the self-concept is congruent with the school's expectations and values, and staying in school is a worthwhile thing to do.

On the other hand, some students may have a similarly clear self-concept, including a sense of future plans, and stay enrolled even though the self-concept is not congruent with the values of the school. For example, an individual may plan to pursue some course of action, such as a job, that requires a high school diploma. Another may view the school as an opportunity to be with peers or to engage in some specific activity such as a sport or club. For these individuals, school represents a necessary, but not sufficient, activity to meet personal needs. On this basis they may choose to stay in school, usually submitting to various rules and regulations, although perceiving little value in most of them. Should the school, for some reason, eventually fail to allow these individuals to meet their specific needs, these students may choose to drop out.

Case 2

Some adolescents have great difficulty resolving the issues involved in the adolescent identity crisis. Their self-concepts are confused inasmuch as they are unclear about their interests, values, personal strengths and weaknesses, and plans for the future. They may also sense that there is no real place for them as yet in the world outside the school as they are unsure about who they are and what they want to do.

These individuals might also perceive accurately that the school is the one place that society generally perceives as an acceptable place for adolescents to be./For them, the school is a kind of haven in which they receive less criticism than they would as school drop-outs in the outside world. Furthermore, these young people may submit to the institutional features and curriculum plans of the school in order to maintain the security that the school offers them. They may simply do what they are told, despite seeing little personal meaning in the school, since they have not yet identified a clear self-concept that would provide a context for finding real meaning in virtually any activity.

The critical issue here is whether the school or some other experience will help these adolescents formulate a clear self-concept. If not, these individuals are likely to continue in both their confusion and their submission throughout school and perhaps even beyond it. On the other hand, they may eventually fail in school activities or sense that school is not helping them resolve their identity crisis, and therefore choose to drop out.

Case 3

As was mentioned in Case 1, some young people do resolve identity issues and, in the process of doing so, also develop clear and realistic self-concepts with regard to values, plans, and the like. For some of these individuals, however, school is not perceived as a supportive or enhancing experience. These adolescents might then choose to physically drop out of school in favor of some other environment or activity which they believe will more likely lead to self-fulfillment. Individuals who fit this case might desire full-time jobs, travel, nontraditional education progams, or other life patterns or styles. A common societal perception of school drop-outs is that they do not feel very good about themselves. This might be the case with some, particularly on the dimension of self-concept as learner, but the activities cited above may often be chosen by young people who feel capable, independent and confident. This includes some who have not done well in school and see no point in finishing, as well as others who have done well academically and socially. In both cases, individuals know who they are and what they want. The point is that they simply do not see the school as the most desirable or significant alternative available for them.

It is true that some of these young people return to school later to complete their formal education; however, doing so is not always convenient because many states prohibit adult participation in daytime school programs. Recent proposals (Shane, 1973) for removing continuous attendance requirements as well as age barriers may make the case of dropping out more common in the future. In any event, school officials must recognize that some young people who choose to drop out of school are doing so for what they perceive to be personally positive reasons, and that these young people may be quite capable of functioning outside the school. In fact, we might do well to encourage some adolescents to leave school if they clearly have plans for themselves and if the school is not capable of supporting those plans. Kelley (1963) put the case for these young people in cogent terms:

> The adult reaction to the young people who cannot become involved in what we have decided they should care about is usually blameful. "If they were any good they would like what I've planned for them." We reward the ones who can and are willing to do what we want and punish those who will not (cannot). Thus while these drop-outs continue to stay in school, their concepts of self continue to take a beating, so that it is possible that they are actually less able for having stayed.

Case 4

Just as some adolescents with clear and accurate self-concepts drop out of school, others who are confused and unrealistic about themselves do so also. Individuals in this case do not have a defined sense of personal interests, values, or plans, and as such they cannot make decisions about school as a viable option in their lives. Once outside the school, these young people may face severe criticism for dropping out and, with no clear sense of purpose, be at a loss for defending themselves. They likely face unemployment or, at best, unsatisfactory employment, and they perhaps become susceptible to negative influences or anti-social behavior standards.

If there is any group about which educators ought to be particularly concerned it is this one, for the simple reason that having left school, feeling confused and unsure about themselves, these young people have left both the protection of the school and the possibility for resolving identity issues with the school's help. In this case it seems logical to suggest that school officials ought to establish some means for keeping in touch with these types of drop-outs and offer continuous opportunities for support or assistance. This might be done through peer counseling services or established contacts with other youth agencies in the local community. Even if drop-outs take advantage of these services they still may not return to school, but at least the school would have assumed its specific responsibility for providing help and support to young people.

The four cases discussed here are not intended to represent a comprehensive treatment of the drop out issue; rather, they serve to illustrate the relationship between self-concept and continuing participation in school. Studies have indicated that school drop-outs tend to have more negative self-esteem as learners than those who stay in school, and that these feelings are a result of cumulative school failure which often begins early in the elementary school (Bloom, 1977). However, self-concept and self-esteem as learner represent only one dimension of self-perceptions. In other words, some young people may physically drop out of school because they believe they cannot succeed within it, but others may leave for entirely different reasons. The latter may perceive that the school does not represent a self-enhancing experience and that other alternatives appear to be more desirable. Further, some young people may physically remain in school, but mentally drop out in terms of submitting to the institutional features and curriculum plans of the school.

That the school has an obligation to enhance self-perceptions should by now be obvious. The fact is that this responsibility is larger than that of regulating attendance; since self-perceptions represent a personal dimension that will outlast the requirements of formal schooling. It seems logical that the school would maintain community contacts with potential employers and youth agencies, as well as in-school counseling services that provide a smooth transition for those who do choose to drop out of school before completion. For example, the type of school and community contact that has historically characterized vocational work-study programs should be extended into contacts for other youth not in vocational programs.

Finally, it is important to remember that clear and positive self-perceptions do not necessarily preclude the possibility of dropping out of school. In the end, the school must do what it can to enhance self-perceptions so that those young people who choose to stay in school will see personal meaning and worth in their school experience, while those who do drop out will do so with a clear sense of who they are and what they want to do.

Teacher Self-Esteem

"I think teachers are people too"—Female, Age 17

While the basic concern of this book is with enhancing the self-perceptions of learners, a related and important issue is the idea of enhancing the self-concept and self-esteem of teachers. Evidence (Jersild, 1952; Combs and Soper, 1963; Walberg, 1968; Linden and Linden, 1969; Fuller, 1969; Combs, 1969) indicates that those teachers with the clearest and most positive sense of self, based on quality professional ideas, are in the best position to facilitate learner self-perceptions. Thus it might be expected that such teachers would develop the kind of classroom learning environment most conducive to clear and positive self-perception development by young people.

The consideration of teacher self-perceptions is also important because of their apparent relationship to the phenomenon of teacher stress or "burn-out." Underlying these feelings of frustration are many factors such as unrealistic expectations of teachers on the part of society, public dissatisfaction with the quality of teaching and teacher competence, threats to job security brought about by financial cutbacks, limitations on support for classroom experimentation, and a general feeling that the job of teaching is overwhelming and unappreciated (Perry, 1976; Macdonald, 1977; Gallup, 1978; Morris, 1978).

In a sense, then, many teachers are faced with ongoing sources of dissonance with regard to the occupational or professional dimensions of self-concept. While the teaching profession is portrayed in teacher education and much of the professional literature as dynamic, rewarding, and of critical importance, the everyday life of many teachers offers a less positive picture (Day, 1959; Rabinowitz and Rosenbaum, 1960; Hoy, 1968; Lagana, 1970; Lipka, 1976). In order to understand the possible consequences of this dissonance, one needs to look first at the dynamics of teacher self-perceptions in light of the general theory of self.

Teachers, like other people, have a variety of dimensions within the overall self-concept. These may include not only the professional role, but those relating to family, friends, community activities, recreational pursuits, and others. While the power of teaching as a priority in the hierarchy of dimensions is unknown, we can speculate that it is probably of higher order since it involves the career commitment the individual teacher has made, as well as other ongoing factors such as source of income, definition of community role, and major time commitment (Lortie, 1975).

Within the teaching role dimension of self-concept, we might also expect teachers to have a variety of related self-perceptions. These might include ideas about self regarding relationships to students, other teachers and administrators, as well as competence in terms of teaching skill (Lipka, 1976; Lipka and Goulet, 1981).

We know also that students and, to a lesser degree, professional colleagues are "significant others" in the lives of teachers; hence their feedback would be a crucial element in the individual teacher's professional self-feelings (Lipka, 1976; Lortie, 1975). Thus teacher self-concept may be viewed as embedded in or related to the theoretical dimensions of the teaching profession, the ongoing life of the school as an institution, and the role expectations and feedback of those with whom the teacher works (Dreeben, 1970; Lortie, 1975; Lipka, 1976).

We have already mentioned the gap between professional ideals and everyday institutional life as a source of frustration. Another concern is the possible variation in role expectations and feedback. Students, for example, might expect the teacher to have a friendly, positive personality (Lipka, Beane, and Ludewig, 1980), while the principal might emphasize the role of the teacher as an authoritarian disciplinarian. The school board may emphasize the teacher's role in cognitive development of learners, while some parents may expect the teacher to stress social learning. Faced with this variation in expectations, the teacher is vulnerable to criticism by one or another group, regardless of what action he or she takes. As a result of this conflict, the teacher may experience a sense of value-confusion or may choose to value one particular kind of expectation. In either case, teacher self-esteem is also threatened unless he or she is particularly confident of professional values chosen.

Underlying all of this is the fact that teaching is a difficult job. The teacher must make literally hundreds of decisions each day (Harnack, 1968; Jackson, 1969) and those decisions may or may not be effective in terms of student learning. Furthermore, accurate feedback about the effectiveness of teaching may require time-consuming and sophisticated measuring devices and may not be clear until years after students leave the school.

In sum, the self-concept and self-esteem of teachers is a complex subject, open to much speculation and vulnerable to many sources of dissonance. Because of their relationship to student self-perceptions, those of the teacher are certainly in need of attention. What will it take to ensure that teachers feel comfortable, competent, and confident in their profession and in working with young people? Perhaps the answer to this question can be found by outlining some possible techniques for enhancing teacher self-perceptions.

One of the characteristics of many new teachers is that they expect to experience a high degree of professional interaction with colleagues (Lortie, 1965; Dreeben, 1970; Lipka, 1976). However, they find in all too many cases that they are cut off from colleagues by scheduling and separated room arrangements. This kind of isolation prevents cooperative efforts by teachers to analyze and solve instructional problems. One way of overcoming this is to promote professional interaction and cooperative planning by arranging schedules and assignments in such a way that teachers have access to one another. One promising variation is the practice of interdisciplinary team planning in which teachers responsible for a common group of students plan and often teach together. In many cases, such teams have responsibility for scheduling, grouping, meeting with parents, and other instructional arrangements. At the elementary level, teachers of the same grade may arrange a similar "teaming" situation. Team planning, particularly where teachers make the type of comprehensive decisions just mentioned, provide teachers with an opportunity to work together, control many aspects of instruction typically reserved for administrators, and develop a broad view of the educational program. In this sense, team arrangements may enhance the feelings of participation and control congruent with the idea of self as a professional educator.

Another way of enhancing teacher self-perceptions is to clarify the role expectations of the teacher. Many schools maintain professional standards committees that pay continuing attention to the state of the profession on a local level. Such groups need to address the expectations held by others for teachers and, where necessary, educate appropriate groups about the complex nature of teaching. A consequence of this considered action should also be the development of a clear statement about reasonable and realistic expectations, as well as the working conditions under which these expectations might best be met. For example, teachers have a right to promote smaller class size since recent research (Smith and Glass, 1979) shows that "in smaller classes, their [teachers'] morale is better; they like their pupils better, have time to plan, diversify; are more satisfied with their performance" (p. 46).

A third technique for enhancing teacher self-perceptions involves placing greater emphasis on worthwhile professional growth activities. It is perhaps a sign of the times that so many school districts spend more on interscholastic football than professional advancement. We believe that professional self-concept and self-esteem are most likely to develop in a professionally supportive environment. The latter may be characterized by opportunities for cooperative curriculum planning, curriculum experimentation, attendance at professional meetings, and teacher participation in all levels of school decision-making. A worthwhile goal might be the opportunity for every teacher to participate in at least one of these areas each year.

Another tact would be for those in higher education to intensify their efforts with teachers when they graduate and assume their first teaching position. Perhaps the signing of the first teaching contract should be accompanied by immediate involvement in a long-term inservice education partnership with university personnel such as those described by Lipka and Jones (1973) and Stoltenberg (1981).

While these and other techniques for enhancing teacher perceptions seem likely to help professionals overcome "burn-out," there remains one other area of possible action. It is conceivable that for some the best form of assistance is a temporary or permanent leave from teaching. No doubt many teachers would find personal and professional renewal in a new assignment at a different level, or a leave of absence or sabbatical to pursue some other areas of interest. Regardless of original intentions, others may have reached a point where teaching is simply no longer a worthwhile commitment. In these cases, schools ought to provide or support assistance in seeking another career.

The emphasis here has been placed on the professional dimension of teacher self-concept. Certainly personal and social problems press on teachers and may be a source of self-concept confusion or negative self-esteem which affects professional feelings. While beyond the scope of this book, these needs require attention and must be a concern of the profession. In any event, much of what can be done to enhance professional self-perceptions can be done by helping teachers clarify their roles and providing a professional atmosphere in the schools. To the extent that teacher self-perceptions may influence those of students, the argument in support of helping teachers is a compelling one.

Summary

The self-perceptions of young people may be influenced by virtually any situation they encounter. Since school plays a major role in the lives of youth, it stands to reason that experiences in and related to school play an important role in self-perceptions. This chapter has involved an examination of how various aspects of life in school affect self-concept, self-esteem, and values.

The analysis was based on the idea that the school is an institution and thus has various institutional features that permeate everyday living within it. These include climate, grouping, decision-making systems, reward/punishment structures, and others. Each may be arranged in ways that may hinder or enhance self-perceptions. Among the former are custodial climate, homogeneous grouping by ability, tracking systems, punitive discipline systems, authoritarian decision making, competitive reward structures, lack of opportunities for interaction, age-isolation, expectation of student failure, lack of parent education, and negative teacher self-perceptions.

In order to enhance learner self-perceptions, institutional features must be thoughtfully planned and should include several characteristics. Among these are the following:

1. Development of a humanistic climate based on democratic principles, personalness, respect for individual dignity, and the like.
2. Grouping based on a variety of variables related to the multi-dimensional structure of self-concept.
3. Emphasis on internal locus of control developed through participatory decision-making procedures like teacher-pupil planning and town meetings.
4. Recognition of peers as "significant others," attempts to help individuals to achieve status in the group, and activities aimed at enhancing the nature and quality of peer interaction.

5. Development of opportunities to enhance self-perceptions as a developing person through interaction with younger and older individuals.

6. Development of expectations that learners can succeed, as well as procedures to enhance their chances for actually doing so.

7. Opportunities for parent involvement in learning through arrangements such as parent workshops, cooperative conferencing, and promotion of the "teaching" home.

8. Efforts to enhance teacher self-perceptions through opportunities for professional interaction, decentralized decision-making, encouragement of experimentation, and clarification of the teacher's responsibilities.

The fact that the school is an institution does not mean that it cannot be structured in such a way that it is likely to enhance self-perceptions of learners. In the end, however, the latter may be most influenced by the curriculum organization and plans that guide the learning experiences students have under the auspices of the school. With this in mind, we now turn to a consideration of curriculum planning to enhance self-perceptions.

3

Curriculum Planning to Enhance Self-Perceptions

In this chapter, we will discuss the form that curriculum planning might take if it is directed toward enhancing self-perceptions. The chapter is divided into two parts, each of which represents a different level of curriculum planning.

Part I involves a discussion of what might be considered the antecedents or foundations of curriculum planning and how these relate to self-perceptions. This includes curriculum theory, development of goals, learning principles, curricular approaches, and other topics.

Part II deals with the enhancement of self-perceptions through curriculum planning for specific teaching-learning situations. Here we will consider selection of organizing centers, objectives, content, activities, and measuring devices.

By this organization, then, we will proceed from general ideas about the curriculum to identifying ideas for use in actual learning situations.

Part I
Curriculum Planning
———————— and Self-Perceptions ————————

Self-perceptions, including the self-concept, self-esteem, and values dimensions, are learned from experiences, or the interaction between the individual and the environment. For young people, school represents both an important environment and a continuing source of experiences (e.g., Macdonald, 1974). For this reason, self-perceptions are an appropriate concern for curriculum planning. Put another way, curriculum planning ought to include consideration of opportunities to enhance self-perceptions.

The word *curriculum* has been used in several ways. One is to define a "structured series of intended learning outcomes" (e.g., Johnson, 1967). Another is to refer to the planned program or activities which presumably lead to learning on the part of students (e.g., Krug, 1957; Smith, Stanley, and Shores, 1957; Phenix, 1958; Taba, 1962; Wilhelms, 1962; Emans, 1966; Saylor and Alexander, 1966). A third is to describe the experiences of learners under the auspices or the guidance of the school (e.g., Anderson, 1965; Oliver, 1965; Harnack, 1968; Gwynn and Chase, 1969; Doll, 1978). The definitions involve more than mere semantic differences inasmuch as they actually reveal theoretical positions about the nature of learning, the value indicators of educators, and the relationship between learners and school plans. If young people in schools learned all or some portion of what is intended for them and if this was essentially all that they learned, then the first and second definitions would suffice to explain curriculum. However, young people do not learn only what is intended, nor is their learning necessarily congruent with what is taught.

Suppose, for example, that Teacher A completes a one-session overview of the War of 1812 and finds that ten minutes are left in the class period. At this point, Teacher A asks for student reactions to a recent wave of vandalism in the community, and an exciting, though short, discussion ensues in which most students participate. For some learners the facts of the War of 1812 may be quickly forgotten while the learning for that day may be centered in the discussion on vandalism.

Suppose that Teacher B sets out to teach students that "good and responsible" parenting requires that both parents be present in the home. Teacher B builds a logical case by describing a scenario of family activities during holidays, vacations, and various moments of family crisis. However, several students live in one-parent homes in which there is a high degree of parent-child respect. Their view of Teacher B's argument is that it not only has faulty logic, but is simply not true. Their learning about family patterns has already taken place, and Teacher B has little or no effect on their perceptions.

The important point of these two illustrations is that what young people learn in school is largely dependent on their perceptions of what is personally important and meaningful, as well as their perceptions of the world around them. What they learn in school is what they perceive to have learned or what actually becomes a part of themselves, and this may or may not be congruent with what the school intended them to learn. In light of this, if curriculum refers to what is learned, the third definition of curriculum appears closest to the mark: the actual experiences of the learners under the auspices or guidance of the school. This definition recognizes that learning may take place in any school situation—in the classroom, on the school bus, in the cafeteria, on the playground, and so on. Furthermore, it takes account of the fact that learning belongs ultimately to the learner and that the school can only supply conditions under which desired learning will most likely take place. It also accounts for the evolving idea of the "hidden curriculum" which recognizes that what is learned from rules and regulations, teacher expectations, school values, and other institutional features is at least as powerful as what is learned from the planned or "visible" program of the school (Snyder, 1973; Jackson, 1969; Overly, 1970; Giroux, 1978). Finally, in clarifying the explicit role of the learner in learning as well as the more subtle role of the "hidden curriculum," this definition includes a recognition of self-perceptions in both the process and outcomes of education.

In the context of "curriculum" as the experiences of the learner, curriculum planning may be defined as the clarification of educational purposes and the subsequent identification of the conditions, circumstances, and situations under which those purposes are most likely to be accomplished. Figure 3.1 shows the components of a framework for curriculum planning. Some curriculum theorists may find disagreement with this framework, but it nonetheless includes the basic components which many agree need to be considered in comprehensive curriculum planning (e.g., Krug, 1957; Macdonald,

Figure 3.1
A Framework for Curriculum Planning

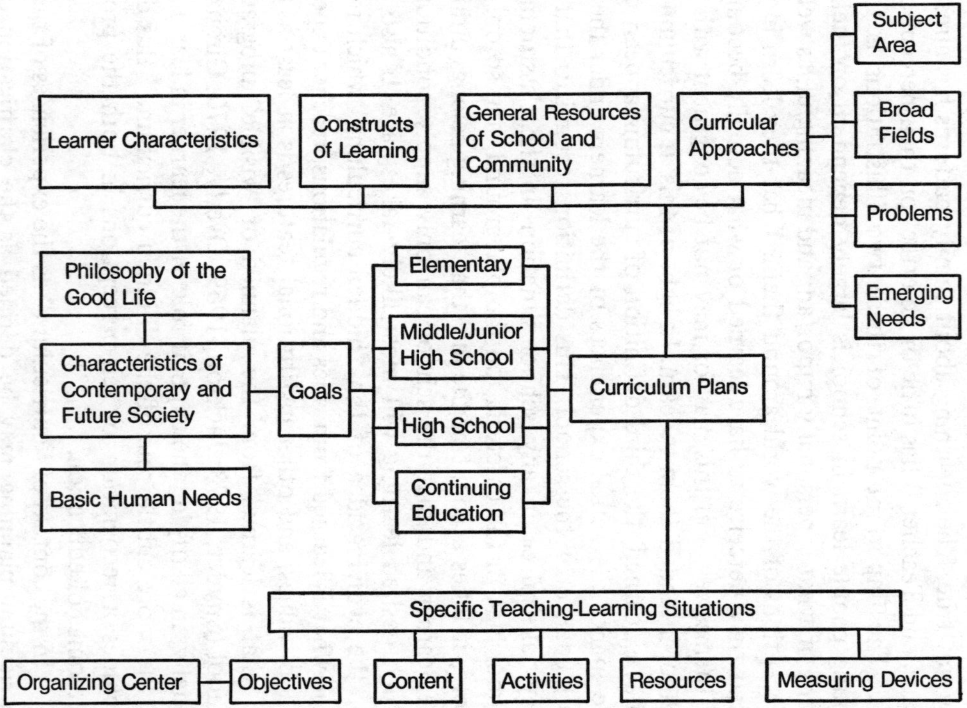

This framework is adapted from Herrick (MacDonald, Anderson, and May, 1965), Krug (1957), and Harnack (1968).

Anderson, and May, 1965; Harnack, 1968; Doll, 1978). While this framework seems to imply that curriculum planning is a linear process, such is not the intention. The framework simply points out the various components that need attention and may be used to guide curriculum planning or analysis. For example, the decision to use certain types of instructional activities at the specific teaching-learning level most likely ought to grow out of their connection to proposed goals for the total school-related educational program. On the other hand, the absence of some type of specific objectives, such as those related to the affective domain, might more logically be questioned if the overall goals imply that affective growth and development are to be a part of the program.

Using the curriculum planning framework, then, the remainder of this chapter will be devoted to a description of how each component might be considered when curriculum planning is directed at enhancing the self-perceptions of learners.

Self-Perceptions and the Good Life

"My biggest dream is to become a professional song-writer—it would make me happy"—Female, Age 14

Educational experiences ought to aim in the direction of helping people lead good lives in both the present and the future. The "good" life may be defined as one which the individual feels to be satisfying and productive. The educational process of the school requires careful attention with regard to whether it is helping learners move toward happy lives.

A good life in our society is not necessarily based on the quantity of goods or materials one assembles. Much more important is the quality of life that an individual experiences in terms of satisfaction with self and relationships with other people (Rogers, 1972). While we may oppose the inequitable distribution of wealth, it appears nonetheless true that many people who are materially poor feel good about themselves while others materially rich lead personally unsatisfying lives. Definitions of the good life may thus be diverse with regard to material content, but consistent in the view that such a life is rooted in an accurate, accepting, and positive view of one's self.

CURRICULUM PLANNING TO ENHANCE SELF-PERCEPTIONS

Kelley (1962) suggests that the person who leads the "good life" might be described as a "fully functioning person." He characterizes the fully functioning person as one who:

1. Thinks well of himself
2. Thinks well of others
3. Sees his stake in others
4. Sees himself as a part of a world in movement
5. Sees the value of mistakes
6. Develops and holds human values
7. Knows no other way to live except in keeping with his values
8. Is cast in a creative role.

This conception of what it means to live the good life has tremendous implications for education and schooling. Much of what goes on in school is aimed at getting ahead, getting a job, and getting into a position of economic security; so much that these aims may become the definition of the good life we portray to young people. Suppose, however, that getting ahead is done at the expense of others, that the job one gets is unsatisfactory, or that striving for economic security hampers the quality of one's relationships with others. In other words, it is possible that the concept of the good life that guides some curriculum planning might grow out of a quantitative rather than qualitative definition. Schooling and education have long been viewed as a means to economic and social improvement and to some extent they are. However, in too many cases this goal has received a disproportionate amount of emphasis. Where this has occurred, too little attention has been paid to how young people view themselves and the quality of their relationships with others. Because this imbalance represents a distorted view of the good life, it should be reorganized in such a way that self-perceptions receive the higher degree of attention that their importance requires.

Society and Self-Perceptions

"I usually watch TV instead of doing my homework"—Male, Age 8

Since self-perceptions are largely a function of environment, those concerned with their enhancement need to be particularly sensitive to the situations in contemporary living that might influence how young people view themselves. Such analysis must focus not only on suggestions that are made with regard to self-concept, but also on the kinds of value bases that might influence self-esteem judgments. At the present time, a number of factors are worthy of our attention in terms of young persons' self-perceptions.

One factor that immediately comes to mind is the nature of commercial media. Studies of television viewing patterns indicate that young people watch television for up to thirty-four hours per week (Winn, 1977). Furthermore, the most popular programs tend to be situation "comedies" and "thrillers," which often present an unrealistic view of life, suggest that physical attractiveness should be a preoccupying issue, and propose value bases that are highly simplistic. As a part of such programming, young people are also subjected to commercials, which even further press the importance of physical attractiveness to a variety of life activities as well as stress conformity and hedonism. If the number of viewing hours is at all connected to a perception of importance, we may well wonder whether the television has become a "significant other" in the lives of young people. If this is the case, then educators need also to worry about whether young people are constructing self-concepts and/or self-esteem judgments on the basis of television content. The analysis of television's impact on self-perceptions might well follow James' (1890) idea that self-esteem is represented by the gap between the ideal self and the actual self. In other words, it is possible that the content of television programming is introducing ideas about the ideal self that are rooted in fantasy rather than reality. Thus the gap between the perceived actual self and the ideal self becomes wider than it might be otherwise. Under these conditions, an individual could be expected to experience negative self-esteem.

A second issue is the conflict arising over the changes in family structure during the past decade. Rosenburg (1965) studied 5,024 adolescents with regard to various self-image issues. Among his findings was the idea that most young persons whose family structure undergoes change from a two-parent to a one-parent home seem to have serious self-perception difficulties. Goodwin and Beane (1978) reported a study of fifth and eighth graders from both conventional (both natural parents present) and nonconventional homes (single-parent homes, foster homes, etc.). Data gathered in the study indicated that young people from unconventional homes evidenced significantly lower self-esteem than those from conventional homes. The authors speculated that, in school, youth from unconventional homes might be subjected to the kind of teacher bias reported by Santrock and Tracy (1978), such as belief that they tend to be anti-social, as well as curriculum bias in cases where the conventional family was portrayed as more desirable. In addition to these school findings, young people who live through a family change (e.g., divorce, death, separation, etc.) often experience feelings of guilt, fear, rejection, and loss. They may also be subjected to ridicule or rejection by neighbors, playmates, and others. In any event, the changes in family structure that characterize our times may be the source of self-perception problems for many young people, although it must be noted that for some the particular change may be bene-ficial (in cases where the "lost" parent was a negative influence).

A third major issue involves the complex network of futures facing our society (Toffler, 1971, 1981). Young people live in an environment that is both novel and ambiguous. Commitments, like material goods, are short-lived and the sense of self in the future may be uncertain at best. The traditional images of the ideal self may seem empty to a generation growing up in a world as awesome as ours, and the reluctance of young people to accept traditional self-concept descriptions as desirable may lead to severe conflict with adults.

Perhaps the most appropriate way in which to view the types of factors just described is to consider them as part of the out-of-school curriculum. Schubert (1981) suggests that educators need to develop a much fuller understanding of out-of-school curriculum, including its sources such as work or occupations, family, homes and communities, media, and peers. Noting that these and other factors have contributed to the "un-schooling of curriculum," he asserts that they must be studied in order to understand contempo-rary youth's perspective on the world.

An analysis of how contemporary life affects youth self-percep-tions could include many issues in addition to the three just described. The idea that such influence is being felt should not be taken lightly in view of the symptoms of confusion and frustration that young people are manifesting. Hardly a day goes by that one does not see in newspapers and popular magazines reports of increasing crime, drug use, alcoholism, and suicide among transescents and adolescents. These behaviors indicate that many young people feel a severe sense of inadequacy and seem to be searching for something to hang onto. One particularly interesting example of the latter is the dramatic increase in adolescent child-bearing. The fact that so many young parents are retaining custody of their children suggests that they perceive the unconditional love of infants as a source of self-worth—a factor that overcomes the frequent sanction by parents, peers, and others.

In sum, then, we may say that young people today are living in a time when the development of self-perceptions is a highly difficult process. Further, we might predict that as social issues continue their present complexity, self-perception difficulties will also continue. For educators this means that the idea of enhancing self-concept and self-esteem will not only be more difficult, but also more imperative. To ignore this need under present circumstances would not only be incomprehensible, but an invitation to a myriad of learning difficulties for the students with whom we work.

Human Needs and Self-Perceptions

"I want to get along with other people"—Male, Age 17

A third foundation for curriculum planning involves consideration of those needs that are basic and common for human beings in order that they may live healthy lives. Among such needs are several that are related to or grow out of self-perceptions. If such needs are not met, the individual may well be faced with a life of frustration, ill health, unhappiness, and even desperation.

Raths (1972) identified eight emotional needs which he hypothesized are common to virtually all people—young and old. These included the need for belonging, achievement, economic security, love and affection, sharing and self-respect, to be free from fear, to be free from intense feelings of guilt, and the need for self-concept and understanding. While the last is obviously directly related to self-perceptions, the others are also related since if they are unmet, the individual may begin to feel unsure or unhappy about himself or herself. On the other hand, we may confidently hypothesize that where such needs are largely met, the individual would probably be confident and satisfied, thus contributing to a positive view of self.

Beyond this, Maslow (1970) described five basic human needs, which he outlined in the order of their relative power.

1. Physiological needs (e.g., hunger, thirst, etc.)
2. Safety needs
3. Love and belonging needs
4. Esteem needs
5. Self-actualization needs (e.g., self-fulfillment)

According to Maslow, an individual cannot successfully approach a particular need until those in previous categories have been satisfied. For example, unless one has a feeling of physiological satisfaction and a sense of security, one cannot begin to approach self-actualization. Of particular concern here are the last three needs, each of which has to do directly with self-perceptions. We can hardly expect an individual to develop a positive self-esteem unless he or she experiences feelings of belonging among family, peers, and other personally significant groups, as well as a sense that those "others" hold the individual in esteem. In addition, the most positive levels of self-esteem are likely to be found in persons who have a sense of self-actualization, "acceptance and expression of the inner core of self . . . and minimal presence of ill health, neurosis, psychosis, of loss or diminution of the basic human and personal qualities" (Maslow, 1962).

Finally, from the theory of self-perceptions discussed in Chapter 1, it is evident that human beings have a basic need to develop a clear and accurate self-concept and a relatively positive self-esteem, particularly with regard to those self-concept dimensions that are most highly valued. Related to this sense of self is a need to maintain a sense of stability and consistency in self-regard, free from serious threat or overwhelming dissonance. Since the individual's environment is particularly influential in the formulation of self-perceptions, we might also add to the internal needs just described, a related basic need: to exist in a setting that enhances the sense of self, provides support in meeting or satisfying needs, and offers opportunities to grow in constructive ways.

In this context, curriculum planning based on the need for a positive view of self and self-actualization is an attempt to help young people experience and develop psychological and mental health. Where this emphasis is excluded from curriculum planning, learners may feel that they have unmet needs. These feelings may lead to those of frustration which, as Raths (1972) suggests, may in turn be manifested in behaviors such as aggression, submission, withdrawal, or psychosomatic illnesses. Such behaviors are hardly unknown in schools. One can only wonder to what degree vandalism, dropping out, drug use, and the like are related to the lack of attention given to basic human needs in the school. Perhaps such speculation might be more serious if we consider that the view one holds of oneself is highly influential in the choices we make, in our behavior, in our attitudes toward others, and in virtually all aspects of social living (of which the school is one). The degree to which a positive view of self is critical is aptly summarized by Combs (1962):

> It is not the people who see themselves as liked, wanted, acceptable, worthy and able who constitute our major problems. . . . It is the people who see themselves as unliked, unwanted, unworthy, unimportant, or unable who fill our jails, our mental hospitals and our institutions (pp. 51-52).

Goals that Support Self-Perceptions

"I go to school—I value education"—Female, Age 19

Previous mention has been made of the fact that comprehensive statements of educational goals should and usually do include one or more that pertain to self-perceptions.

At the national level, such goals can be found as early as the Educational Policies Commission (1938) inclusion of self-realization among its four "purposes of education in American Democracy." At the state level, a typical example is Pennsylvania's inclusion among its goals that "quality education should help every child acquire the greatest possible understanding of himself and an appreciation of his worthiness as a member of society" (Pennsylvania Department of Education, 1973). That educators should support development in this area makes a great deal of sense since this is an integral aspect of the human beings with whom they work. To deny the importance of self-perceptions is to ignore their power as an ongoing influence in living and learning. In previous chapters we have seen that self-perceptions developed within and outside the school loom large in growth and development. Thus curriculum plans to enhance self-perceptions actually have two temporal dimensions: to assist learners with views of themselves in their present lives and to continue developing healthy self-images which will help learners live more satisfying lives later on.

Typically, goal statements related to self-perceptions indicate that learners will be helped to:

"Develop a positive sense of self-worth."

"Build a healthy self-esteem."

"Develop a positive view of themselves."

Such vague statements may often confuse rather than guide the process of curriculum planning. In order to make the place of self-perceptions clear and useful within an overall statement of educational goals, it is necessary to develop a framework in light of concepts and definitions already discussed. The following is an example of how self-perception related goals might appear, as well as clarifying statements that would help bridge the gap between goals and practice:

School experiences will be developed in such a way that they enhance self-perceptions of learners. In order to do this, learners will be helped to:

1. Develop a clear, realistic, and accurate self-concept.
2. Clarify and develop values upon which a positive self-esteem may be based.
3. Understand the nature and importance of healthy self-perceptions in living and learning.
4. Develop skills required for self-evaluation.
5. Understand the social, cognitive, and physical aspects of their present age around which self-perceptions are developed.

At first glance, the sample goal and clarifying statements may seem to fall under the affective domain or that area of human development concerned with valuing, feeling, perceiving, and the like. However, it is important to note that we form self-perceptions around the cognitive and psychomotor domains and that cognition in the sense of introspection or thinking about self is critical to self-evaluation, self-concepting, and valuing. In this manner, self-perceptions cut across all three domains and are critical to development in each. Furthermore, concern for self-perceptions and their enhancement cannot be delegated to any one or a few subject areas such as psychology, home economics, or social studies. As we have seen, self-perceptions account for at least some of the variance in virtually any task or endeavor taken on. In this sense, enhancing self-perceptions represents an authentic educational goal as it permeates all areas and activities of school life.

The broad goal statements may be further refined and clarified by considering how each level of education will apply them to its curriculum plans. This consideration may result in the formulation of general objectives or statements less broad than the goals and less specific than instructional objectives. The purpose of general objectives is to help bridge the gap between goals and specific objectives, thus clarifying their relationship. For example, elementary level curriculum plans may focus on the self in relation to the concrete environment or as a source of feelings, while the middle or junior high school may focus on the self in relation to peers. The high school may wish to focus on the self in terms of developing independence or as a part of the global community. Since schools are maintained for the education of all citizens, young and old, consideration may also be given to how the goals might guide efforts to enhance the self-perceptions of adults through community or continuing education. The latter general objectives may lead to adult discussion groups, parenting courses, counseling services, or other programs and activities for self-enhancement. In discussing possible general objectives, curriculum planning groups may wish to consider the developmental task scheme (Havighurst, 1972)—the identification of organizing centers appropriate for various developmental levels of self-perceptions or other topics related to curriculum sequence. Several of these will be described more fully later. In any event, the goals concerning self-perceptions and the actual curriculum plans carried out in specific teaching-learning situations are often incongruent. The formulation of general objectives is perhaps a way to bring the two into closer connection.

Self-Perception Characteristics of Learners

"If you knew me you wouldn't ask that" (in response to the statement "Tell me about yourself")—Male, Age 16

In formulating curriculum plans, close attention must be paid to the characteristics of the learners for whom the plans are intended. This means that teachers need to be aware of interests, concerns, problems, cognitive levels, and other dimensions of learners. With regard to self-perceptions, teachers may make certain assumptions, but specific characteristics cannot be known until the time a unit is actually undertaken. As we shall see, curriculum planning at this stage must

Table 3.1
The Developmental Tasks of Havighurst

DEVELOPMENTAL TASKS OF INFANCY AND EARLY CHILDHOOD
1. Learning to walk.
2. Learning to take solid foods.
3. Learning to talk.
4. Learning to control the elimination of body wastes.
5. Learning sex differences and sexual modesty.
6. Achieving physiological stability.
7. Forming simple concepts of social and physical reality.
8. Learning to relate oneself emotionally to parents, siblings, and other people.
9. Learning to distinguish right and wrong and development of a conscience.

DEVELOPMENTAL TASKS OF MIDDLE CHILDHOOD
1. Learning physical skills necessary for ordinary games.
2. Building wholesome attitudes toward oneself as a growing organism.
3. Learning to get along with age-mates.
4. Learning an appropriate masculine or feminine social role.
5. Developing fundamental skills in reading, writing, and calculating.
6. Developing concepts necessary for everyday living.
7. Developing conscience, morality, and a scale of values.
8. Achieving personal independence.
9. Developing attitudes toward social groups and institutions.

DEVELOPMENTAL TASKS OF ADOLESCENCE
1. Achieving new and more mature relations with age-mates of both sexes.
2. Achieving a masculine or feminine social role.
3. Accepting one's physique and using the body effectively.
4. Achieving emotional independence of parents and other adults.

(continued)

Table 3.1
Continued

5. Achieving assurance of economic independence.
6. Selecting and preparing for an occupation.
7. Preparing for marriage and family life.
8. Developing intellectual skills and concepts necessary for civic competence.
9. Desiring and achieving socially responsible behavior.
10. Acquiring a set of values and an ethical system as a guide to behavior.

DEVELOPMENTAL TASKS OF EARLY ADULTHOOD

1. Selecting a mate.
2. Learning to live with a marriage partner.
3. Starting a family.
4. Rearing children.
5. Managing a home.
6. Getting started in an occupation.
7. Taking on civic responsibility.
8. Finding a congenial social group.

DEVELOPMENTAL TASKS OF MIDDLE AGE

1. Achieving adult civic and social responsibility.
2. Establishing and maintaining an economic standard of living.
3. Assisting teen-age children to become responsible and happy adults.
4. Developing adult leisure time activities.
5. Relating oneself to one's spouse as a person.
6. Accepting and adjusting to the physiological changes of middle age.
7. Adjusting to aging parents.

DEVELOPMENTAL TASKS OF LATER MATURITY

1. Adjusting to decreasing physical strength and health.
2. Adjustment to retirement and reduced income.
3. Adjusting to death of spouse.
4. Establishing an explicit affiliation with one's age group.
5. Meeting social and civic obligations.
6. Establishing satisfactory physical living arrangements.

be considered preplanning, prior to the moment when final plans are formulated by the teacher and learners together.

Several ideas offer helpful clues for thinking about possible topics, objectives, types of activities, and so forth. One is the concept of developmental tasks suggested by Havighurst (1972). A developmental task is defined as "a task which arises at or about a certain period in the life of the individual, successful achievement of which leads to his [or her] happiness and to success with later tasks, while failure leads to unhappiness in the individual, disapproval by society, and difficulty with later tasks." According to Havighurst, developmental tasks arise from physical maturation, cultural pressure from society, and personal values or aspirations which are part of the self. An examination of the tasks for each age group (see Table 3.1) may help teachers to identify the kinds of needs they might expect a particular group of learners at a given stage of development to have. One way of interpreting these needs is to imagine that each is a possible dimension of self-perceptions for learners. For example, children may have self-perceptions about themselves with regard to physical skills or getting along with age-mates, emerging adolescents with regard to their changing physique, and adolescents with regard to their sense of independence.

Another source is the concept of "persistent life situations" developed by Stratemeyer et al. (1957). Persistent life situations are "those situations that recur in the life of the individual in many different ways as he [or she] grows from infancy to adulthood" (p. 115). Presumably, the degree to which individuals are able to meet these situations successfully leads to outcomes similar to those expected when developmental tasks are accomplished. In thinking about curriculum plans, teachers may thus wish to consider the kinds of persistent life situations shown in Table 3.2 and how self-perceptions might emerge from the nature of the situations for a particular age group.

Still other sources for self-perceptions that might commonly be expected in a particular group of learners may be found in the large body of literature on self-concept and self-esteem (e.g., Yammamoto, Thomas, and Karnes, 1969; Rosenburg, 1979; Wylie, 1979; Hamachek, 1978) and in many sociological sources.

More specific information might be found by using various techniques for gathering self-perception information such as observation of behavior, interviews, interest inventories, and the like. In some

Table 3.2
Persistent Life Situations

Persistent Life Situations	Early Childhood	Later Childhood	Youth	Adulthood
Adjusting to personal strengths and weaknesses	Becoming aware of individual strengths and weaknesses	Finding ways of using or adjusting to individual capacities	Growing in ability to use individual capacities	Making constructive use of individual capacities
Developing individual capacities for social ends	Finding how one's contribution can make for group welfare	Deciding what individual contribution to make to the group	Establishing more adequate bases for determining what is the most effective contribution to the group	Making a maximum contribution of individual abilities for the good of the group
Dealing with success and failure	Finding ways of meeting successes and disappointments	Learning how to plan next steps after meeting success and failure	Extending ability to make constructive plans in situations involving success and failure	Making constructive use of success and failure
Achieving constructive expression of emotions	Exploring acceptable ways of expressing emotions	Developing constructive channels through which to express emotions	Extending ability to control and direct emotions	Achieving constructive and mature expression of emotions
Securing balanced satisfactions	Finding sources of emotional satisfaction in daily activities	Learning to use varied sources of emotional satisfaction	Extending the range of constructive sources of emotional satisfaction	Using constructive sources of emotional satisfaction

Reprinted by permission of the publisher from Florence B. Stratemeyer, Hamden L. Forkner, Margaret G. McKim, and A. Harry Passow, *Developing a Curriculum for Modern Living.* (New York: Teachers College Press. Copyright © 1957 by Teachers College, Columbia University.) All rights reserved.

cases, teachers who have previously worked with the same learners may provide valuable insights, although these must be approached with caution. Individual learners may have different self-perceptions than those they had when working with previous teachers due to changes within themselves or because previous teachers had different expectations. In the end, accurate and up-to-date information about learners' self-perceptions cannot be had until the learners are actually present. Whether or not real self-perceptions match those predicted or assumed in preplanning should be a concern of teachers since

---

Case 3.1

Jefferson County Open High School*
Guidelines for Initial Advisory Interview

The first session with each advisee should facilitate the development of a relationship of mutual trust and responsibility. Advisors will work on this in ways that are most comfortable for them. There are, however, three specific areas that every advisor should be sure to cover.

Documentation. Be sure each advisee understands the general system of evaluation as well as your expectations for the individual documentation. Emphasize our goal that every student become capable of realistic self-evaluation.

Personal Profile. Each advisee should be made aware that the following questions have two major purposes. First, they should help you, as an advisor, get to know the student so that you can advise in the development of the educational program. Second, the responses will become the initial self-evaluation, against which the student will be able to measure growth during the time at the Open High School. It is for these reasons that you will be taking notes during the interview.

1. Are you satisfied with the way you handle most situations? In what sort of situations do you feel most comfortable? In what sort of situations do you feel uncomfortable?   SELF-CONCEPT

2. Do you try to see the other person's point of view. Kids your own age? Parents? Other adults?   SOCIAL INTERACTION

3. What is something that you feel you really do well? Why is doing it well important to you?

SELF-CONCEPT—SPIRITUAL DOMAIN

4. Was it your choice to come to the Open High School? If so, how did you make the decision? If not, who made the decision and what part did you play in the process?

DECISION MAKING

5. In terms of school-type activities, what are your strengths and weaknesses?

A STUDENT VIEW OF SELF

6. If you could do anything that you wanted, if you were not restricted by age or money, what would you like to do?

PROGRAMS FOR THE FUTURE

Parent Conference. Upon completion of the initial advisory interview, ask the advisee, to arrange a meeting for you and him with his parents. Try to have as many of these as possible at school during the day, but be willing to meet in the home if that is necessary.

---

*Courtesy of Arnold Langberg, Jefferson County Open High School, Evergreen, Colorado.

plans may need to be modified if they do not. However, the sources suggested here offer worthwhile insights, and their consideration may help to keep the idea of self-perceptions on the curriculum planning agenda.

Self-Perceptions and Constructs of Learning

"I like school—I'm really good in school—it's fun"—Female, Age 12

Curriculum plans developed by teachers and others ought to be based on principles of learning; that is, concepts and ideas about how and under what conditions learning most likely occurs. A good deal has already been said about the relationship between self-perceptions and learning, and it remains here to identify those learning principles that guide the formulation of curriculum plans to enhance self-perceptions.

Construct 1. Individuals are most apt to want to learn those skills and knowledges that they perceive to be most self-enhancing. Skills and knowledges that are personally satisfying are thus of highest priority.

Construct 2. The way in which individuals perceive themselves affects the perception of what is worth learning. The most desirable learning is that which grows out of the salient dimensions of self.

Construct 3. Self-perceptions influence the type of learning activities in which individuals are willing to engage. Learners tend to have perceptions of their skill or probable success in various kinds of activities and tend to choose those that they believe will be most self-enhancing or the least debilitating.

Construct 4. Self-perceptions may influence the degree to which individuals are willing to participate as members of a group. Learners may vary in the degree to which they have confidence in the ideas or skills they might contribute to group activities.

Construct 5. Self-perceptions may influence approaches to problem solving. Learners having various degrees of confidence in themselves may also vary in the extent to which they are willing to invest themselves and take risks in solving problems.

Construct 6. Self-perceptions of ability account for some degree of variance in learning. The degree to which individuals have confidence in their ability to learn may influence the degree to which learning actually takes place.

Construct 7. Self-perceptions of ability may be necessary, but are not sufficient to ensure learning. In some cases, the nature of what is to be learned may require skill or background beyond the present level of the individual. Thus the design of learning situations must be connected to the present ability of the learner or risk failure and consequent self-perception problems.

Construct 8. Self-perceptions are most likely enhanced in

democratic learning situations. Individuals who have an opportunity to participate in planning and whose ideas and needs are otherwise respected have a greater opportunity to experience personal meaning and satisfaction.

Construct 9. Self-perceptions are most likely enhanced when their role in what is to be learned is clear and immediate. The more obvious the relationship between curriculum plans and self-perceptions, the greater the likelihood that learning with regard to the latter will be internalized.

Construct 10. Self-perceptions are most likely enhanced when individuals knowingly assume responsibility for their own learning. Activities in which learners assume greater responsibility and in which they are aware of personal efforts in this regard add to personal meaning and satisfaction.

Construct 11. When situations are incongruent with self-perceptions or when they are perceived as threatening to the self, learning efforts are more likely to fail and related activities avoided. Almost no one wants to fail and thus will try to avoid situations where failure is imminent. This includes both the nature of the proposed learning experience and the expectations of the teacher.

Construct 12. Self-perceptions are most likely to be enhanced when high priority is placed on interaction. Those learning situations in which individuals have opportunities to try out new roles, test ideas, and get feedback from others are most congruent with the interactive nature of self-perception development.

Construct 13. Self-perceptions are most likely enhanced in situations in which individuals experience success and achievement. The degree to which we have confidence in our ability to succeed is largely dependent on our past experiences in similar situations.

Construct 14. Self-perceptions of ability are multidimensional and hierarchical. Confidence in the ability to succeed may depend on what is to be learned as it relates to the previous experience *in the same area* of learning. The degree to which individuals perceive that area of learning to be personally salient influences the desire to succeed and interest in the area.

Construct 15. Self-perceptions are most likely enhanced in situations where there is a variety of activities and resources.

The availability of alternative learning modes allows individuals to select those that are perceived to hold the greatest probability for success and self-enhancement.

General Resources to Support
Self-Perception Enhancement

"I know where the nurse's office is and the library too"—Female, Age 6

Since curriculum plans will be carried out within the context of the local school and community, it is helpful to identify available resources that relate to self-perception enhancement.

Almost every community offers a wide variety of resources, both human and material. The former may include human service agencies and organizations, helping professions, and individuals who may offer young people exemplary role models in terms of "full functioning." In addition, local libraries and other resource clearinghouses typically provide free or inexpensive materials related to aspects of physical, social, and personal growth.

Similarly, schools are staffed by various professionals who may assist teachers and learners in thinking about self-perceptions. Libraries or instructional resource centers usually contain a variety of books, magazines, pamphlets, films, tapes, and other materials directed at that topic. Where information about self-perceptions is sought, parents can be of great help, as can various instruments and inventories designed for that purpose and housed in counseling offices. In the latter case and the school libraries, some search may be required since the materials related to enhancing student self-perceptions may be stored in a place reserved for "little used" items.

Other possible resources involve descriptions of curriculum plans and programs already designed to enhance self-perceptions, as well as the people involved in the programs. Professional journals, convention sessions, and innovative project pamphlets frequently describe programs and related activities that are intended for that purpose. Care must be taken, however, to avoid the temptation to simply replicate an existing program since self-perceptions of learners in one locale may differ from another. Also, local curriculum development provides teachers with an opportunity to develop a clear understanding of ideas that lie behind curriculum plans and promotes higher degrees of commitment to actually carrying out the plans. Nevertheless, other programs may offer valuable suggestions, the "wisdom of experience," and savings in terms of curriculum planning time.

The use of resources will be more thoroughly discussed in relation to specific instruction. In any event, teachers engaged in curriculum planning need to inventory both school and community to identify possible resources related to self-perception enhancement.

Self-Perceptions and Curricular Approaches

"I don't see how all these subjects are helping me"—Male, Age 16

In formulating curriculum plans that are likely to enhance self-perceptions, consideration must be given to the kind of curricular approach or organizing pattern that might be most appropriate.

Historically, curricular approaches have been delineated in four types (e.g., Krug, 1957; Macdonald, Anderson, and May, 1965). These include the following:

1. The *subject approach* in which curriculum plans are organized around separate subjects or disciplines of knowledge

2. The *broad-fields approach* in which curriculum plans are organized around concepts related to two or more subjects (e.g., humanities or art history)

3. The *problems approach* in which curriculum plans are organized around major social problems (e.g., environmental problems, community problems)

4. The *emerging needs approach* in which curriculum plans are organized around personal and social needs of learners (e.g., human growth and development, human relations)

At one level, the type of curricular approach used is independent of self-perception enhancement since self-perceptions are involved in all aspects of school life and their enhancement is the responsibility of all educators regardless of the approach they use. At another level, the choice of curricular approach or the balanced use of all four is very important since obviously the emerging needs and

95

problems approaches are specifically directed at helping learners to understand themselves and their environment. To clarify their relationship to self-perceptions, each of those approaches needs further elaboration.

The subject approach and the broad-fields approach, in which separate subjects still retain their identity, typically draw objectives and subject matter from within an organized field of knowledge (e.g., history, English, science, mathematics, etc.). More importantly, the objectives often involve only the mastery of that subject matter in the form of facts and principles. The problem with the latter idea is that learners may perceive the content from a particular subject area as having little if anything to do with their real lives. To the degree that teachers and textbook authors avoid making such a connection, the learner perception is probably accurate.

To remedy this problem, teachers who use the separate subject approach should use two procedures simultaneously. First, they should work toward the various types of self-enhancing techniques described in Chapter 2. In all cases, those procedures function independently of the type of curricular approach used. For example, positive teacher expectations, cooperative learning, teacher-pupil planning, and cooperation with parents may characterize the subject approach as much as the needs approach. Second, such teachers should also identify "psychological meaning" within their particular field (Jersild, 1952). Included here are some illustrations related to various subject fields.

Social Studies

While social studies courses are often carried out simply as history courses, their actual purpose is to help learners examine the nature of social problems experienced by people. For example, the facts and principles associated with the American Revolution or the Civil War begin to take on real meaning for learners when studied within the context of how human disagreements arise, why people revolt, and how conflict evolves from feelings of frustration. These concepts are not only a part of national events, but also of conflict with parents, friends, teachers, and so on. By exploring the relationship between historical, social events and the real, contemporary lives of students, social studies teachers offer opportunities for learners to think about themselves within the context of this subject area.

English/Language Arts

Technically, the language arts, including reading, writing, speaking, listening, and observing, represent functional skills that enhance opportunities for people to "send" ideas to others and properly interpret "messages" from them. Inasmuch as interaction is the crucial element in formulation of self-perceptions, the development of language arts skills promotes the possibility of enhancing self-concept and self-esteem through clearer and more constructive interaction patterns. However, language arts activities ought to focus as much as possible on understanding self and others so that the connection described above is not left to chance. The teaching of interpersonal communications skills as described in Chapter 2 is an excellent illustration of this process. In addition, the facts and principles of language arts may take on real meaning if analyzed through a study of commercial media, including how these portray and influence young people. (See Chapter 4 for a sample unit on this topic.)

Teachers of English or literature courses should likewise emphasize materials in which authors and artists express ideas about themselves. This is not a difficult task since most novels, poems (including the lyrics of some contemporary music), short stories, and all autobiographies are essentially media for self-expression. Again, however, the teacher must make certain that curriculum plans include direct questions and activities through which learners may use literature for self-thinking so that this issue is not left to chance.

Science

The study of science offers several opportunities for dealing with self-perceptions. First, the process of self-perceiving is greatly enhanced when characterized by careful analysis, thinking, and decision making. In science courses, learners have opportunities to develop skills in making inferences, organizing and classifying information, identifying chains of events and causal relationships, and the like. If the emphasis in science is on learning these processes, young people may sharpen some of the skills they need for clarifying and analyzing their self-feelings. To be more certain of this connection, however, science teachers need to take time to engage in discussions with learners in which they actually make the application of the learned processes to their own lives.

Science courses might also include units that have direct relationships with the lives of learners. Many science teachers continue to include as part of their programs units dealing with environmental problems. Some of these involve extensive study of local problems, including the social aspects, as well as opportunities for young people to improve their own attitudes and behaviors regarding pollution, diminishing resources, and so on. Other science teachers have developed units that help students to learn about futures and futuring. For example, students may explore technological advances in technology in areas such as medicine, communications, and transportation, with special attention given to how these may influence lifestyles, values, attitudes, and so on. In this case, learners have a chance to think about themselves in the future as well as the social and moral implications of science.

Finally, many science teachers retain responsibility for learning about human growth and development, often including psychological and physical aspects. Here, the emphasis should be on extending the relatively "safe" facts into opportunities for learning about themselves. In particular, the focus of human growth and development units should be on the developmental stage that the learners are currently experiencing. By helping to clarify issues involved in the particular stage the students are in, the science teacher may make a valuable contribution to the clarity and accuracy of their self-perceptions. Without such discussions, however, the facts may represent little more than meaningless additions to others accumulated in school.

Mathematics

The issue of how self-perceptions might be enhanced in mathematics courses is largely related to whether the courses involve abstract or applied mathematics. In higher-level courses, the nature of the subject matter tends to be largely theoretical, and thus self-perception enhancement is basically a matter of using the techniques described in Chapter 2. In applied mathematics, such as computation and problem solving, emphasis should be placed on functional use of skills in ways that improve learners' lives. Computational skills may be applied to unit buying, managing service jobs such as baby-sitting or newspaper routes, keeping records for clubs, saving for special purposes, and other real-life situations. As young people develop proficiency in these situations, they may also feel more personally competent and confident. Some mathematics teachers also develop interesting problem-solving units around topics such as managing family budgets, studying economic problems in the community, keeping records on sports, building scale models, and so on. The first of these is sometimes planned as a simulation so that students use both problem solving and computational skills as part of learning how to purchase homes and automobiles, buying insurance, balancing checkbooks, and other family budgeting situations. Here again, young people may be helped to feel more competent and confident in dealing with real-life issues, thus enhancing their self-perceptions in that dimension.

Exploratory Areas

The so-called exploratory courses offered in most schools not only have the potential for numerous self-enhancing opportunities, but usually actually include them. Physical education programs, for example, frequently emphasize physical fitness, weight control, lifelong sports, and other topics aimed directly at helping learners improve their physical selves. In addition, some programs also involve learners in looking at personal attitudes toward competition, aggression, and similar social aspects of sport. Home economics courses, often misinterpreted as simply cooking and sewing, usually include extensive work on family living, human growth and development, child care, human relations, and nutrition. Art and music courses should typically (although curiously they do not always) focus on creative self-expression through their respective media. Industrial arts and vocational education courses often emphasize creating projects, repairing home appliances, and learning how to secure work. In this case, young people have the chance to develop and use skills that are personally satisfying and sometimes economically rewarding in terms of part-time or work-study jobs. Finally, foreign language courses, with both a bicultural and bilingual focus, allow young people to compare and contrast their development to that of age-mates in diverse cultural settings. This process has the potential of encouraging young people to reexamine their personal sources of attitudes, beliefs, and values.

Examples such as these are well known to educators and have a longstanding history in the curriculum field. As Dewey (1915) noted:

All studies arise from aspects of the one earth and the one life lived upon it. We do not have a series of stratified earths, one of which is mathematical, another physical, another historical, and so on. We should not be able to live very long in any one taken by itself. We live in a world where all sides are bound together. All studies grow out of relations in the one great common world. When the child lives in varied but concrete and active relationship to this common world, his studies are naturally unified. It will no longer be a problem to correlate studies. The teacher will not have to resort to all sorts of devices to weave a little arithmetic into the history lesson, and the like. Relate the school to life, and all studies are of necessity correlated (p. 91).

Recent studies (Brandt et al., 1979), however, have indicated that subject teaching is still largely tied to textbooks and facts, in which case self-perceptions of learners are mostly ignored and enhanced only for those who learn the facts. Even in this latter instance, enhancement is limited to self-concept of ability in the particular subject area.

--------------------------------- Case 3.2 ---------------------------------

The New Model Me*

One of the most popular programs in the area of affective education is entitled "The New Model Me." Originally developed in 1968 by the Lakewood, Ohio, School System and the Educational Research Council of America, the program is included in the U.S. Office of Education's National Diffusion Network.

The aims of the curriculum are twofold: first, it attempts to help students build an understanding of human behavior; second, it helps to provide a framework that will enable students to make positive decisions about their behavior and apply these decisions to their everyday lives.

The goals of the curriculum are:

1. To assist students in understanding the human motivations underlying behavior

2. To assist students to realize how their personal resources and physical and social environments can influence their behavior.

3. To help students realize the nature of frustrations, the sources of frustrations, and constructive methods for resolving them

4. To help students understand that there are many alternative ways of responding in a particular situation

5. To provide students with guidelines for determining which behaviors are constructive and which are not

100

6. To assist students to learn to make decisions in terms of the effects of various courses of action on both themselves and others

7. To help students understand the nature of aggressive behavior and the forms it may take

8. To assist students in applying their knowledge about behavior and constructive problem-solving methods in their everyday living

In practice, The New Model Me program is a K-12 program. At the elementary level, curriculum plans focus on dealing with the causes of behavior, while at the middle school/junior high level, the program revolves around dealing with aggressive behavior. The high school strand of The New Model Me consists of six units: an introductory unit on human behavior and related units dealing with social controls, the real self, values clarification, human responses to situations, and change in human behavior and relationships. The units may be used as a separate course or integrated into other courses which focus on human development or behavior.

From a curriculum standpoint, The New Model Me program illustrates use of an emerging needs approach inasmuch as students have the chance to analyze and evaluate the personal view of problems which are a part of their daily life as young people.

---

*See Florence Beatty, "The New Model Me" *American Education* (U.S. Office of Education) 13, 1 (February 1977): 23-26.

If those who emphasize use of the subject or broad-fields approaches were to reorganize instruction along the lines just described, the enhancement of self-perceptions would certainly become more likely in schools. However, a more appropriate effort might be made by placing increasing emphasis on the use of the problems and emerging needs approaches. By definition, these approaches involve a more direct method to helping learners understand themselves and their environment. Specifically, they draw both objectives and subject matter from the real lives of learners, the former particularly aimed at aiding learners in learning about and resolving real-life issues. Curriculum plans organized around these approaches might involve unit topics such as "Living in Our School," "Getting Along with Others," "Life in Our Community," "What It Means to Be Thirteen," "Everyday Superstitions," and so on. In each case, learners would obviously have an opportunity to learn about themselves, to see how their ideas and opinions fit together and hold up under scrutiny, to try out new roles, and to think about their personal self-perceptions.

Curriculum research suggests that learners involved in programs using these approaches seem to fare better on indicators of more positive self-regard (Aiken, 1941; Alberty, 1960; Jennings and Nathan, 1977). Perhaps the best known study in the curriculum field related to effects of curricular approaches is the Eight Year Study (Aiken, 1942). In that study, 1,475 secondary students involved in experimental high school programs were compared over eight years to the same number of students participating in traditional, subject-centered programs. While many variables were studied, several were directly related to affective development. Data gathered in the Eight Year Study indicated that, when compared in terms of college experiences, graduates of the experimental programs demonstrated the following characteristics relative to graduates of the control settings:

1. A higher degree of intellectual curiosity and drive
2. More clear and well-formulated ideas concerning the meaning of education
3. A higher degree of resourcefulness in meeting new situations
4. Greater effectiveness in approaching adjustment problems.
5. More frequent participation in student groups
6. A more active concern for what was going on in the world

These differences emerged even though some of the experimental programs tended only slightly in the direction of the approaches suggested here. Even more enlightening is the direction these data took when graduates from the most experimental schools were separately compared to graduates of the control schools. Here, the difference was much greater, favoring experimental school graduates on the preceding indicators. In light of this kind of evidence and the theory of curricular approaches, it is clear that curriculum planning aimed at enhancing self-perceptions must give greater attention to the use of the problems and needs approaches. The systematic inclusion of these approaches in the school program is not without precedent. In fact, today, as in the past, one can still find examples of a program specifically intended for this purpose; namely, core curriculum.

By definition, core programs attempt to meet the common needs of learners and the society, without regard for subject area lines (Lurry and Alberty, 1957; Faunce and Bossing, 1958; Alberty and Alberty, 1962; Vars, 1969). In practice, core programs were to use the problems and needs approaches in a block-time or self-contained setting with emphasis on teacher-pupil planning, home-base counseling, and other arrangements related to enhancing self-perceptions. Not to be confused with so-called "core" movements aimed at specifying a series of required courses, the authentic core arrangement described here never reached the level it ought to have, given its support in curriculum research (Wright, 1958; Jennings and Nathan, 1977). Alberty (1960) summarized that research by noting that "in the area of attitudes and values, there is fairly good evidence that a core program, organized in terms of common needs and problems of adolescents, is distinctly superior to the conventional subject-centered program." Perhaps, then, one useful step in planning to use the problems and needs approaches might well be a careful review of the large body of literature on theory and practice of the core curriculum.

At present most secondary schools (Beane, 1975; Tubbs and Beane, 1981) and an increasing number of elementary schools are organized around the subject approach. So long as this trend remains intact we can only hope that various techniques are used to enhance self-perceptions. When this trend is changed, we might then expect curriculum planning and teaching to realize their fuller potential with regard to how learners view themselves.

Part II
Curriculum Planning for Specific
———— Teaching-Learning Situations ————

Until this point we have considered several areas that are antecedents to curriculum planning for specific teaching-learning situations. Presumably, decisions related to the development of specific curriculum plans, such as characteristics of learners and general curricular approach, are affected by those made during the antecedent phase. In this case, then, the curriculum plans discussed below represent those that the teacher uses to guide day-to-day activity with learners. The idea held by some educators that the broad areas or antecedents have little to do with the everyday life in schools is unfortunate, since they offer a context or set of guidelines that ought to illuminate specific teaching-learning situations. Furthermore, given the definition of curriculum as all of the experiences of the learner under the auspices or guidance of the school, ideas developed within the broad areas should be applied to analysis of any situation in which learners may develop self-perceptions. These situations include not only those in classrooms, but also those encountered in out-of-class activities such as clubs and sports.

Specific teaching-learning situations have been characterized as having many aspects, but typically such descriptions have six common areas:

1. Organizing Center—a topic, theme, or problem that serves as a unifying source around which the remaining five components are developed.

2. Objectives—the intended or possible learnings for students

3. Content—the important facts, principles, and concepts related to the objectives and with which learners are to become familiar

4. Activities—possible situations in which learners may engage in order to accomplish the objectives

5. Resources—material and human resources related to the objectives

6. Measuring Devices—the means by which accomplishment of the objectives can be determined

Since these six items characterize teaching-learning situations, they may also be used as the components of actual curriculum plans.

Before discussing the place of self-perceptions in each of the six components, one important point needs to be considered. The development of specific plans discussed here actually represents a type of preplanning. The final planning, if one is concerned with self-perceptions, is carried out cooperatively with learners. As pointed out earlier, the participation of learners in curriculum planning or teacher-pupil planning is particularly crucial in the sense that it emphasizes to learners that they are capable and responsible (Waskin and Parrish, 1967). Further, as noted in Chapter 2, it facilitates internal locus of control, the feeling on the part of learners that they have some control over their own fate.

In practice, each of the six components represents a decision point at which teachers and students together, teachers alone, or students alone may select a specific course of action to be followed. For this reason, the development of curriculum plans by teachers, prior

-- Case 3.3 --

Jefferson County Open High School Walkabout Program*

Walkabout is a program which will help today's young people to prepare for adulthood in a manner similar to the rites-of-passage in less-developed societies. The term itself is taken from the Australian Aboriginal rite.

Our school program develops the Pre-Walkabout skills through the process of self-directed learning and the advisory system. Activities are chosen which identify and utilize the basic skills areas. These areas include personal, life-long learning; consumer, citizenship, career, family, leisure time; and investigative skills.

Projects are then proposed by the student to an advisory committee which represents a challenge to one of the six passage areas of competence. Each challenge, or passage, contains the following components and necessary conditions: initiated by the student, experiential, an extension of capabilitv, an element of risk, intense, out-of-school interaction with persons out of the student's age group, balance, pre-planning, and allowing instances of the unexpected (life's happy accidents).

The six passage areas of JCOHS are:

1. **Adventure.** Display courage, endurance, and coping skills in an unfamiliar environment.

2. **Career Exploration.** Develop a marketable skill that could lead to sustained employment, or projects a fantasy beyond recreational skills.

3. **Creativity.** Explore, cultivate, and express one's own imagination artistically.

4. **Global Awareness/Volunteer Service.** Identify a human need for assistance or a concern of global impact; become actively involved in making others aware of the problem by providing the necessary assistance or showing evidence of responsibility to the community through voluntary action in the area of impact.

5. **Logical Inquiry.** Identify, use, and evaluate a variety of resources to systematically gain information which is useful to the student (investigation and research); show evidence of an independent, in-depth study in one of the academic disciplines.

6. **Practical Skills.** Develop proficiency in a skill for which the student was formerly dependent on others.

It is possible to develop a challenge which incorporates one or more of the passage areas. Each student is expected to attempt at least one passage on his own and at least one passage with someone else.

----

*Courtesy of Arnold Langberg, Jefferson County Open High School, Evergreen, Colorado.

to working with students, should take the form of a resource unit. (See Chapter 4 for sample resource units.) Teachers may identify a wide range of possibilities for each of the six components from which specific choices may later be made in conjunction with learners. For example, the teacher may suggest twenty or thirty objectives related to a particular topic and subsequently identify with students those that will be carried out by the whole group, small groups, or individuals. Some objectives may not be addressed, new ones may be added, and so on. A variation of this kind of cooperative planning is that in which the teacher makes virtually no decisions prior to meet-

Table 3.3
The Role Definitions

Role	Teacher Behavior	Student Behavior
Planner	Prepares and collects material Organizes items, spacing, sequence of materials Constructs own materials Provides time and space for planning Writes or Selects purposes and objectives	Prepares and collects material Organizes items, spacing, sequence of materials Constructs own materials Provides time and space for planning Writes or Selects purposes and objectives Plans and consults with teacher and peers
Introducer	Presents materials to lead to inquiry and discussion Selects appropriate material at appropriate time Creates problematic situations	Student inquiry may lead to recycling of teacher role Student follow-up Creates problematic situations
Questioner Sustainer	Asks question (or makes statement) that stimulates (i.e.) open-ended divergent questions Provides room for student opinion Encourages explanation of different alternatives regarding problem Redirects questions so as to maintain interaction	Responds Explores Asks Redirects

(continued)

Table 3.3
Continued

Role	Teacher Behavior	Student Behavior
Manager	Recognizes students Makes announcements Engages students in planning Keeps records Maintains order Provides optimum use of space, hardware, time (See Planner)	Recognizes students Makes announcements Engages students in planning Keeps records Maintains order Provides optimum use of space, hardware, time (See Planner)
Rewarder	Consults with student (expresses intent and concern) Constructively criticizes student work Evaluates and reports progress to parents Recognizes students (compliments, shares, etc.) Allows time for all progress	Evaluates self in reliable fashion Progresses at a steady rate for self Shares information with peers, teacher, etc.
Diagnoser	Analyzes previous achievement (standardized achievement tools and aptitude tests) Administers diagnostic devices (skill, content, attitude) Identifies and places student on instructional skill level or in comfortable materials Shares results of diagnostics with student and parent	Evaluates self progress and placement Accepts judgment and results of tester and testing devices Works with materials at instructional level Progresses at a steady rate for self from known to new

Courtesy of Karle E. Wicker, Amherst Junior High School, Amherst, N. Y.

ing with learners. In this case, cooperative planning takes on a more sophisticated form in which students participate fully in all decisions—from the identification of topics to the design of possibilities within each of the five components (Hopkins, 1937; Alberty, 1953). While the first form of teacher-pupil planning described here offers more teacher security, the second may provide even greater opportunity in terms of learner self-perceptions since students have unlimited possibilities for suggesting topics and processes that represent their interests and ideas.

Many educators object to this kind of cooperative planning, believing that it results in loss of authority and control. If sharing means losing, this is probably so. The fact is that cooperative planning means that both teachers *and* students assume responsibility for learning. A group of teachers and administrators at the Smallwood Drive School in Amherst, New York, conceptualized these responsibilities in terms of roles for teachers and students in conducting mini-courses (Wicker et al., undated). Tables 3.3 and 3.4 illustrate their ideas of role definitions in learning. Note that many of the specific responsibilities included are similar to those discussed throughout this book as being likely to enhance self-perceptions. The most important feature of this work, however, is the obvious attempt to help learners develop a sense of control over their own environment.

As we now turn to a consideration of how self-perceptions fit in each of the six components of teaching-learning situations, we will be concerned not only with processes that will enhance self-perceptions, but with ideas that represent salience in learner self-perceptions (Lipka, Beane, and Ludewig, 1980).

Organizing Centers

"I wish I knew myself better"—Female, Age 13

The kind of curriculum planning described here is based on the historical idea of unit teaching as well as the modern concept of mini-courses (Heitzman, 1977), particularly of the type characterized by "experience" units (Hopkins, 1937, 1941; Hanna, Potter, and Hagaman, 1963). An experience unit is defined as one centered around some topic or problem that has personal meaning in the life of the learner and that is aimed at enhancing both attitudes and behaviors. In describing the experience curriculum, Hopkins (1937) noted that:

1. It is centered in learners.
2. It promotes all-around growth of learners.
3. It is controlled and cooperatively planned by learners and others in the learning situation.

Table 3.4
Characteristic Roles in a "Unit" of Work

Teacher Roles	Pupil Roles
1. Basic *planning* of the "unit" including general *objectives*, rationale, essential vocabulary, etc.	1. *Selection* of unit to be studied
2. *Motivating* the pupil to action concerning unit (if necessary)	2. *Reading* background information on topic (rationale, general information)
3. *Consulting* with the pupil on topic and objectives of unit	3. *Consulting* with teacher on topic and objectives of unit
4. *Selecting/making* objectives with pupil that are pertinent to pupil's needs and interests	4. *Selecting/making* objectives with teacher that are pertinent to topic, interests, and needs (teacher-pupil, pupil with teacher consultation)
5. *Consulting* with pupil on unit as to: objectives and format, materials, activities, etc.	5. *Selecting* materials and activities to represent fulfillment of objectives
6. *Aiding* in the gathering of media necessary to fulfill pupil's objectives	6. *Working* (reading, writing, charting, etc.) through unit in prescribed and agreed upon time, manner, and form (pupil-teacher agreement)

7. *Guiding* pupil (if needed)
  a. through materials
  b. through problems that arise
  c. through form (proof-reading)
	7. *Reporting* in some agreed upon manner the information, facts, findings, and learnings of the unit, or testing self in self-directing, self-testing, self-correcting devices

8. *Evaluating* pupil progress:
  a. records and anecdotal writings
  b. testing
  c. discussing
  d. appraising
	8. *Evaluating* self-progress (records, charts, conclusion in terms of stated objectives)

Courtesy of Karle E. Wicker, Amherst Junior High School, Amherst, N.Y.

4. It places emphasis on meaning which will function immediately in improving living.

5. It places emphasis on building habits and skills.

6. It places emphasis on understanding and improving through the process of learning.

This concept suggests that the curriculum plans developed by teachers for and with learners ought to be life-centered. Put another way, the use of the problems and needs approaches manifested in experience units offers an opportunity to base curriculum plans in those dimensions of self-perceptions that learners perceive as most salient. This means that topics selected for units and procedures used to carry out the unit may derive from what learners view as most important to them and most congruent with and enhancing to their self-perceptions (Holt and Sonstegard, 1971). Furthermore, as Gwynn and Chase (1969) point out, "the student selects his activity or center of interest and then brings to bear upon it all the subject-matter fields he needs for the solution of problems in that activity or area."

The lives of learners as a source of organizing centers is a long-standing concern in the curriculum field (Mosher and Sprinthall, 1972). Dewey (1902) suggested that ". . . the lack of any organic connection with what the child has already seen and felt make the material purely formal and symbolic." Such early twentieth-century reasoning set the stage for the larger progressive movement in education in which curriculum plans were to be made to fit the learner rather than the reverse. More specifically, the use of the needs approach and related life-centered organizing centers evolved from criticism that traditional approaches were too remote from the needs and concerns of youth (Taba, 1962).

When the organizing centers for teaching-learning situations are derived from the learners' own lives and experiences, they have the opportunity to seek their own solutions to personal problems of living and to become aware of their uniqueness and individuality (Venable, 1967). Furthermore, they can use their learnings in present, meaningful experiences both in and out of school.

There is perhaps nothing more life-centered for learners than their perceptions of themselves and the sources of those perceptions (Combs, 1971). As suggested in Chapter 1, self-concept, self-esteem, and values represent the central feature of the human personality and its development. While the identification of organizing centers is

———————————————————————— Case 3.4 ————————————————————————

Social Studies Simulations in the Middle School Classroom*

The social studies curriculum at the middle school level is an ideal format for simulation development. In the case of the social studies curriculum at the Galvin Middle School in Canton, Massachusetts, the students in the sixth grade have a course in World Cultures. The seventh and eighth graders respectively have the first and second parts of American History. The structure of the curriculum for all three grades lends itself to the use of the simulation technique, and, in the past several years, it has been used. In the sixth grade, simulations have been developed in the area of African cultures, and in the seventh grade with respect to the establishment of colonization in early America.

In the following descriptions, the organization and structure of the simulations will be covered at the sixth- and seventh-grade levels. It is important to note that in each of the following simulations, the organization and format are developed by the students with the teacher acting as a facilitator. As problems are encountered in the simulation process, the students must feel, through decision making, that the simulation is their creation.

The African Simulation

The sixth-grade African tribal simulation consisted of two major concerns: the physical building of the African village, and the preparation of worksheets for each of the tribes represented. The first step involved meetings with all sixth-grade classes to determine the physical set-up of the African village. (In this case four classes were involved.) It was decided that four life-size huts would be constructed in one classroom, one hut by each class. Each hut would represent the culture of one distinct African tribe. The four tribes represented were: the Ibo from Nigeria, the Tiriki from Kenya, the Kepelle from Liberia, and the Tiv from Nigeria.

Each of the huts was constructed with a frame of two by threes with old bed sheets stretched over the frames for stability. The size of each frame was eight feet by eight feet by six feet high. The roofs were constructed by extending insulated wires from the top of the hut frames to the ceiling supports in V-shaped patterns. Brown construction paper was cut into strips, feathered, and placed over the wires and outside the frame to give the appearance of layered thatching.

Inside each of the huts, benches, and tables were constructed out of two by threes and plywood to accommodate six to eight students. The interior walls were covered throughout the project with ceremonial tribal masks, maps, charts, and any artifacts which pertained to the particular tribe.

111

Each class was divided into four groups. Each group spent two weeks in each tribal hut. During this period, each of the students spent one week in research and completed a five-page worksheet.

In the second week, each student had to demonstrate knowledge of the tribe through questioning by the tribal council. (The tribal council was made up of the other students who were studying that particular tribe.) These students took their places on the tribal stand, while the student to be tested stood in front of them. After a period of questioning, the student had to provide entertainment dance, complete with a ceremonial mask. Authentic tribal music was played to help with the dancing.

After this performance, the student being tested returned to the hut, while the tribal council voted to admit the student into the tribe. If the vote was favorable, the student passed the worksheet in and went on to the next tribe. If the vote was unfavorable, the student had to review the worksheet, and complete another ceremony.

The length of time for this simulation was nine to ten weeks, depending on the time involved in construction. In most cases, the physical construction of the village was accomplished after school and on weekends.

The Colonial Simulation

The seventh-grade colonial simulation consisted of the construction of a colonial village and written descriptions of the development of a colonial settlement. Meetings were held with the four classes concerned to determine the physical structure of the colonial village. It was determined that three life-size log cabins would be constructed in one classroom. These log cabins included: a trading post, complete with horse hitching posts and watering trough; a village jail with stocks; and a combination family log cabin and schoolhouse. In the center of the colony was a village well.

Each log cabin was constructed of two by threes with old bed sheets stretched over the frames. The size of each cabin was eight feet by eight feet by six feet high. Brown construction paper was rolled to form simulated logs and attached to the outside of the frames. Inside the trading post, tables and benches were constructed and shelves were built to hold a variety of goods. Inside the schoolhouse/family log cabin, tables and benches were constructed along with shelves for the library. The library included books on life in the colonies and a fifteen-volume set on colonial occupations. The interior of the jail consisted of real bars on the window and crude benches and tables for the unfortunate occupants.

Each class was divided into four groups. Each group was charged with the writing of a term paper on the construction of a colony. The members of each group had to write detailed descriptions of the development of a colony as if they had just landed in the New World.

Summary

The success of these simulations has been overwhelming. The enthusiasm and interest of the students have proved its educational value. Many students who were evaluated as "slow learners" produced as well as other students, and in some cases even better. The physical building of the simulations, and the experiencing of the *environment* of the area studied seemed to generate interest for *all* students.

In the past five years, the local news media has covered the simulations in various newspapers. Last year, a local TV station video-taped the sixth-grade African village with special interviews with the students. This video-tape was shown in a two-part series on a regular evening newscast.

---

*Excerpted from Robert B. Stromberg, "Social Studies Simulations in the Middle School Classroom," *Dissemination Services On The Middle Grades*, 1980. Reprinted with permission of Robert B. Stromberg and Educational Leadership Institute, Inc.

alone a critical event in curriculum planning, it is particularly important when planning is aimed at enhancing self-perceptions. When life-centeredness becomes a criterion for selection of an organizing center, curriculum plans are immediately more sensitive to self-perceptions of learners. Furthermore, since the other components of the teaching-learning situation evolve from the organizing center, the idea of life-centeredness represents a commitment to weigh both intentions and actions in that direction. In this way, a bridge is built between the broad areas and antecedents of curriculum planning and the real curriculum—the actual experiences of the learners.

There are many sources from which ideas about possible life-related organizing centers might be gleaned. These include the developmental tasks (Havighurst, 1972), persistent life situations (Stratemeyer et al., 1957), community problems, moral issues, out-of-school curriculum factors, school problems, and many others including spontaneous suggestions by learners themselves. As has been noted frequently, the final selection ought to be made in consultation with learners. In addition, if the learners are part of a fixed group in a classroom, provision ought to be made for subgroups to simultaneously address different units with different organizing centers.

Figure 3.2 illustrates some of the organizing centers that might be considered in relation to dimension and sources of self-perceptions.

Figure 3.2
Sources of Organizing Centers

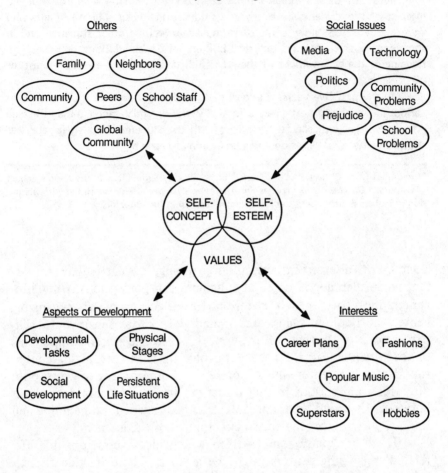

Objectives

"I like to know what I'm doing"—Male, Age 10

It is important that learner self-perceptions be seriously considered in the development of specific objectives since these represent the immediate and open agenda in teaching-learning situations. Accounting for self-perceptions should be done in two ways: by developing objectives that will involve self-perception enhancement and by using the teacher-pupil planning previously described.

There have been many ideas expressed about the way objectives ought to be written (e.g., Mager, 1962: Raths. 1964: Tyler, 1964: Esbensen, 1967; Macdonald and Wolfson, 1970; Eisner, 1969). Objectives implying that learners openly engage in self-perception improvement aim at self-concept clarification, self-reflection, self-esteem analysis, and valuing. To be effective, objectives need to suggest that during the course of a unit, learners will have opportunities to think about the topic or problem at hand in relation to their own lives and to engage in problem-related activities that will enhance self-perceptions. Suppose, for example, that a group is working in a unit centered around the topic of "Contemporary Media," involving study of television, newspapers, radio, and the like. The teacher and students in this case might wish to pursue self-perception objectives such as the following:

1. To evaluate the impact of commercial media on lifestyles of youth (e.g., values, nutrition, physical health)
2. To analyze the intent of commercial advertising in relation to developmental tasks or self-perception problems
3. To identify the self-perception problems of people characterized in situation dramas
4. To develop ideas for media to use in improving self-perceptions of consumers
5. To describe the social, sex, ethnic, and racial roles that media portray and suggest
6. To identify the values that are portrayed by various types of programs or by the content of news analysis
7. To identify the self-perception messages reflected in media intended for certain age groups (e.g., young children)

These objectives would of course represent only a portion of the many instructional purposes that could be undertaken in such a unit. Others might involve cognitive outcomes such as learning about media production, laws governing media, and various types of media. The objectives listed, however, involve learners in analyzing the effect of media on their own lifestyles, aspirations, and values. In pursuing these objectives, learners clarify their self-concepts and values as they begin to see those depicted by various media. If such objectives are ignored in curriculum planning, the place of self-perceptions in ongoing unit activities becomes a matter of chance, leaving learners to their own devices for determining the relationship between the topic and themselves.

Beyond the content of objectives, those attempting to enhance self-perceptions must also be concerned with the form objectives take. Much effort has been expended during the last two decades to promote the idea of behavioral or performance objectives. Some advocates would seem to have us believe that unless objectives include specification of a terminal behavior, they are not really objectives. The problem with this exclusive approach in the context of self-perceptions is that the latter are both personal and perceptual. While self-concept and self-esteem appear to influence behavior, behavior or performance may not necessarily reveal feelings about the self. Thus curriculum plans ought also to include some objectives that are "expressive." Eisner (1969) defines expressive objectives as those that describe an "educational encounter." Rather than specifying a behavior or performance, expressive objectives indicate a situation or activity in which learners are to be involved and thus leaves open the possibilities for outcomes. For example, Eisner illustrates expressive objectives as "to visit the zoo and discuss what was of interest there" or "to develop a three-dimensional form through the use of wire and wood." In pursuing the objectives, the learner is left free to create his or her own meanings and products. By definition, then, expressive objectives provide learners with opportunities to think about themselves and to try out ideas, opinions, beliefs, and the like. Since these processes are congruent with the process of formulating self-perceptions, expressive objectives should have an important place in curriculum plans.

The outright inclusion of self-perception objectives is only one method for taking self-reflection into account. A second is the use of teacher-pupil planning, the general idea of which has already been described. In considering the selection of specific objectives, however, some additional points are important. Let us assume that the teacher or group of teachers has preplanned a resource unit. Among the components would be a list of many possible objectives that learners might pursue. This then leaves the selection of objectives that will actually be undertaken to the teacher(s) and learners in the actual setting. Decisions about which objectives will be pursued by all or most learners, small groups, or individuals must be made. At this point, a good deal of discussion ensues and personal preferences are suggested

Table 3.5
Advantages of Teacher-Pupil Planning

1. It provides a model of democratic living based on cooperative and participatory decision making.

2. It supports mental health by providing opportunities to have a feeling of belonging.

3. It enhances teacher-student relations by the suggestion that learning is a mutual adventure.

4. It offers a chance for teachers to know what is important and interesting to learners.

5. It enhances social competence by offering opportunities to participate.

6. It offers learners a chance to express their own ideas and interests.

as the group formulates plans. This kind of deliberation gives individuals a chance to think about their own interests and ideas; in other words, to determine the relationship between the unit topic and salient dimensions of the self. In addition, learners may feel a sense of control over that portion of their lives that will be devoted to the unit. As the teacher takes student ideas seriously and ideas become actual objectives and activities, he or she is suggesting an expectation that students are capable of and responsible in making decisions—that student ideas count for something.

Some of the advantages of teacher-pupil planning are listed in Table 3.5. Those advantages imply that teaching-learning situations in which this technique is used are democratic, open, and humanistic. The kind of setting in which proposed objectives obviously show a concern for self-perceptions and in which student ideas are seriously considered, is the kind that offers a real chance for the enhancement of self-concept, self-esteem, and values.

Content

"I don't know anything"—Female, Age 9

The content or subject matter in specific teaching-learning situations designed to enhance self-perceptions is found in the connection between the topic under consideration and the actual self-perceptions of the learner. This differs from the view of content as a body of facts, principles, concepts, and understandings that reside outside of the learner, usually in some subject area, and that ought to be mastered simply for their own sake. The selection of content in the former situations is based on two criteria: first, what content will broaden the perceptions of learners so as to introduce new possibilities to the self-concept and, second, what content will help learners to develop accuracy and clarity in those concepts of themselves already held? Such questions address Dewey's (1915) idea that "to become integral parts of the child's conduct and character they [subject matter] must be assimilated—not as mere items of information, but as organic parts of his present needs and aims—which in turn are social."

To illustrate the application of these criteria, we may return to the previous unit example centered around "Contemporary Media." The first criterion, content selection to broaden self-perceptions, might be applied through a focus on roles, ideas, situations, or events portrayed in the media as opportunities for self-involvement. By studying this kind of media "content," learners may discover new possibilities for themselves in terms of new roles or interests. This process might be facilitated by helping learners to ask questions like "Would I feel better about myself if I tried that role?" or "What would I feel like if I were in that situation or if that event were happening to me?"

The second criterion, content selection to clarify self-perception, might be applied through analysis of media content. Again focusing on roles, situations, and events portrayed, learners might ask questions like "Do I tend to act like a given character in a particular situation?" or "How do I feel about a particular event and why?" The content of commercial advertising offers an interesting topic for analysis on this basis. In this case, learners might start with the assumption that advertising is based on the idea that people are dissatisfied with their lives and want to improve them. Learners may analyze various commercial advertisements through such questions as, "What does that ad assume about my values?" "Does the ad accurately predict aspects of myself with which I am dissatisfied?" or "If I acquired a particular product would I really be held in higher esteem by others?"

The content embedded in some unit topics is more directly related to the criteria for selection. For example, the content of a 'human growth and development unit done with a group of emerging adolescents offers these learners facts and concepts about the physical and social changes they are actually experiencing. In this case, the content would by its very nature broaden knowledge about the self and promote clarity and accuracy of the personal changes around which current self-perceptions may be formed. Even in these cases, however, teachers need to help learners ask self-questions such as, "Where do I stand with regard to physical development?" so that integration of the content with self-perceptions is not left to chance.

In other cases, the connection between the unit topic at hand and the self-perceptions of the learners may not be as readily obvious. Here, teachers must help learners develop these relationships through content focus. For example, in studying other cultures or historical periods, continuous attention must be paid to how young people in those places or times occupied themselves, how they were viewed by the society in which they lived, and how the present group of learners would feel about themselves if they lived under the same conditions.

The crucial point in content selection to enhance self-perceptions is whether the content can be or is connected to the real lives of the learners. When it is, the content may then come alive for learners and begin to add to the breadth and clarity of their self-concepts. Under these circumstances, content may not only be of real worth, but more readily internalized as well.

Activities

"I like working with handicapped kids"—Female, Age 17

The kinds of activities used to accomplish objectives offer numerous opportunities to enhance self-perceptions. In fact, of all the aspects of curriculum planning and teaching-learning situations, this one is most crucial in that regard since the activities represent the action phase of learning and are most salient in learner self-perceptions in school (Lipka, Beane, and Ludewig, 1980).

Since self-perceptions grow out of social interaction and personal efforts, the greatest emphasis should be placed on small-group and independent learning activities. Large group activities must of necessity involve almost entirely the dissemination of information. They may provide ideas for learners, but eventually fall short of interaction and individual thinking. In taking on problems or tasks alone or with other learners, students have the chance to be self-directed and thus may try out personal skills and ideas (Della-Dora and Blanchard, 1979). As these are carried out, learners are apt to develop a sense of competence, adequacy, and independence, all related to the notion of the "fully functioning person."

The idea of using small group and independent activities is hardly new in education, and many teachers successfully do so. Others, however, believe that students are incapable of working on their own, that the only worthwhile activities are those solely teacher-directed, or that these latter are most expedient. Of these three points, only the last can be taken seriously, but expedience should not necessarily be equated with effectiveness. The problem with the first and second objections is that they may well contribute feelings of irresponsibility and incompetence to learner self-perceptions. We have noted that self-perceptions are learned and this is also true for the skills and attitudes that constitute self-concept of competence in learning. For this reason, teachers must help young people learn how to work on their own and to participate as a member of a group. Initial attempts at small group or independent work may require a large degree of teacher guidance. Over time, however, learners may take on greater degrees of responsibility for their own learning. One might speculate that if this idea were taken seriously, adolescents might acquire self-direction skills that would facilitate fuller exercise of their desire for independence, thus supporting self-perception development at that stage and perhaps reducing the conflict that arises out of the premium placed on adult domination in high schools.

Another way of enhancing self-perceptions through learning activities involves more frequent use of projects—activities that culminate in dramatizing or debating ideas, action to improve the school or community, and others. The development of projects by learners provides an opportunity to enhance feelings of pride and personal accomplishment much more so than the use of paper-pencil tests as culminating activities.

One particular type of project deserves special attention; namely, community service projects. Community service projects involve students in activities intended to improve the local community, including the school. Specifically, students may engage in such activities as helping older people with various jobs, conducting surveys of community attitudes, working on environmental projects, assisting in day-care centers, and the like (National Commission on Resources for Youth, 1974). These projects contribute to a sense of power and participation for learners (Anderson, 1969; Dollase, 1978; Hamilton, 1980). Research to date indicates that those who participate in community service projects demonstrate considerable gains in general self-esteem and self-esteem in social situations (Hedin and Conrad, 1980).

A third source for identifying activities that are likely to be congruent with learner self-perceptions is the identification of those that are most salient for the learners themselves. In the research by Lipka, Beane, and Ludewig (1980) mentioned earlier, students suggested some useful clues about salience. When describing themselves as engaged learners, children most frequently placed higher value on "fun" type activities such as those typically found in learning centers or which they perceived as games. Adolescents, on the other hand, most highly valued activities that were congruent with life plans (e.g., work, college, etc.) and that involved interaction with peers. In both cases, low premium appeared to be placed on teacher-directed activities. Thus, if activities are to be designed that are congruent with salience in learner self-perceptions, they ought to involve active engagement with an eye to "fun" at the elementary level and peer interaction at the secondary level.

In sum, then, we can attach certain characteristics to the activities that may most likely enhance learner self-perception. Such activities ought to offer opportunities for:

1. High levels of interaction—the chance to try out ideas and roles with others and thus to test the self-concept

2. Leadership—the chance to assume and feel real responsibility

3. Responsibility—the chance to be self-directed, to try out new skills and follow through with ideas

4. Development of projects—the chance to do something worthwhile, to develop personal ownership and pride

As Dewey (1902) pointed out:

If the subject-matter of the lessons be such as to have an appropriate place within the expanding consciousness of the child, if it grows out of his own past doings, thinkings and sufferings, and grows into application in further achievements and receptivities, then no device or trick of method has to be resorted to in order to enlist "interest." The psychologized is of inter-

est—that is, it is placed in the whole of conscious life so that it shares the worth of that life. But the externally presented material, conceived and generated in standpoints and attitudes remote from the child and developed in motives alien to him, has no such place of its own. Hence the recourse to adventitious leverage to push it in, to factitious drill to drive it in, to artificial bribe to lure it in (p. 27).

Resources

"I like to read books and watch filmstrips"—Male, Age 8

Many, if not most, of the resources used in schools are designed to show young people aspects of the world around them, both past and present. However, these resources are typically developed in such a way that their content is delimited to some particular subject area or field. Admittedly one aspect of self-perception development is a simple understanding of the world outside the self, but the more complete process of self-perceiving depends on interaction with that world. Thus, one problem with those kinds of resources is that they fail to offer opportunities or suggestions regarding how young people might think about themselves in relation to the resource content. This gap leaves teachers with two alternatives: to find resources that do offer insights about the self in relation to the environment, and to identify ways to supplement available resources with activities that encourage self-thinking.

Both human and material resources for student use are available and may offer assistance in the area of self-perceptions. These include books, films, filmstrips, video-tapes, and cassette recordings. For example, at the primary level many books are available that portray children dealing with problems such as fears, moving, going to the hospital, and so on. At the emerging adolescent level, a growing number of books are available that deal with characteristic problems and perceptions (e.g., those by Judy Blume). In addition to these, practically every library or resource center contains a collection of biographies, in book and audio-visual forms, that describe how various people have approached and dealt with life problems. A variety of resources of this type are listed in conjunction with sample resource units in Chapter 4. Merely listening to, viewing, or reading material resources is obviously not enough to ensure that learners are using them in thinking about self. Much depends on discussion of the materials or independent work in which such analysis is directly encouraged.

Beyond this type of material resource, others are also available that purposely elicit self-thought and analysis, such as those found in values clarification sourcebooks (e.g., Bessell and Palomares, 1973). When these are used, however, the teacher must be aware of some cautions. One is that some of the exercises that are supposedly designed for values clarification have little to do with the real lives of young people. For example, an exercise in which participants are asked to select from a list of various occupations some lesser number whom they would have survive an airplane crash, may sound interesting but it is abstract in terms of the more pressing concerns of youth. If these kinds of values clarification activities are used, the problem addressed might better have to do with school conflict, local community issues, peer interaction, and the like.

Another caution is that these materials often appear as the sum and substance of values education. Unfortunately, this has led some teachers to believe that values education is a discreet and differentiated curriculum area to be addressed only during some particular set-aside time of the day or week. Research on this approach to values education offers little in the way of support (Lockwood, 1978). However, these activities and materials may offer a way to get discussion started in relation to some ongoing issue or topic that a group of learners is studying. In this way, values clarification materials become part of the larger curriculum context of which values education is a part.

A third source of materials that may support self-perception development is the collection of personal items young people and their families have collected. Personal memorabilia may provide an opportunity to look back at experiences and events and to examine how these may influence present and future thinking about the self. For example, learners may be interested in developing a personal timeline complete with photographs, sample toys, and the like to depict major personal and family events, significant others at various times, hobbies, interests, and other meaningful aspects of their lives. The timeline can then be analyzed by answering questions like, "What did I feel like when this happened?" "Why was that hobby interesting to me?" or "Why did I like that person so much?" Young people might also be encouraged to keep journals and diaries as a source of continuing self-knowledge, to interview parents and other relatives about important past events, or to develop family trees. These and similar activities offer an excellent opportunity to use personal materials to clarify and analyze self-concept, self-esteem, and values.

Another resource for helping with self-perceptions is peers—both older and younger. Many young people wonder about what life will be like at the next stage of their development. For example, younger children are quite likely to wonder what life will be like in the middle or junior high school as they hear rumors or stories from older brothers, sisters, and friends. Since such questions are often very troubling and may lead to fear or anxiety, they need to be addressed. An excellent resource for helping to answer these questions is, of course, well-adjusted older youth who can talk about their recollection of similar apprehensions, how they made the stage transition, and what techniques they currently use to manage their lives. By the same token, young people at any given stage may find it helpful to talk with younger peers in order to help them recollect their own earlier apprehensions and how those were overcome.

In addition to peers, self-perception issues might also be addressed by a variety of community resource persons. Members of helping professions, for example, are frequently happy to spend time with young people to talk over questions about mental and physical health, peer relations, and so on. To facilitate the use of community resources, many teachers have constructed local community resource guides, listing the names of persons who are skilled or knowledgeable in various topics and how they may be contacted.

A final consideration with regard to resources and self-perceptions involves the question of how various materials portray people. The way in which persons are depicted may be interpreted as accurate simply because it appears in print and thus suggests personal perceptions of self and others. In addition, learners may interpret such depictions as representative of the teacher's ideas, particularly if the teacher originally selected the materials. Much has been said elsewhere about the need for responsible portrayal of racial and ethnic minorities as well as sex roles (Gay, 1970; Miller, 1970; Banks, 1974). Gall (1981) offers insight and suggested methods for analysis of curriculum materials to identify such bias.

In addition to these important issues, educators concerned with self-perceptions need to analyze materials to be certain that they reflect young people as responsible, competent, and adequate human beings, capable of self-direction and "full-functioning." Furthermore, the portrayal of older persons should reflect the same qualities in order that learners be helped to develop healthy and optimistic views of the future selves. Earlier, a strong case was made regarding the power of teacher expectations in student self-perceptions. Among the ways that such expectations are communicated is through the resources available to learners. For this reason, then, the material and human resources offered to learners should be those that not only help to enhance self-perceptions, but do so by depicting the diversity and adequacy of persons the same and other ages.

Measuring Devices

"Grades don't mean anything to me"–Male, Age 16

Perhaps nothing has been more detrimental to the serious consideration of self-perceptions in curriculum planning than the attitude that, since self-perceptions are so difficult to measure, they ought not to be addressed. This idea seems to grow out of a belief that all learning must be quantitatively measured and recorded by using some norm-referenced, incremental growth scale. The current vogue of testing has encouraged that idea, suggesting that measures of growth must involve specification of whether a student is above or below grade level, like those from similar schools, and so forth. The fact is that self-perceptions are highly personal and just do not necessarily follow any particular group trend as they develop and change. To say that the self-perceptions of a learner are or are not what they should be for a particular age or grade is antithetical to the individual and personal nature of the self.

On the other hand, teachers are often highly aware of and sensitive to the self-perceptions of young people with whom they work. When they observe a youngster who is withdrawn or highly submissive, who refuses to take a risk or avoids making personal contributions to discussions, teachers are apt to say, "That student doesn't feel very good about himself or herself." By the same token, another learner might be characterized as feeling good about self if he or she volunteers ideas or opinions, assumes leadership, takes on ambiguous problems, and so on. In other words, self-perceptions are often regarded as difficult to measure, yet many teachers seem quite aware of the quality of student self-regard and are willing to say so.

Our position is that quantitative measurement of self-perceptions ought to be avoided in working with students, but the teachers should make an effort to identify systematically the nature, quality, and improvement of self-attitudes as part of an ongoing evaluation of students and their work. By this we mean that teachers should be aware of, and hopefully record, indications that students are developing

Table 3.6

Behaviors that May Indicate the Quality of Self-Perceptions

The person who is developing and maintaining clear and positive self-perceptions typically:

is willing to take risks

expresses opinions and ideas, even when they may be unpopular

is eager and willing to take on new problems

is willing to become involved in group interaction

asks questions in search of self-understanding

can function in an ambiguous and flexible environment

is willing to assume leadership

brings in materials from hobbies or interests

draws examples from his or her experiences in expressing ideas

is willing to assume responsibility

shows interest in new ideas and is willing to examine them openly

is concerned about the feelings of others

avoids situations that have self-destructive potential

is willing to deviate from the group if the group is seen as nonconstructive

cares about personal physical health

enjoys seeing others succeed

follows through with tasks

shows confidence in his or her work

is willing to show personal work to others

refers to self in positive terms

accurately assesses his or her work

is optimistic about his or her future

(continued)

Table 3.6
Continued

The person whose self-perceptions tend to be unclear and/or negative frequently:

is overdependent on teachers and other "authorities"

is obsessed with conforming to others' standards

avoids expressing personally held ideas or opinions

rejects new ideas or alternative explanations

criticizes others to make himself or herself look better

avoids new or complicated problems

is reluctant to meet new people or interact in a group

avoids leadership roles, even when asked by the group

refuses to talk about personal interests, hobbies, and the like

rarely asks questions that search for personal meanings

has few or no interests other than those assigned by others

ignores the feelings of others

unthinkingly exposes self to destructive situations

does not take care of self physically

constantly demonstrates a need to prove self-worth

easily gives up when problems or difficulties are encountered

depends on others for answers or solutions to problems

refers to self in negative terms

over- or underestimates his or her own work

is pessimistic about his or her future

is very inconsistent, constantly changing his or her mind

cannot make decisions

---

clarity of self-concept, improved self-esteem, and higher levels of values thinking.

There are many ways of doing this. Probably the most prominent is through observation of student behaviors that indicate enhanced self-perceptions. We have already mentioned indicators like submissiveness and withdrawal on the one hand and volunteerism and leadership on the other. Table 3.6 lists a number of behavior indicators that are typically associated with the quality of self-perceptions. As teachers observe students working in groups, interacting in clubs or at play, and engaging in independent projects and other settings, lists like these may be used as checklists to note momentary indications of self-perceptions or changes over a period of time. However, some cautions must be recognized in using observation of this type as a measuring device.

One warning is that behavior at a given moment does not necessarily equate with general or persistent perceptions of self. In a particular situation like group interaction, a student may be demonstrating self-perceptions on that one specific dimension of self; furthermore, that dimension may have relatively low priority and thus not enter significantly into broader self regard. A second precaution is that the teacher cannot confidently infer any ideas about self-perception if no obvious behavior is demonstrated. In some cases, learners may choose to remain neutral or inactive for casual reasons about which the teacher need not be overly concerned. Third, behaviors demonstrated in school may be different from those outside the school and thus observation may lead to unwarranted conclusions. (Many of us have known a young person who was quiet and reserved in school, but outgoing at home, and vice versa.) Despite these cautions, observation is nonetheless a valuable device for measuring quality of, and change in, self-perceptions. Over time, teachers may become highly skilled in this technique. Its use in conjunction with other devices, including ongoing conversations with students, may offer many worthwhile clues about how learners view themselves. (See Table 3.7.)

Beyond observation, teachers can use other unobtrusive devices to gain insights into self-perceptions (Webb et al., 1966). Miller (1978) suggested that there are numerous opportunities to gather information using unobtrusive or nondirect measures, and listed a substantial number including many that are related to enhancing self-perceptions. By letting students know that teachers care about them and are willing to talk over problems, students may well volunteer reasons for their actions. As these relate to self-perceptions, such conversations may offer teachers valuable insights and information they can use to work with students.

Another worthwhile measuring device is the use of self-report materials that students may periodically be asked to complete. Young children may be asked to show how they feel by matching their feelings with happy or sad faces or by completing sentences such as (Fox, Luszki, and Schmuck, 1966):

I feel best when _____.
I feel worst when _____.
I wish I could _____.
My friends like me when _____.

Older youth may be asked to write stories about themselves, outline their personal plans, and so on. If self-reports are done periodically or as pre- and post-inventories in connection with a particular unit, teachers may use them to note changes or improvements in self-perceptions.

With regard to evaluation roles, it has been said that "in our society we grade meat, eggs, and students." In most cases, students have about as much to say in that process as the other two, even though the latter are inanimate. A clear and adequate self-concept depends on the skill of self-evaluation; thus, to enhance self-perception development we must help students learn how to evaluate themselves. The following procedure serves to illustrate this process.

1. Have students keep a daily and weekly log or diary, recording what and how they do in school as well as insights gained and problems encountered.

2. At the time that reports are sent to parents, have the students review their logs in light of the objectives they set out to accomplish during the preceding period of time. The teacher should help with guiding questions such as "What did I set out to do or not to do?" "What problems did I encounter and how were they overcome?" "What was the highlight of learning?" and so on.

3. On the basis of the questions and the journal review, ask the learners to write a few self-evaluation paragraphs.

4. Meet with each student and review the written statement. If the teacher agrees, he or she simply signs the statement under the student's signature. If not, the teacher prepares a statement showing points of disagreement. These statements should be sent to parents along with progress reports. In this way, parents are provided with comprehensive information, personal comments from their child, and the kind of anecdotal report many teachers know ought to be used, but which is too time-consuming if done by the teacher alone.

Table 3.7
*Examples of Unobtrusive Measures**

Number of situations in which students are:

1. Voluntarily remaining after school to chat with teachers
2. Making significant choices
3. Involved with realia
4. Involved with resource people
5. In active roles
6. Involved in planning learning activities
7. Involved in planning social events
8. Rewriting, rehearsing, and polishing their efforts
9. Making bulletin boards, displays, or models
10. Choosing what is to be studied
11. Reporting to the class
12. Clarifying values
13. Asking questions
14. Learning from other than the written word
15. Working independently
16. Attempting to understand themselves with teacher assistance
17. Learning in areas off the school site
18. Learning from other students
19. Learning salable skills
20. Evaluating their own progress with teacher assistance
21. Smiling
22. Laughing
23. Playing
24. Using supplementary instructional materials
25. Examining current topics or issues
26. Carrying and/or using paperbacks which are not textbooks
27. Using their own funds to buy books
28. In risk taking situations (that is, doing new things)
29. Using interest centers

(continued)

Table 3.7
Continued

Data about students:

1. What percentage of students are participating in a community or school service program?
2. What percentage of students drop out each year?
3. What percentage of students skip each day?
4. What percentage of students are tardy each day?
5. How many students have been arrested this school year?
6. How many students run away from home each year?
7. How many students know the principal's name?
8. How many students don't return to class after a fire drill?
9. How many students left school because of pregnancy the last school year?
10. How many students were high or nodded off because of substance abuse yesterday?
11. What percentage of students participate in extracurricular activities?
12. How many shake downs of students by other students occurred last week?
13. How many students attend optional school events?
14. How many students have well thought through educational or vocational plans for next steps after termination of their secondary education?
15. What percentage of students eat the cafeteria lunches?
16. What percentage of students participate in more than one extracurricular activity?

*W. C. Miller, "Unobtrusive Measures Can Help in Assessing Growth," *Educational Leadership* 35 (1978): 264-269. Reprinted with permission of the Association for Supervision and Curriculum Development and W. C. Miller. Copyright © 1978 by the Association for Supervision and Curriculum Development. All rights reserved.

The self-evaluation may also serve as a basis for parent-teacher-child conferences. For the student, this procedure provides an opportunity for legitimate role evaluation, a systematic means for self-evaluation, and a context in which to learn and apply self-evaluation skills.

Case 3.5

Jefferson County Open High School*
Evaluation

A major goal of JCOHS is to help students become capable of realistic self-evaluation. Advisors and teachers will assist students, but it is the student who must take the responsibility for evaluation.

There are three levels of evaluation required for all students:

1. At the end of each activity, either class, trip, or apprenticeship, the student is expected to evaluate the experience and to share the evaluation with the person who led the activity. That person will respond in writing as part of the procedure. If the student fails to do an evaluation, the leader of the activity has no obligation to evaluate, and, therefore, no record of the activity will exist. Evaluations that will come under category #1 would be at the conclusion of the disorientation, at the end of block one, and at the end of block three.

2. Twice a year, in January and May, each student is required to write an extended self-evaluation covering the previous half year.

3. During the final year, every student is required to write a transcript which describes the entire experience at JCOHS. The student is also expected to get supporting statements since the transcript will be the official school record which could be sent to colleges or prospective employers. Guidelines for writing the transcript are available from the office.

   In addition to the three levels of self-evaluation, the advisory portfolio will include the student's Pre-Walkabout grid, APL test results, notes on the initial advisory interview and the initial parent interview, and anything else the student would like to include.

---

*Courtesy of Arnold Langberg, Jefferson County Open High School, Evergreen, Colorado.

To the extent that self-evaluation is necessary for developing clear and realistic self-perceptions, this method is an imperative procedure for those concerned with enhancing the sense of self as learner.

Related to the issue of measuring devices is that of grading or marking of students. Self-perceptions are largely influenced by the environment and particularly by feedback received from others. One consistent source of feedback for students is teacher reaction to their work. In most schools this is based on competition with other students and reported through some kind of letter grade or number.

Additionally, the feedback typically accentuates the negative rather than the positive accomplishments of learners. Each of these issues presents problems with regard to student self-perceptions.

From middle childhood on, young people place a high premium on social connection and acceptance. Learning to get along with others through constructive patterns of social interaction is not only a developmental task for individuals, but an imperative need for building a humane society. Thus, the use of competitive reward systems is not only antithetical to the personal development of students but also an obstacle to pursuit of broad social cooperation. Some persons argue that the competitive system is a realistic representation of our society. Such a claim is highly questionable when one considers that, for example, we tend to value those neighbors and friends who are cooperative rather than those who compete against us. The claim is particularly strange when it comes from educators who, themselves, work in a profession in which salary increases are granted "across the board" rather than on a competitive basis—a factor that is true for the vast majority of federal and industrial employees as well. As such, then, emphasis on competition in school may introduce to students self-concept characteristics that are unrealistic and which in real life may seem rejection by others.

The grading system used in most schools is equally tenuous. When coupled with competition, the assignment of grades typically results in some kind of grading curve, which means that most students are told that their work, in summary, is average or worse than that of their peers. These students develop concepts of themselves based on this feedback and thus may come to accept it as personally appropriate. Snygg and Combs (1949) stated this powerfully by pointing out that "it is a profligate waste of our national resources to teach millions of people to think of themselves as mediocre, incompetent, or failures at activities which are socially desirable and even essential." Furthermore, as the grade may be the only or the most significant communication the teacher has with the student, the latter may perceive that this represents the teachers' judgment of one's general human worth (LaBenne and Greene, 1969).

The way in which teachers react to the day-to-day work of learners is also often perilous to self-perceptions. For example, after observing a group discussion, a teacher may meet with a particular participant and point out several things the individual did not do well, ignoring those that were done well. Other teachers may return worksheets in mathematics indicating how many problems were missed, failing to note how many were done correctly. Some others may return student essays covered with red ink of criticism. The common use of these procedures is a curious paradox when one hears so often that teachers resent supervisory evaluations that emphasize negative rather than positive teacher behavior. The substantive effect of such feedback for students is the suggestion that they ought to have negative self-esteem as learners based on self-concepts constructed from a sense of the things they cannot do well.

Suppose that at this moment one of our own family members or good friends were rating us by listing all of our personal characteristics that he or she perceived as negative. Imagine that we were confronted with such a list and told that this constituted our evaluation. Furthermore, in order to regain our status we would have to correct each shortcoming. Such a deficit analysis could only suggest that we are consumed with debilitating features and ought to feel negative about ourselves. The deficit-model suggests negative self-esteem and makes for poor human relationships among family members and friends. Unfortunately, it does the same for learners in schools.

None of the policies listed here is necessary for effective learning, and those concerned with enhancing self-perceptions need to move toward other alternatives. First, the competitive reward structures ought to be replaced with cooperative procedures whereby students are rewarded for working together. Specifically, learners ought to be asked to work together on school activities, helping and teaching one another, and to aim toward projects that are the result of cooperation. One particular case of this method, discussed in Chapter 2, is team learning, in which students work in cooperative settings throughout the school day and year (Slavin, 1981).

Next, the use of letter or number grades ought to be replaced with methods that comprehensively describe what the student has done. For example, through the use of teacher-student planning, work ought to begin by generating a mutually understood list of objectives and a plan for activities, resources, and measuring devices. At the end of the unit, the list and related plan can serve as a checklist for indicating what may be yet unaccomplished. This method has not only the advantage of comprehensiveness, but recognizes the need to be specific about the nature of evaluation—a factor consistent with the multidimensional aspect of self-perceptions. This record also shows what the student has and can do rather than what he or she cannot do, thus contributing to self-concepts based on adequacy rather than shortcomings.

Finally, in this whole area of measuring devices and reporting, teachers must carefully avoid the pitfall of conditional acceptance of students' self-regard. Self-perceptions are highly personal and often fragile. They belong to the student, not to the teacher, and are often based on conditions such as physical development—over which neither has any control. We can hope that all of our students have clear and positive self-perceptions, but we cannot afford to accept or reject them or their work on that basis. Rather, we must accept and try to understand all young people with the whole diversity of their self-perceptions and to offer help in that regard wherever possible.

Summary

Enhancing self-perceptions is one of several issues with which curriculum planning must be concerned. Among others are cognitive development, transmission of the cultural heritage, and preparation for future roles and responsibilities. However, even the other areas are closely tied to self-perceptions inasmuch as the way an individual perceives himself or herself is critical in achievement, acceptance of physical attributes, and concepts of the self in the future. Thus curriculum planning to enhance self-perceptions has a dual function. On the one hand, it aims to clarify self-concepts, improve self-esteem, and promote more effective thinking about values; in short, it helps learners understand and feel good about themselves. On the other hand, this kind of curriculum planning serves as a supporting basis for the variety of school goals and purposes which are more effectively achieved if learners believe they can succeed and if they perceive personal meaning and value in them.

In theory, the curriculum consists of the experiences of the learner under the guidance or auspices of the school. Curriculum planning is the clarification of educational purposes and the subsequent identification of the conditions, circumstances, and situations under which those purposes are most likely to be accomplished. These definitions correctly imply that curriculum planning is a broad field. It includes a number of components such as goal identification, consideration of learner characteristics, learning principles, and curricular approaches and planning of specific teaching-learning situations. Virtually all areas of school life are subjected to scrutiny when using these components since the curriculum includes all learner experiences.

The enhancement of learner self-perceptions is hardly a new topic in the field of curriculum planning. Most reference works in the field include consideration of this important topic, especially those that are a part of the continuing movement for person-centered and life-centered education. However, the majority of such work has been based in philosophic-moral-ethical reasoning while giving limited, if any, recognition to the growing body of empirical research, which offers equally substantial support.

Curriculum planning to enhance self-perceptions may be broadly characterized as that which is based on the salient dimensions of learner self-perceptions and which maintains those as a central focus of each curriculum planning component. This means that goals are identified that commit curriculum planning to enhancing self-perceptions and that the commitment is carried through. Attempts are made to identify student self-perceptions, the problems and emerging needs approaches are used, and plans for specific teaching-learning situations include direct attention to enhancing self-perceptions.

That such curriculum planning is possible is proved by the many teachers and schools that have made serious and sincere attempts to focus on student self-perceptions. Exemplary programs and anecdotes along these lines abound. The fact that these continue to be reported as innovations should, however, be a concern to those involved in curriculum planning.

4

Illustrative Curriculum Plans

This chapter includes illustrative curriculum plans designed to enhance self-perceptions in specific teaching-learning situations. In Chapter 3 we discussed the components of this level of curriculum planning, including organizing center, objectives, content, activities, resources, ane measuring devices. It was also pointed out that an effective way to organize such plans is through the use of resource units, a format that facilitates the techniques associated with unit teaching. The illustrative curriculum plans in this chapter are therefore presented in resource unit form.

A Format for Curriculum Plans

In theory, resource units consist of a wide variety of possible ideas for each of the specific teaching-learning situation components. In fact, the number would ordinarily exceed those that a group might actually be able to use. This is done so that teachers and students might select those ideas that seem most suitable or appropriate for their own group. Comprehensive resource units would thus be beyond the scope and focus of this book. The intention here is to provide examples of resource unit topics and components that deal directly with self-perceptions. Specifically, each sample includes:

1. An organizing center selected for its salience in self-perceptions

2. A rationale indicating how the topic relates to self-perceptions
3. *Sample* objectives within the topic which are directed at enhancing self-perceptions
4. *Sample* content matter relating the topic to self-perceptions
5. *Sample* activities which encourage self-thinking and analysis
6. *Sample* resources which deal with the topic in terms of self-perceptions
7. *Sample* measuring devices for assessing self-concept, esteem, and value growth in the unit.

Given the fact that the samples reflect only one part of what would be a full resource unit, the measuring devices consist of a series of questions that may be used by the teacher to structure obtrusive (e.g., face-to-face interviews) or unobtrusive (e.g., making note of library and cafeteria behavior) observation of students. For this component of the resource unit, we would encourage teachers to resist the temptation to scale items for some sort of total score. As Jersild (1952) noted:

> *In some of our procedures for testing personality we use an instrument, say, with fifty items and then assume that a student who marks forty-five items "right" is better adjusted than the one who marks only thirty-five "right." We usually assume that each quantitative item has about the same value. From an objective point of view this makes good sense, but from the standpoint of the subjective state of the individual learner it may not make any sense at all. On a list of fifty items there may be one (or several) items bearing on the matter of self-confidence. To a certain student this matter of self-confidence may be something of supreme importance. For him to have gained in this respect may be of great significance. From his point of view this item may mean as much as all the other forty-nine items combined" (p. 110).*

Teachers who wish to use these or similar unit plans would need to add items in each component dealing with cognitive, psychomotor, and additional affective aspects of the topic. Additional items might also be developed pertaining to self-perceptions since those included here are limited in number. It should also be noted that the activities are not intended to be used independently of the other components. In most cases, affective education loses effectiveness because it not only is separated from learning in other domains, but is done simply as activities without guiding objectives, supporting resources, and thoughtful evaluation. The resource unit format illustrated here relates the affective domain to others and encourages planning and teaching in this domain as part of a comprehensive curriculum planning framework.

Finally, the addition of new items, refinement of items, and/or selection of items that are actually used ought to be done through teacher-student planning. As previously pointed out, this technique has great promise for enhancing self-perceptions. Its use is thus assumed to be an integral part of unit plans, which are directed toward self-concept, self-esteem, and values.

Sample 1: The Family

Self-perceptions develop in a social context and are mainly influenced by the environment. The development of clear self-concept and positive self-esteem is enhanced when the individual understands the nature of the environment and his or her role in it. The environment is actualized in social interaction, while self-perceptions depend mainly on the quality of the interactions. The primary unit through which a sense of self, belonging, and participation are promoted is the family. At each stage of development, the "family" takes on a larger definition. In childhood, the primary family is the nuclear family, which consists of parents or guardians, siblings, and other relatives. In older childhood and transescence, peers become a kind of "family" in the sense of approval, values, behavior standards, and the like. As adolescence proceeds, the "family" broadens to include the community, and finally (also, hopefully) all humankind around the world.

The illustrative resource units included here are intended to help young people develop and improve their sense of self as a member of the "family" at each stage. The units proceed from the nuclear family to the family of peers, the community family, and the global family. Each is designed for the particular stage at which the type of family is an important part of the environment.

The Nuclear Family (Childhood)

Objectives

1. To describe roles and responsibilities of members of my family
2. To identify my rights and responsibilities in my family

3. To describe ways in which I am like and unlike other members of my family
4. To describe family events that make me happy or sad
5. To identify ways in which my school is like and unlike my family

Subject Matter (for the teacher to use in planning with students)

1. Children are basically "products" of their family. The family shapes behavior, attitudes, and self-perceptions.

2. Parents tend to be the most "significant others" in children's lives in terms of self-perception development.

3. In most families, each member assumes certain roles and responsibilities. These may include economic provider(s), decision maker(s), individuals responsible for household jobs, and so on.

4. Members of a family have characteristics in common and others that are unique to individuals. Either category may include interests, attitudes, likes and dislikes, physical attributes, etc. Such similarities and differences contribute to the dynamics of family living. Children should be helped to see how their characteristics are like and unlike those of other family members.

5. Family life involves both happy and sad events (plus many that are mainly neutral). Single events may have different effects, causing some members of the family to be happy and others to be sad or unhappy. Children should be helped to realize that both happy and sad times are a part of family living and that one sad event need not be viewed as an overly negative problem.

6. The early years of schooling ideally blend the interests of the school with the characteristics of the family. This is done to provide an easy transition for the child and in recognition of the fact that young children are still highly family oriented.

7. Family patterns vary widely. While many children live in homes where both natural parents are present, many others are from single-parent homes, live with guardians, and so on. Children from families in which there is divorce or separation often feel rejected or guilty and thus feel depressed or frustrated. In addition, such children may feel left out of family-oriented school activities or confused by holiday-related activities such as making crafts for Mother's Day or Father's Day.

Activities

1. Develop a personal family time-line showing major events in your life as well as major family events. Attach pictures, newspaper clippings, party invitations, and other items to illustrate events. Events might include birthdays, parties, trips, special activities, memorable holidays, the day you learned to ride a bicycle, and so on.

2. Interview your parents about important family events to find out what they remember. These might include happy or sad events, interesting stories about when you and brothers and sisters were born, and how your family is like your parent's family when they were young.

3. Keep a diary for a week. Write about things your family does together, jobs you do around the house, things that make you or others happy, projects you work on, and so on.

4. Make a daily time chart and show a typical schedule for a day in your family. What time does each member wake up and go to bed? What time are meals? What do family members do at various times of the day?

5. Make a list of responsibilities of various members of your family. For example, who cleans the house? Who does the food shopping? Who takes care of the yard? Who feeds pets? And so on. Count how many responsibilities each family member has. Who has the most and least? How are responsibilities assigned?

6. Make a list of words or phrases used in your family to show happiness, anger, love, and other feelings. Also, draw pictures to show how faces look when people in your family feel each way. For each feeling, give an example of an event or time when someone in your family felt that way.

7. Make a list of things that make each member of your family happy. These may include hobbies, activities, games, jobs done, and so on. Then make another list showing things you might do or say to help other members of your family feel happy.

8. Develop a list of family members including roles and responsibilities. Next to each, indicate a person in the school who carries out similar roles and responsibilities. Discuss how people and places in school are like your family and home. (Persons

141

and places that might be thought about in this activity include the teacher, the nurse, the library, the playground, the cafeteria, etc.)

Resources

About Myself (picture-posters, stories). Glendale, Calif.: Bowmar Publishing Co.

Children Need Families; Animals Have Families, Too; Neighbors Are Places Where People Are Friends. New York: William H. Sadlier, Inc.

Finding Your Roots (booklet with ideas, charts interview forms, directions for personal timeline). Carson, Calif.: Education Insights.

Getting to Know Me (filmstrips and records). Chicago: Society for Visual Education, Inc.

Jaynes, Ruth. *The Littlest House.* Glendale, Calif.: Bowmar Publishing Co., 1967.

Jaynes, Ruth. *The Biggest House.* Glendale, Calif.: Bowmar Publishing Co., 1968.

Keats, Ezra Jack. *Whistle for Willie.* New York: Viking Press, 1964.

Meeks, Esther K. *Families Live Together.* New York: Follet, 1969.

Robert and His Family (filmstrips and records). Chicago: Society for Visual Education, Inc.

Scott. Ann Herbert. *Sam.* New York: McGraw-Hill Book Co., 1967.

Sendak, Maurice. *Where the Wild Things Are.* New York: Harper, 1963.

Simon, Norma. *All Kinds of Families.* Chicago: Albert Whitman and Co., 1976.

Udry, Janice May. *What Mary Jo Shared.* Chicago: Albert Whitman and Co., 1966.

Understanding Your Feelings (filmstrips and cassettes). Boulder, Col.: Learning Tree Filmstrips.

What Are Parents for Anyway?; Who Do You Think You Are?; Brothers, Sisters, Feelings and You (filmstrips and records). Pleasantville, N.Y.: Guidance Associates.

Measuring Devices

Since this portion of the unit plan is directed toward enhancing the self-concept, work done by the students should be accepted unconditionally. The teacher, however, should be alert to the following kinds of criteria in observing and reviewing student work:

1. Does the child evidence clarity of his or her role in the family or does he or she seem uncertain or confused?
2. Does the child seem to have a clear and accepted place in his or her family?
3. Does this family do things together as a group much of the time, occasionally, or almost never?
4. Are there any family problems to which the child is particularly sensitive or which seem to be a source of unhappiness or frustration?
5. Does the child feel that the school is like the home in the sense of being a friendly place, providing help when needed, and so on?
6. Does the child experience mostly happy times at home or is the home an unhappy experience?

In answering these questions, the teacher will gain a sense of the child's view of the family, which may help to identify difficulties, if any exist. Ideas determined in this way may lead to personal conferences with the child, or perhaps to parent conferences in which the teacher might alert parents to potential problems.

The Family of Peers (Upper Childhood Transescence)

Objectives

1. To analyze reasons why peers are important
2. To identify ways in which the peer group influences attitudes, behavior, and values.

143

3. To compare and contrast peer values with those of adults
4. To identify reasons why friends are chosen
5. To analyze the clique and status structure in the school
6. To compare and contrast the values and standards of various cliques
7. To describe personal contributions one makes to the peer group

Content (for the teacher to use in planning with students)

1. One characteristic of older childhood and transescence is emergence of the peer group. For some dimensions of self-perceptions (e.g., dress, body build, language), feedback from the peer group becomes more influential than that of parents.
2. Acceptance by peers is probably the most preoccupying motive for behavior of older children and transescents.
3. The standards of the peer group often conflict with those of adults, including teachers. This conflict is typical for the age group, but often leads adults to react harshly or angrily.
4. Developing social connections with peers is one of the initial steps toward developing emotional independence from parents and other adults.
5. Even though acceptance by peers is important, older children and transescents often need the assurance of adult support on highly emotional issues.
6. Individuals are often so immersed in peer group dynamics that they are not clear about the degree to which they are being influenced by the peer group.
7. The overall peer group in older childhood and transescence typically divides into smaller cliques, each one with its own set of specific standards. Competition among cliques is often acute, and even though they are accepted in one clique, individuals may wish they were members of another.

Activities

1. Develop a series of sociograms for a group of peers. Base each one on a different idea:

a. Whom would each person like to do a school project with?

b. Whom would each person choose as a partner for an athletic event?

c. Whom would each person like to have as a best friend?

For each sociogram, discuss with a small group the reasons why people were chosen. Also look for differences in choices among the sociograms and discuss why different choices were made for different events or ideas.

2. Develop a list of cliques among the peer group in the school. For each one, cite the outstanding ideas that the clique has about behavior, attitudes, values, and the like. Also identify how one is accepted into the clique and under what conditions a member might be rejected. Compare the analysis with others.

3. Prepare a skit or play that dramatizes a major school event. Develop characters on the basis of caricatures or stereotypes of cliques.

4. Describe events, language, or behavior that are generally approved and disapproved by the peer group.

5. In a small group, develop a series of "Ann Landers" type responses to typical problems of your age group. For example:

a. How does one resolve a fight with a good friend?

b. How should one explain to friends that he or she has been grounded by parents a few days before a major social event?

c. What does one do if he or she is at a party where drugs or alcohol are being used and he or she doesn't want to use them?

6. Role play conflict events among peers. Try to use such interpersonal techniques as reflective listening, paraphrasing, and clarifying responses.

7. Develop a list of the behavior standards, attitudes, and values of your own clique. Note those that you have initiated. Rank standards in order of priority to the group and to yourself. Think of one or more issues on which you would take a stand against your clique.

Resources

About Me (booklet with activities, charts, and ideas for self-evaluation). Chicago: Encyclopedia Britannica Educational Corporation.

Alexander, Arthur. *The Hidden You: Psychology In Your Life.* Englewood Cliffs, N.J.: Prentice-Hall, Inc., 1962.

Bread and Butterflies. Agency for Instructional Television (series of fifteen programs designed specifically for emerging adolescents).

The Family You Belong To; The Friends You Make; The Person You Are (booklets with activities for analyzing self and environment). New York: Follet Publishing Co.

Living With Others (cassettes). South Holland, Ill.: Wilson Corporation.

Physical and Emotional Targets for Teenagers (cassettes and filmstrips). Q-ED Productions (a division of Cathedral Films, Inc.).

Self-Incorporated. Agency for Instructional Television (series of fifteen programs designed specifically for emerging adolescents).

Measuring Devices

Since the objectives in this unit plan are directed toward enhancing self-perception, work done by students should be accepted unconditionally. However, the teacher should be alert to the following kinds of criteria in observing and reviewing student work:

1. Does the student evidence understanding of the peer group as an influence?
2. Does each student feel accepted by at least one or two peers?
3. Are the analyses of clique structures and clique standards accurate and complete?
4. Does the student seem willing to accept others, especially those who are not particularly "best" friends?
5. Are cliques based on generally pro-social values and standards. If not, are students aware of this?

6. Do individuals perceive themselves as contributing members of their cliques or are they simply followers?

7. Are students developing skills in constructive interpersonal communications? Are they evident in activities other than role-playing, such as those that take place outside the classroom?

The Community Family (Transescence)

Objectives

1. To analyze the qualities of a "good" citizen as perceived by the local community

2. To identify community customs that youth are expected to honor

3. To analyze the local community's view of youth

4. To identify racial, ethnic, and religious characteristics in the local community

5. To identify community groups or agencies that provide services to youth

6. To identify services that youth provide to the community

7. To analyze ongoing or current problems that face the local community

8. To identify contributions that individual youths might provide to the community

Content (for the teacher to use in planning with students)

1. Different communities may have similar or unique ideas about characteristics of "good citizenship." These may include participation in civic groups, involvement in solving community problems, participation in local government, and other social contributions. They might also include, in some communities, passive acceptance of a local power structure, economic self-sufficiency, membership in a profession, or involvement in a certain social group. The two views are somewhat polar and may offer values viewpoints. Within a given community, both views might be held as well as others between the two.

2. Local communities tend to have certain views of youth, which may range from optimistic to pessimistic. These views may be manifested in newspaper editorials, availability of youth-activity facilities, and youth services. They might also be manifested in expectations that youth follow certain customs, such as participation or acquiescence in civic government. Youth often sense the reality of these views and develop a feeling that they are wanted or unwanted, belong or do not.

3. Many communities have a variety of religious, ethnic, and/or racial groups within them. Individual youths belonging to one or another may have self-perceptions about their place in the community, depending on how the group with which they are affiliated is generally viewed by peers and others.

4. Many towns, cities, and counties have a variety of groups or agencies that provide services to youth. These may include drug or alcohol centers, recreation councils, social services offices, employment centers, and others. It is important that youths be aware of these services as a source of help or guidance in times of difficulty.

5. Schools and/or local youth groups often sponsor community service projects intended to improve local communities. These may include environmental projects, citizen surveys, projects to improve recreation facilities, help for older persons, and the like. Youth also provide other services (sometimes on a paid basis) such as delivering newspapers, assisting fire departments, playing in community orchestras, and so on. The activities are, in fact, services that youth provide to the community and that enhance community life.

6. Virtually every community faces problems such as those related to the environment, social services, traffic, land-use, zoning, energy resources, as well as periodic conflicts over issues or events. Young people should have an opportunity to study these problems and, where appropriate, to share findings or recommendations with appropriate groups. This kind of activity helps youth to feel a sense of participation and worth in the local community.

7. Related to the study of youth services and community problems is the potential for identifying possible contributions that individual youths might make. These may include helping older

persons or children, serving on community task forces, assisting community agencies, and others. Such activities offer opportunities for action or experiential learning and help individuals to develop a sense of belonging, participation, and self-worth.

Activities

1. Develop a survey form that asks citizens to identify the characteristics of people who enhance or detract from community life. Conduct the survey by mail, phone, or door-to-door interviews. Tabulate the findings and develop a profile of each type of citizen. Discuss such issues as how many citizens of each type there are locally or personal opinions about the profiles.

2. Develop a directory of community groups or agencies that offer services to youth. Include name, address, telephone number, type of service, and contact person. The directory might then be printed and distributed to other persons. Also, analyze the directory to determine areas in which services are not provided and discuss how steps may be taken to see that they are in the future. An excellent example of a format for such a directory is *Adult Education Opportunities in Berkshire County* (researched and edited by the Learning Connection, 73 North St., Pittsfield, Massachusetts 01201).

3. Develop a list of local laws or customs that pertain specifically to youth. Discuss the list with reference to what the laws or customs mean, how they affect youth, whether they are just or not, and so on. Organize a formal debate on controversial items, contact youth in other communities to compare lists, or interview adults about their views of the list.

4. Acquire the results of the most recent federal or local census. Identify racial, ethnic, and/or religious groups represented in your community. Interview local leaders of these groups about how they believe the community perceives their group and what, if any, problems the group has in the community. Collate the results of the interviews and discuss issues that emerge from them. Students representing any group or local group leaders might be asked to make presentations on the ideas, beliefs, and customs that are unique to their group, or to express public opinions that reflect misperceptions of their group.

5. Develop a list of services that youth, in groups or individually, provide to the community. Interviewing or surveying other students in the school may add to the list. Try to determine the percentage of young people in the community who are involved in such services. Develop a scenario of how the community would look if youth-services stopped. Identify service areas not included in the list but which should be, by contacting local groups or agencies.

6. Analyze recent newspapers or other reports to identify problems that the local community faces. Interview or survey citizens about their views of a particular problem and conduct a class or small group analysis of the problem. Conduct a debate on a problem with students representing two or more views. Develop one or more position papers regarding how a particular problem might be solved. You may wish to make these available to appropriate persons or groups.

7. Contact local groups or agencies to identify services for which they need help. Determine one or more that young people might help with and find out what would be involved. Take on one or more of these as a project and/or make a list of them available to other students with a request for volunteers. (Be sure to provide information about the need, the group, or the individual involved and how to contact them. Or, set up a clearinghouse in the school for helping student volunteers and groups or individuals needing help in making contact with each other.)

8. Develop a student exchange program with age-mates from a different type of community (e.g., rural-urban, black-white). Construct all necessary committees to carry out the exchange, including orientation, housing, recreation, etc. Before the actual exchange, role play and discuss perceptions and expectations of individuals and life in the other community. Share these during the exchange.

Resources

Citizen Involvement (film using exemplary communities in Seattle, Philadelphia, and Arkansas, depicting the process of citizen involvement and how it can contribute to better decisions at the local level). New York: R. H. R. Filmedia, Inc.

The Citizen's Role in Aiding Law Enforcement Officials (series of 4 videotapes). Richmond, Ken.: Eastern Kentucky University Division of Television and Radio.

Dissent in Action (tape in which Ramsey Clark discusses his views on an individual's right to dissent and what should be done to dissenters who flout the law). Chicago: American Library Association.

The Individual in the System (film examining what the future holds for the students of today). Florida: Modern Talking Pictures.

It's a Nice Place to Visit, but I Wouldn't Want to Live There (series of 13 cassettes, exploring the environmental and social problems of the big city). Chicago: Canadian Consulate General.

Lord, Clifford L., ed. *Teaching History with Community Resources.* Bureau of Publications, Teachers' College Columbia University.

Los Angeles: What the City Means to Its Youth (film contrasting the lives of affluent, white, middle-class youth in Los Angeles with those of underprivileged black youths of the suburbs). New York: Time Life Films.

Post, Langdon W. *The Challenge of Housing.* New York: Farrar, Straus and Cudahy.

The Quiet Summer (film describing how, in 1965, a summer project operated by youth ended annual youth rioting in Hampton Beach, New Hampshire). Washington, D. C.: National Audiovisual Center.

Three Young Americans: In Search of Survival (film). St. Paul, Minn.: 3M Company.

Toward A Quality of Living (2 filmstrips focusing on the interdependent relationship of the family with the behavioral , man-built, and natural environments). J. C. Penney Co.

Twain, Mark. *The Man that Corrupted Hadleyburg and Other Stories and Essays.* New York: Harper and Brothers.

What Can You Do? (a documentary film on community health care). Florida: Modern Talking Pictures.

Your Space and Mine: A Behavioral Approach to Environments (filmstrip investigating the interrelationship of personal space, sensory cues, environmental messages, and behavior settings). J. C. Penney Co.

Youth Tutoring Youth: Why? (article describing how to set up such a program in the community). New York: National Commission on Resources for Youth.

Zu Tavern, A. B., and Bullock, A. E. *The Consumer Investigates.* Chicago: H. M. Rowe Co.

Measuring Devices

The sample objectives are directed toward improving the sense of self as a member of the community. Teachers should observe students and review their work related to these objectives, paying attention to the following kinds of criteria. In addition, students should evaluate their own work with regard to the objectives and the criteria.

1. How do students perceive how the local community views them? Do they feel that they belong or have a respected place? Do they feel they are treated justly?

2. Do students care about the problems or quality of living in their local community or do they tend to be apathetic or indifferent?

3. What prejudices do students have about ethnic, racial, or religious groups? If so, what are they based on? How strong are they? Have they dissipated during the unit?

4. Do students volunteer to help with community needs? If not, are their reasons justified or do they grow out of feelings of incompetence, apathy, or rejection?

5. Do students tend to participate in established service projects or groups?

The Global Family (Adolescence)

Objectives

1. To define the terms *global* citizen and *global interdependence*
2. To describe the life of cohorts in other societies
3. To analyze the "rites of passage" to adulthood in other societies
4. To describe the role of communications technology in creating and promoting global interdependence

5. To compare the views of western society toward developing nations and developing youth

6. To analyze the idea that the history of humankind is similar to the process of individual human growth and development

7. To develop a sense of potential future lifestyles and values that might be available to individuals

Content

1. A global citizen is one who perceives himself or herself as a part of a world, in addition to a local or national society, and who is concerned about problems and issues that have global implications. The global citizen tries to understand other cultures and cares about the needs of humankind around the world.

2. Global interdependence refers to the concept that people from various nations and cultures depend on each other for resources, services, ideas, support, and communications. To see oneself as a global citizen depends on an understanding of global interdependence.

3. The "rites of passage" to adulthood vary among cultures. In western and westernized societies, the rites are related to the completion of adolescence, willingness to accept adult roles and responsibilities, and maintenance of economic self-sufficiency. In other cultures, the rites may involve some symbolic ritual, upon achieving pubescence, which automatically qualifies the individual for adulthood. Symbolic rites such as the Jewish bar mitzvah and the Catholic confirmation are maintained by Western Society, but do not literally allow the individual to have the rights and privileges of adulthood in society. Adolescents in Western Society often face confusion and ambiguity in self-perceptions since they are not considered adults even though their physical development is adult-like and they often assume adult responsibilities.

4. Modern communications technology has brought real meaning to the concept of global interdependence. Interactive and non-interactive television, radio, satellite communications, and other devices constantly remind us of events and problems in distant places. Such technology also encourages "instant" analyses of issues so that we can see how actions in one country affect those

in others. This means that self-perceptions are constantly exposed to large and powerful issues, the complexity of which often promote feelings of helplessness in individuals. On the other hand, lack of such knowledge may cause people to remain ignorant about global issues and largely ego- and ethnocentric.

5. In many ways the view of Western Society toward "developing" nations is similar to its view of "developing" youth. Both are typically considered immature, irresponsible, unsophisticated, and in need of constant guidance. Perhaps as a consequence, both often encounter conflict in attempting to exercise or assert their independence and both frequently feel misunderstood.

6. Some historians have likened the history of humankind to individual human growth and development. They point to similar beginning stages in which the environment controls humans, developmental stages in which the balance begins to shift, and later stages in which humans finally control their environment. The quality of self-perceptions similarly becomes related to locus of control, particulary in adolescence.

7. As we have begun to understand values in other cultures, the latter have become influential in our own. For example, Eastern religions have attracted attention in Western Society in terms of such practices as meditation and also in terms of various life philosophies. In like manner, Eastern Societies have adapted many Western customs and practices. The interchange of societal values has opened up new possibilities for people as lifestyles and values from other cultures have become more acceptable and more widely practiced. Thus in thinking about future lifestyles and self-perceptions, contemporary youth may think beyond local and national norms.

Activities

1. Contact a local or national agency that sponsors a pen-pal or similar program. Select adolescent individuals from various countries and write them letters requesting information about pertinent topics. These might include school topics, popular music, clothes, interests, responsibilities, problems, and so on. Develop a group chart that shows information about each topic by country. Analyze the chart to identify similarities and differences

across cultures. (Be sure to include our society.) Also, develop one or more statements of value dilemmas and ask pen-pals to react to them.

2. Interview persons from other countries who have recently migrated to the local community. In addition to gathering information similar to that in Activity 1, find out why they migrated, problems they encountered, and first impressions upon arriving. Some might also be invited to visit a class to discuss these issues. (Keep in mind that a language interpreter may be necessary in this activity.)

3. Keep a log of international news reported by various media for one or two weeks. Select several problems or issues reported, and have small groups attempt to identify how those might affect adolescents in the particular country where the problem occurred. Have each group identify how they would react if they were in that situation and how their lives would be affected.

4. Contact local, state, or federal agencies that have information about programs designed to help persons in need in other countries. Establish a class project to participate in one or more programs. These might include sponsoring a destitute child or family, or collecting foods to be sent to a country where some natural disaster has occurred. Have the class or small groups construct projects that depict the purpose for their participation in the assistance program and their personal feelings as a result of the participation.

5. Select one or two "developing" nations. Identify, historically if possible, the role that a "developed" nation (e.g., United States) has played in the former's development. Then collect information about how the developing nation has been portrayed in media and how government agencies and citizens view that nation. Compare this information with the general view of our society toward adolescence. The comparison may involve issues such as independence, responsibility, privileges, lifestyles, values, and so on.

6. Research the area of human growth and development, concentrating on the relationship between the individual and the environment (e.g., infant dependency on others). Try to identify the nature of the relationship in infancy, childhood, early and later adolescence, and early, middle, and late adulthood. After de-

picting this development on a chart, try to identify times in history when humankind has been like each stage of development. Also, discuss what happens when an individual is placed in a new or unfamiliar situation, and compare this to stages of human development. In each activity, discuss such issues as conflict between the individual and the environment and the consequences of not resolving the conflict.

7. Make a list of various aspects of the adolescent subculture. The list should include items such as dress, music, recreation activities, and so on. For each one, identify how, if at all, the item has been influenced by other world cultures. Use this discussion to initiate a larger analysis of how values and lifestyles in other cultures are influencing our society in other age groups.

8. Using the same format as Activity 7, analyze adolescence in previous generations.

9. Contact the local ACTION agency and arrange an interview with a recently returned Peace Corps volunteer about value dilemmas that he or she faced in working in another culture. Also, raise questions about adolescent life in the other culture.

10. Interview a former local or regional VISTA volunteer who had responsibilities in the refugee program about problems faced by immigrants entering our culture, particularly adolescents. (Compare information with that received from the Peace Corps volunteer noted in Activity 8 if that activity is used.)

11. Contact the Peace Corps about their "Partnership" program. This involves sponsoring development of a school in a Third World country.

12. Gather information about past recipients of the Nobel Peace Prize. Compare the biographies to a list the group has developed of characteristics of a global citizen.

13. Establish a volunteer program to tutor recent immigrants from other countries.

14. Contact a foreign student group at a local university. Request opportunities to interview members or invite them to do a presentation on their home country.

Resources

One excellent source of global education resources is the Peace Corps Information Collection and Exchange, 806 Connecticut Avenue, N.W., Washington, D. C. 20525. That office can provide information about programs, resources, and so on. Other helpful sources include:

Africa (series of 3 films: *Where the Brides Do the Choosing; Magicians of the Black Hills; Journey to the Magic Valley).* Troy, Mich.: Time Life Films Series.

Asia (6 color films on customs, cultures, and traditions of Asia). Troy, Mich.: Time Life Films.

Australian Aborigines: Men of the Dream Time; People Out of Time; The Roaring Serpent of Arnhem Land. Troy, Mich.: Time Life Series.

Baker, Liva. *World Faiths: A Story of Religions.* Abelard-Schulman, 1965.

Bay Area Global Education Project. Director, Mezzanine Floor, Hotel Claremont Office Park, Berkeley, Calif. 94705.

Center for Global Studies. Indiana Univeristy, 513 North Park Ave., Bloomington, Ind. 47405.

Center for Teaching International Relations. Director, University of Denver, Denver, Col. 80208.

Central and South America (5 color films on the customs, cultures, and traditions of Central and South America). Troy, Mich.: Time Life Films.

The Energy Crisis: Questions and Answers (booklet discussing energy shortage problem; offers possible solutions). New York: American Jewish Committee.

The Faces of My Brother (documents the hunger, poverty, and sickness common to the Third World nations). New York: Maryknoll Film Library.

The Family of Man (series of 7 color films that investigates and contrasts family life from birth to death in five different cultures). Troy, Mich.: Time Life Series.

Global Perspectives in Education, Inc. Director of Program Development, 218 E. 18th St., New York, N. Y. 10003.

The Heart of Apartheid (describes how South Africa's blacks feel about segregation). Troy, Mich.: Time Life Film Series.

Our Poisoned World (5 films on environmental pollution). New York: Time Life Films.

Race to Extinction (a film describing the present-day Lacandon Indians, the last of the Mayan Civilization). Troy, Mich.: Time Life Film Series.

The Road to Progress (long and short versions; addresses the question of how to deal with world food problems as well as other community and economic problems).

A Simple Cup of Tea (film about an AID agricultural advisor working in East Pakistan). Washington, D. C.: National Audio-visual Center.

Social Studies School Service. 10,000 Culver Blvd., P. O. Box 802, Culver City, Calif. 90230.

When Other People Hurt (filmstrip narrated by a teenager; takes a look at world hunger and what can be done about it). New York: CROP.

The Witch Doctor. Troy, Mich.: Time Life Series.

Young Citizens (film showing youth of world, particularly of India, in search of ideals). New York: Information Services of India.

Measuring Devices

The sample objectives are directed toward helping learners develop a sense of global citizenship and interdependence, in other words, a sense of self as a member of the global family. Students should be observed and should evaluate themselves with regard to the following kinds of questions:

1. Have students changed their attitudes toward other cultures in terms of their values and philosophies?

2. Do students demonstrate empathy toward the problems and issues faced by other nations and cultures?

3. Do students demonstrate clarity and accuracy in discussing the nature of adolescence with regard to human development, societal attitudes, and the like?

4. Do students show inclination toward continuing positive attitudes toward global citizenship beyond the completion of the unit?

5. Do students show curiosity and sensitivity toward other cultures' values, philosophies, lifestyles, etc.? Are they open-minded about value information from other cultures?

Sample 2: The Self and Contemporary Media
(Transescence, Adolescence)

Media technology has increased the opportunities for young people to see and hear about the lifestyles, attitudes, values, and ideas of other people around the world. In short, it has put them in touch with much that was unknown to previous generations. Commercial media have become a widely used source for entertainment and information. At the same time, however, they have developed real influence in the lives of young people. In some cases, dramatic characters assume the role of "significant others" in developing self-perceptions. Commercial advertising is also powerful in that it is based on the need to maintain or improve self-perceptions and social standing. For these reasons, young people need opportunities to understand their roles as consumers of commercial media. The following illustrations are from a unit that would serve that purpose.

Objectives

1. To evaluate the impact of commercial media on lifestyles of youth
2. To analyze the intent of commercial advertising in relation to self-perceptions
3. To identify self-perceptions of people characterized in situation dramas
4. To identify ways media might improve self-perceptions of consumers
5. To describe the social, sex, and ethnic/racial roles that media portray and suggest
6. To identify values portrayed by various characters in dramatic and comedy programs

159

7. To identify the self-perception messages of commercial media that are intended for certain age groups

Content (for the teacher to use in planning with students)

1. Young people watch television up to 15,000 hours by the time they leave high school. In addition, they may spend numerous hours listening to radio and records, attending films, and so on. The commercial media are intended for entertainment, but they also influence values, lifestyles, attitudes, and beliefs. In this sense, they are also teaching devices.

2. Lifestyles and values are suggested by commercial media through character portrayals, program topics, and advertising. The latter, for example, may influence nutritional habits, career choices, standard-of-living aspirations, and consumer attitudes.

3. Commercial advertising is largely based on the idea that people are either dissatisfied with aspects of their present life or wish to maintain their status.

4. Situation dramas offered by commercial media are intended to portray either real or fantasy conceptions of life. Characters involved in these dramas demonstrate various types of self-perceptions, attribute satisfaction, negative or positive self-esteem, confused or clear self-concept, and anti-social or pro-social values. Self-perceptions of dramatic characters may be identified through personal dialog, observed behavior, relations with others, and perceptions others have of them.

5. In some cases, commercial media portrays characters and events in terms of racial, ethnic, and sex stereotypes. In the sense that commercial media influences attitudes, these stereotypes may come to life in the beliefs of media consumers. One crucial value issue for media is whether it should contribute to the end of stereotyping by purposely counteracting prejudicial views of groups held by some persons and groups in our society. This might be done by portraying typically stereotyped groups in situations, occupations, and so on that conflict with the stereotyped attitude. Characters in nonstereotyped situations also offer role models for the self-perceptions of young people.

6. Assuming commercial media have an effect on self-perceptions, programs might be developed that encourage open-mindedness,

human relations, positive interpersonal communications, and nonstereotyped views of age groups, sexes, racial and ethnic groups, persons with handicapping conditions, and socio-economic groups.

7. Programming on commercial media, including advertising, is frequently aimed at a particular age group. This focus makes assumptions about the interests, values, and self-perceptions of a given age group. Perhaps the most controversial example of this concept is the programming intended for young children on Saturday morning television. Questions have been raised about the influence of violent scenes, nonnutritional advertising, and so on. If concerned citizen groups are correct, then young children must be viewed by media programmers as prone to violence, nutritionally inept, and gullible to attractive advertising.

Activities

1. Establish a standing committee (with rotating membership) in the class, responsible for review of special programs on various media. These may include newspaper features, television and radio programs, and movies at local theaters. The committee should develop a guide for worthwhile, up-coming programs, and then present reviews, including summaries of those by professional critics. Analysis should focus on programming intended to enhance self-perceptions and promote pro-social values.

2. Develop a rating system for commercial programming based on whether programs enhance self-perceptions and values. Ask groups to review programs and apply the rating system over a period of time. Disseminate the ratings on a school-wide basis and publish them in local newspapers.

3. Describe the self-perceptions of characters in situation dramas on television, radio, and in short stories. Discuss how the self-perceptions were identified. Compare the techniques on the basis of media used (e.g., Did the nonvisual aspect of radio hinder the identification of self-perceptions? Does the written word add depth to such identification? Which allows for the broadest interpretation? Which is most suggestive of one interpretation?).

4. Develop a situation drama based on the local peer group. Include

characters who portray typical types of peers engaged in typical events (e.g., parties, classes, clubs). Also include characters who try to improve self-perceptions and values of peers. Record the drama on cassette or video-tape and have other students analyze it in terms of character development, self-perceptions, and the like.

5. Analyze video-tape or cassette recordings of various commercial advertisements. Discuss questions such as: Who is it aimed at? What does it assume about consumer self-perceptions? What value does it portray? What are the characteristics of people who would be influenced by it? Survey students to determine how their lifestyles and values relate to frequency, timing, and content of the commercials.

6. Systematically select a sample of commercial advertisements and situation dramas. Record the frequency of ethnic/racial characters portrayed, as well as the by-sex and by-age proportion of characters. Keep track of such characteristics of the characters as occupation, social standing, socioeconomic status, attitudes, interests, and others. Analyze these to determine whether they reflect stereotyping or bias.

7. Survey other students to determine favorite commercial programs, films, records, etc. Ask for reasons why particular ones were chosen as favorites. Compare responses by age groups, sex, and other variables. Develop and publish lists of favorites in each media category.

8. Try to keep a log of examples of media permeating people's lives. Note times when peers or others quote commercials, sing "jingles" or songs from commercials, or imitate popular characters. Compare the log with those kept by others. Try to determine why certain commercials or characters are more popular than others.

Resources

In addition to those listed below, several excellent resources are available from the National PTA TV Action Center, 700 North Rush St., Chicago, Illinois 60611. These include program reviews, curriculum guides, and other timely information.

Consumer Power: Advertising (film). BFA Educational Media.

Feedback (cassette series). Network Project. New York: Radio Free People.

Freedom of the Press–Today (filmstrips and cassettes). Pleasantville, N. Y.: Guidance Associates.

Inside Radio and Television (cassette). Hollywood, Calif.: Center for Cassette Studies, Inc.

Johnson, Nicholas. *How to Talk Back to Your Television Set.* Boston: Little, Brown and Co., 1970.

Label for the Voiceless: The Wired City and Those Careless Promises. Washington, D. C.: National Education Association.

Mass Media: Impact on a Nation (filmstrips and cassettes). Pleasantville, N. Y.: Guidance Associates.

Mass Media: Their Role in a Democracy (filmstrip and record). New York: New York Times.

Mitchell, Malcolm G. *Propaganda, Polls and Public Opinion: Are People Manipulated?* (concepts, activities).

Schrank, Jeffrey. *TV Action Book* (includes activities and log forms). Evanston, Ill.: McDougal, Litell and Co., 1978.

Skinner, Stanley. *The Advertisement Book* (activities and concepts). Evanston, Ill.: McDougal, Littell and Co., 1976.

TV News: Measure of the Medium (film). Santa Monica, Calif.: BFA Educational Media.

Measuring Devices

The purpose of the objectives in this sample unit is to help students understand how media influence their self-perceptions and values. Through teacher observation and student self-evaluation, the following kinds of questions should be addressed:

1. To what extent do commercial media influence learner self-perceptions and values? Are they analytic as consumers or is the influence overly powerful?

2. What are the values portrayed in the most popular media programming? Are these pro-social or anti-social?

3. Do learners know why they are media consumers? Are they interested or is it simply an escape?

4. To what extent are students made to feel adequate or inadequate by the media of which they are consumers?

5. Do learners accurately identify media use of stereotypes, bias, and fantasy? Are they critical of this? Do they have ideas for changing it?

6. Are learners' media interests focused on fantasy programs and characters? If so, why? Do they understand this? Is it related to self-perception problems?

Sample 3: Living In Our School (Elementary)

From the time children enter school it becomes a major part of their lives. For most, formal education will continue through high school at least and learning, hopefully, through the entire lifespan. It is thus important for children to develop early a clear sense of themselves in school, in other words, to get a good start. Children learn directly about many things in school, but most learning about school itself is left to experience. For this reason, many children develop confused or negative feelings about various aspects of school life. Some of these feelings may become more or less permanent ideas and influence the perception of school as a social institution. The unit of which the following sample might be a part is directed at helping children to develop clear and confident self-perceptions with regard to school. It is also intended to make life in school a visible part of the curriculum agenda.

Objectives

1. To identify the reasons why children are required to go to school
2. To describe what it takes to do well in school
3. To identify the roles of various people in the school
4. To investigate the reasons behind school and classroom rules
5. To compare and contrast the school with the home
6. To identify some of the problems faced by children in coming to school

7. To describe how different events in school influence how children feel about themselves

8. To develop confidence in participating in school life

Content (for teachers)

1. Children may believe there are many reasons why they have to come to school—because their parents work, to learn, because their older brothers and sisters have to, and so on. The fact is that they are legally required to attend. They need to understand primary and secondary reasons so that they have a sense of purpose in coming to school. The reasons need to be immediate, however, since children probably do not understand remote reasons (e.g., "so you can go to college or get a better job").

2. Children may hear from siblings, teachers, parents, and others ideas about what it takes to do well in school. Some of these ideas may conflict and the child may develop a confused sense of expectations. Children who do well in school tend to have a clear sense of purpose as well as a sense of certainty about what is expected of them.

3. Children are often uncertain about what various adults do in school. They may know their teacher well, but be less certain of roles and responsibilities of administrators, cafeteria workers, secretaries, maintenance personnel, and others. Children tend to feel more confident when they know the people around them, what they are like, and what to expect of them. Being familiar with adult roles in the school may therefore help children develop confidence in themselves in school.

4. Schools tend to have two kinds of rules: those required by legislation and those developed locally. In addition, interpretation of rules may vary from one adult to another. Confusion growing out of these concepts may contribute to a sense of self-confusion in children. Their confidence and understanding may be enhanced by understanding the reasons behind rules, as well as which are fixed by law and which are local and thus negotiable. They may be helped in this regard even more if they have a chance to participate in rule making.

5. Children tend to be highly family oriented. The family is typically familiar and thus is a useful device for comparison in learning

new ideas and information. Ideally, the school blends its own interests with the characteristics of the family in order to accommodate and build upon the family orientation of children. Understanding how the school is like the family may help children develop a sense of security and confidence in the former.

6. Children face many problems in school. Whether any one is simple or complex depends on how the child perceives it, regardless of adult views. Problems may involve getting to and from school, relating to teachers, fear of cafeteria crowds, contacts with other children, remembering assignments, and so on. Undue concern or worry about these may cause children to dislike or fear school and to question their ability to survive or do well within it. They need to be helped to understand that these are common problems that can be solved, as well as knowing they will receive support when problems do arise.

7. Life in school usually involves both happy and unhappy feelings. Children typically experience such feelings as they engage in various events and activities from day to day. In some cases, an unhappy experience may become an obsession in their feelings, evolving into dislike for school. Children need opportunities to consider how they feel about aspects of school life and that other children probably feel the same way. This will likely add to the clarity and confidence of their self-perceptions.

Activities

1. Have the students develop a list of the reasons why they think they have to come to school. Also ask them to interview members of their family for additional reasons. Discuss which ones are most important and why. (Using the lists, ask them to make up stories about children who do not go to school.)

2. Invite various adults in school to describe to children what they do in terms of roles and responsibilities. Adults should also tell about themselves personally: hobbies, interests, families, trips, and so on. Ask each adult to take children in groups of four or five to their school workspace and familiarize them with what is done there. Develop a list of possible problems that could arise in school, and for each problem, note the person to whom children might turn for help.

3. Have children engage in some activity in which they can all succeed. Ask them to list the reasons why they think they succeeded and why. Relate the reasons to other school activities, particularly those that will soon be undertaken. As the latter develop, remind the children of the previous discussion and use the list as a checklist.

4. Develop a list of school and classroom rules, the latter with the help of children. For each rule, ask the children to identify what happens if the rule is followed or not followed. Focus on natural consequences such as physical injury to self and others, and so on. Have the children think of ways that they can remember the rules.

5. Have children develop personal time-lines of their lives in school. Use pictures, notes, reports, and so on to illustrate events. Ask the children to indicate which ones were happy or unhappy and why. Extend the time-line for two or three months into the future and have the children write in (with illustrations) things they hope will happen during that time.

6. Develop a list of family members, including roles and responsibilities. Next to each, indicate a person in school who carries out a similar role or responsibility. Discuss how people and places in school are like those in the family or home. (Persons and places that might be thought about include the teacher, the nurse, the library, the playground, the cafeteria, etc.)

7. Take children on a tour of the school, paying particular attention to physical facilities. Along the way, ask for suggestions about how they might improve facilities. Record these ideas, as well as positive or negative comments about various aspects of the school facility in general. Afterwards, discuss these comments and develop a list of needed improvements. (These might include access to places, playground equipment, size of furniture, and so on.) Send the list to the school principal and ask for reactions.

8. Develop a set of procedures for welcoming new students to the school. Form a committee that would carry out the procedures when necessary. They might plan tours, introduce new students to classmates, and construct packets of materials such as papers, pencils, and the like.

9. Develop a project centered around the history of the school. Have students construct a time-line depicting the history, draw pictures about the school's history, interview adults who attended the school, and so on. Also have students suggest ideas through stories or pictures about what the school might be like in the future.

Resources

The resources learners use in this unit should be derived from the local setting (e.g., teachers, parents, nonteaching staff, school board members, etc.). These local resources are particularly important since they may likely be "significant others" for the learners.

Measuring Devices

The aim of the objectives in this sample unit is to help children understand themselves as participants in school life. Teachers should observe students during the unit in terms of the following kinds of questions:

1. Do the children evidence clarity in their school self-concepts or are they confused?
2. Do children indicate a sense of clarity and confidence in terms of family expectations for their school experience?
3. Do children seem to understand that various rules exist and why? Do they seem confident that they can live within them?
4. Do children seem to know what adults in school do? Do they appear comfortable with these adults or are they fearful of some? If so, are the fears realistic or unrealistic?
5. Do children know whom they can turn to for help with various school problems?
6. Do children feel that the school is like the home in the sense of being a friendly place, where help is available when needed? If not, does this arise out of home or school confusion?
7. Do children seem confident in participating in school activities? If not, why? Are they shy, timid, fearful?
8. Do children seem to have a clear idea of what is supposed to happen in school, why they are there, and so on?

In answering these kinds of questions, the teacher will gain a sense of the child's view of self in school. Problems should lead to supportive action by the teacher or, in some cases, to conferences with parents or other adults in school to clear up confusion, allay fears, and so on.

Summary

In Chapter 4 we have presented samples of resource unit sections that are focused on the idea of enhancing self-perceptions in school and through school experiences. In each case, the samples could and should be extended to include cognitive, psychomotor, and additional affective components. They should, however, offer initial ideas for curriculum planning to enhance self-perceptions.

Beyond this, it is assumed that teachers who undertake such units are inclined toward the ideas of unit teaching, including such aspects as teacher-student planning, small group work, problem solving, and project development. Finally, it is important to note once more that resource units are intended to provide suggestions for teachers and students in a format that is congruent with the components of a teaching-learning situation. The various sections are open to revision, addition, and deletion, but are to be viewed as interrelated and not dealt with separately outside the context of the whole unit.

5

State of the Art and Hope for the Future

In this final chapter we will undertake two tasks. Part I is a description of the state of the art with regard to theory, research, and practice related to self-perceptions. In light of these, a summary view of the self-enhancing school in terms of ideas discussed in previous chapters will also be presented.

Part II involves a look at what we see as some of the roadsigns that offer hope for developing self-enhancing schools in the future. We will describe some of the recent advances in technology, exploration of human relationships, learning, and school processes, which, when taken together, provide encouragement for an optimistic point of view.

Part I
State of the Art

It is obvious from the many references cited in this and other volumes that theory and research on self-perceptions have enjoyed increasing popularity in recent years. We certainly know much more about these topics than we did a decade or two ago. However, work in this area is far from completed and efforts to date often seem to raise as many questions as they have answered.

A good deal of the theoretical consideration regarding self-perceptions was done earlier in this century, and while this does not immediately suggest that it is questionable, much has changed in our society since. For example, many of the conditions of our environment have been reconstructed by rapidly advancing technology. We have always thought of "significant others" mainly in terms of those persons with whom the individual has relatively immediate contact. Now, however, communications technology brings individuals into daily contact with persons who are from other cultures, who have varying lifestyles, and who, in commercial media, are often polished and stylized to portray "ideal" personalities. Furthermore, technology has often advanced at the expense of human interaction and reflection. In short, technology has created fundamental changes in the environment in which self-perceptions are formulated. It may be the case that technology has only a very limited place in this environment, playing a minor role compared to the more immediate "others" with whom the individual has contact. On the other hand, technology may play a greater part, thus broadening the traditional notion of the "environment" and bringing more complex and ambiguous aspects to it. If this is the case, the kinds of role models that have typically been studied as environmental aspects may need considerable rethinking as we attempt to develop an adequate theory of self-concept and self-esteem.

Another problem, already alluded to, is the imprecision of terminology and instrumentation used in theory and research on self-perceptions. We are constantly confronted with research studies and school programs that purport to deal with self-concept, self-esteem, self-worth, self-regard, self-image, and myriad other variables that undoubtedly represent aspects of self-perceptions. However, one is often unsure about exactly which aspect is under consideration since terms are used interchangeably and imprecisely. For example, one may be reading a fascinating study of how adolescent boys describe themselves on an adjective checklist and suddenly be told by the authors that some of these boys have negative self-esteem. As we have seen, this kind of inferred conclusion about self-esteem is unwarranted unless the researcher makes some effort to determine whether the adolescent boys are happy or unhappy about their self-description. Confusion on the part of the researcher regarding what is being studied thus detracts from the report and limits its potential contribution to our understanding.

In like manner, school goal statements frequently speak to the need for improving some aspect of self-perceptions. Suppose, though, that the school undertakes to improve self-esteem, extending great efforts to help students feel that they should accept themselves as they are. What does this mean for individuals who have confused or unsure self-concepts or who are convinced that they are incompetent? Furthermore, what does this mean for the school if some students perceive that school is worthless or meaningless? In one case, the school purports to help students be satisfied with unclear and inadequate self-concepts, while on the other hand, students are to accept self-perceptions that are opposed to the school itself. The lack of precision in self-perception "language" in schools is probably representative of the lack of understanding of the concepts behind this area of development. Until some effort is made to remedy this confusion, however, programs that are directed toward enhancing self-perceptions may be expected to lack clarity in purpose and procedure. Lack of clarity, of course, also leaves these programs open to the criticism that they are the "soft" side of the curriculum and thus not on par with the so-called "rigorous," cognitive curriculum.

Another example of the definition problem in education to enhance self-perceptions is the lack of specificity in recognizing self-perception dimensions. Wylie (1979) has pointed out the lack of conclusiveness in studies that examine the correlation between "self-concept" and school achievement. This observation emerges largely from the number of studies that attempt to relate global self-perceptions with specific areas of academic achievement. One can hardly expect an individual's general sense of self (e.g., "I am a pretty good person") to have very much to do with his or her success on a mathematics test. On the other hand, the individual's self-concept of ability as a mathematics student when the test is given may have a great deal to do with relative success on the test (e.g., Brookover, Thomas, and Paterson, 1964). Unfortunately, as Rosenberg (1979) notes, most of the instruments used in school achievement studies deal with global rather than specific dimensions of self-perceptions.

Similarly, educators frequently attempt to enhance academic achievement through global self-perceptions. A student with reading problems may be confronted by a teacher who says, "You're a good person, you can do it!" This supposes that global and specific self-perceptions are one in the same, or that the learner could establish some kind of mystical relationship between the two. One can hardly fault teachers for this situation, however, since their view reflects the confusion that seems to reside in the research.

Besides the imprecision issue, instrumentation used in self-perception research may also be subject to question in terms of its reactive nature. In Appendix A, we discuss this problem in detail, but the point is worth making more than once. Basically, the instruments used to identify self-perceptions consist of lists of items to which the respondent reacts. Depending on the response, judgment is then made about the relative sense of self-worth the individual has. The first problem with these instruments is that one cannot be sure that the items are the same as those that the respondent considers personally salient. Thus the researcher may gather lots of information about how a student describes himself or herself on items that he or she rarely, if ever, thinks about. The second problem is that researchers often use such instruments to judge the self-esteem of the respondent without asking whether he or she is happy, unhappy, or indifferent to the self-description. Such judgments can only be made on the basis of the researcher's personal values or some notion of "conventional" values. Since self-perceptions are personal, inferred judgments of them must remain speculative at best. Reactive instruments are attractive partly because they lend themselves to convenient statistical analysis, and also because inferences based on conventional values sound "sensible" to other adults. Until researchers and others use less expedient methods to find out how individuals really feel about themselves in terms of their own values, conclusions about self-perceptions will fall short of comprehensiveness.

This problem is further compounded by the shortcomings of alternative methods for identifying self-perceptions. Beyond the difficulties of reactive instruments, self-reports are also subject to question since one can never be wholly sure that respondents are revealing their deeper feelings about themselves. Observations of behavior may also be faulted since a particular way of acting might reflect a temporary feeling not representative of more constant self-perceptions. In addition, the observed behaviors of others are perceptions and thus represent what the viewer sees or chooses to see and not necessarily what the behavior is actually intended to mean. A researcher, for example, may observe a student being overly aggressive during a class and conclude that the student is frustrated by lack of success in whatever is being undertaken. The student, however, may be reacting out of boredom or on the basis of some unmet emotional need that has nothing to do with school. However, teachers and other educators have the advantage of working with students on a consistent basis over extended periods of time and hence may engage students in the kinds of conversations through which real self-perceptions are revealed.

In the end, self-perceptions may defy generalization and analysis since they are deeply personal, often temporary, and enormously complex. The field of self-perceptions has been explored by theorists on a moral/philosophical basis, by researchers seeking scientific precision, by artists reflecting on the meaning of self-expression, and by persons, such as educators, trying simply to find a better way to help others grow and develop. Often one group engages in criticism of another. Philosophers may criticize scientists for trying to quantify a dimension of humanness that they believe is beyond science. Scientists may criticize philosophers for engaging in what is perceived as pure speculation without attempting to empirically validate ideas. Artists may criticize both groups for wasting time analyzing something that should simply be expressed. Finally, practitioners may criticize all three groups for the perceived failure to base their work in "reality."

Criticisms of these kinds are largely unproductive. Without empirical study, the theory must remain at the idea stage, subject to the "any opinion is as good as any other" notion. Without ongoing practice, both philosophers and researchers lack the basis for identifying new issues that need consideration. And without all three, we would lack the insight for understanding the place of art and other forms of self-expression in our culture. The point is that each group has much to offer to the others in the way of ideas, evidence, insight, and analysis. Self-perceptions have both qualitative and quantitative dimensions and we need to explore both if we are to develop a clear understanding of the nature and meaning of self-concept and self-esteem. The question is not "Who is right?" but "What is right?"

There is no argument that we have an enormous collection of information about self-perceptions; however, this does not mean that we also have an adequate theory about them. New research appears almost daily showing the influence of self-perceptions on some area of life or, just as often, counteracting some previous research. With time and effort, the theory of self-perceptions and the means for researching it will undoubtedly become more thorough and clear. Along the way, though, attention will need to be paid to:

1. Reexamining the traditional theories of self in light of contemporary life

2. Developing more precise and consistent terminology for talking about and studying self-perceptions
3. Determining acceptable means for identifying self-perceptions
4. Clarifying the interrelationships among fields that are concerned with self-perceptions
5. Respecting the complex nature of self-perceptions

Self-Perceptions
as an Educational Issue

The basic premise upon which this book is based is that self-perceptions can and should be enhanced through the educational programs and procedures of the schools. This premise, however, is based on what may be a tenuous assumption; namely, that self-perceptions represent a prominent issue in ongoing planning and practice in schools.

Throughout the twentieth century, many educators such as Dewey, Rogers, Combs, Raths, and others have consistently pointed to self-perception enhancement as a real and compelling educational need. However, the gap between theory and practice has remained wide and the prominence of their ideas has been uneven at best. The major reason for this has been the preoccupation with academic achievement, particularly in the areas of reading and mathematics. The vulnerability of self-perceptions as a valuable educational focus is evidenced by the periodic demise of various programs intended to enhance self-concept and self-esteem following events such as the launching of Sputnik in 1957 and the more recent back-to-basics movement of the 1970s. Given the apparent relationship between academic achievement and self-concept of ability in academic areas, such occurrences are not only curious, but tragic.

Compounding this problem is the fact that so much of the research on self-perceptions in school has explored the self-concept/ academic achievement connection. Generally lost in all of this is the idea that self-perceptions involve more than academic issues. As noted in the first chapter, relationships have been established between self-perceptions and a variety of other variables, including behavior and perceptions of others. Furthermore, clear and positive self-perceptions represent a basic human need antecedent to a "fully-functioning" life. Thus, self-perceptions ought to be an educational issue not only because they are related to academic achievement, but because they are an integral part of human growth and development.

To say that the school will enhance self-perceptions is to say that the school will help young people clarify their self-concepts and improve their self-esteem. It also means that young people will be helped to develop independence, self-confidence, social competence, and other characteristics associated with"full-functioning." These are aspects of individual happiness, security, and self-actualization. In other words, the enhancement of self-perceptions constitutes no less than participation in helping young people live full, productive lives.

Perhaps some educators who resist this concept are concerned about what it may mean for the institutional character of schools. They may sense that independent young people will be less likely to submit to custodial features such as adult control. They may understand that curriculum planning to enhance self-perceptions is more work than simply disseminating information. A few may be very unhappy and dissatisfied with their own lives and thus resent the idea that young people should be happy and satisfied in theirs. Certainly some also hold the belief that the sole function of schools is the development of academic skills. Whatever the reasons, it is unlikely that self-perceptions will assume a prominent role in schools by unanimous agreement within the profession. It is possible, however, that a substantial number of educators will begin to think seriously about this issue—enough to bring it closer to reality in curriculum planning and teaching.

For those who are serious about enhancing self-perceptions in schools, certain broad questions still lack sufficient answers. One has to do with identifying a clear connection between thinking and self-perceptions. Assuming the validity of Piaget's cognitive stages, one may wonder, for example, whether perceptions of the self in childhood actually represent the real meaning of self-concept. The kind of reflective thinking and introspection associated with self-concept and self-esteem seems to be most closely related to formal operations, a stage not reached until at least transescence. If this is so, what is now called "self-concept" in children might more appropriately be referred to as "self-feelings." Certainly the kind of thinking described by Raths, Harmin, and Simon (1978) in the valuing process involves formal operations, and thus the self-esteem of persons who do not function at this level is perhaps based more on value indicators such as attitudes, interests, and beliefs. If these ideas are valid, then educators who attempt to enhance self-perceptions must be alert to the nature of thinking associated with learners at each developmental stage and formulate curriculum plans appropriate to those stages.

A second question involves clarifying the relationship between self-concept and achievement in various developmental tasks. A good deal of evidence exists to support the idea that "success leads to success." However, more specific issues remain cloudy. For example, what constitutes success and what qualities of successful or unsuccessful experiences are most critical? We might speculate that success has two components: achievement and a clear perception of personal contribution to that achievement. If this is so, then success involves both external reality and internal self-perceptions. Following this line of thinking, we might further suppose that both are necessary as critical qualities of success. If an individual believes he or she has succeeded, but in reality has not, then self-concept of ability may again be confused or inaccurate. Such reasoning, however, is largely speculative. The development of effective curriculum plans and teaching methods to enhance self-perceptions depends on further clarification of these issues. As this happens, educators will have the opportunity to develop more confidence and skill in building on the connection between self-concept and success.

A third question has to do with clarifying the power of school in influencing self-perceptions. Many young people have self-perception problems which, while not directly growing out of school experiences, nonetheless influence their chances for success in school. Such problems may develop as a result of experiences in the home, with peers, or in other settings. Theory and research on self-perceptions suggest that they are largely influenced by significant others, yet it is unlikely that teachers themselves will always be perceived as "significant" enough to make a direct and substantial difference for many learners. Thus teachers are faced with the need to identify and work through those persons whom the learner does perceive as "significant others." While rapidly emerging, methods for systematically working with parents are still relatively untested and ways of working through peers are even less developed. The notion of influencing media role models looms as a larger task, assuming some of these are viewed as "significant others." Until these issues are more clearly resolved, teachers face the frustrating task of trying to assume significance in the lives of learners, but always risking failure in that regard.

We may add to these needs the development of professional skill in the areas of curriculum planning and teaching, which are described in the next section. However, the point remains that a great deal of work remains to be done in promoting the area of self-perceptions as an educational issue. While not necessarily sufficient, it would seem necessary that those concerned with the school's role in enhancing self-perception continue to:

1. Point out the need to consider self-perceptions as a prominent and legitimate concern of education
2. Study the nature of self-perceptions in learning and living
3. Test various curriculum plans and teaching methods that may influence self-perceptions
4. Develop the professional attitudes and skills that are most effective in enhancing self-perceptions

A View of the Self-Enhancing School

"I like my teacher a lot—he talks nice to me."—Female, Age 7

Throughout this book we have made numerous suggestions regarding ideas, activities, and attitudes that we and others believe will help to enhance the self-perceptions of learners. In almost all cases, suggestions have been supported with research or considered opinion. In this section we will attempt to reconstruct those suggestions by way of describing the "self-enhancing school." This task is not an easy one since there are still wide gaps in the theory and research on self-perceptions and understanding of how these function in schools. The best that can be done at this point is to describe the characteristics of such a school in somewhat piecemeal fashion. At one level, such a description may be sufficient since as self-perceptions themselves are not static, so the self-enhancing school might best be viewed as developing rather than developed. For this reason, each of these characteristics of the self-enhancing school will be defined here as moving *from* some debilitating feature *to* an enhancing feature (see Table 5.1).

From self-perceptions as a low priority to self-perceptions as a focus. In a school where self-perceptions are ignored or deemphasized, we

Table 5.1
Moving toward the Self-Enhancing School

From	To
Low priority on self-perceptions	Self-perceptions as a focus
Custodial climate	Humanistic climate
Attribute grouping	Variable grouping
External control	Self-direction
Self-isolation	Peer interaction
Age isolation	Multiage interaction
Accepting failure	Expecting and assuring success
Avoiding or blaming parents	Working with parents
Negative expectations	Positive expectations
Debilitating teacher self-perceptions	Enhancing teacher self-perceptions
Vague self-perception goals	Clear self-perception goals
Confusion about learners	Clear understanding of learner characteristics
Vague learning constructs	Learning constructs to enhance self-perceptions
Subject-centeredness	Life centeredness
Teacher-exclusive planning	Teacher-student planning
Textbooks and tests	Problems and projects
Maintenance of the status quo	Continuous development

can hardly expect them to be enhanced. More likely, if self-perceptions are not perceived to be of importance, the chance for feelings of belonging and participation are minimized. On the other hand, where self-perceptions are a focal point of the school, learners may feel that they have an important place. This means that in developing curriculum plans, making decisions about institutional features, and interacting among faculty or with learners, care is taken to act in ways that will enhance the clarity of self-concept and the quality of self-esteem. It also means that educators will make serious professional attempts to understand theory and research on self-perceptions as those relate to living and learning.

From custodial climate to humanistic climate. Self-perceptions may be seriously threatened and their development restricted in settings that are characterized by impersonalness, lack of respect, autocratic governance, and low emphasis on personal dignity. Where priority is placed on personalness, respect, participation, and human dignity, we can expect learners to sense that they are worthy and accepted as human beings. They may take risks, try out roles, attempt to resolve problems, and feel free from fear or guilt. These actions and feelings are characteristic of the kind that function in humanistic climates and that lead to clear self-concept and positive self-esteem.

From attribute grouping to variable grouping. When learners are grouped or tracked according to some supposedly homogeneous attribute such as ability, they become subject to stereotyping, teacher bias, and self-fulfilling prophecies. Single attribute grouping defies the diverse and multidimensional character of self-perceptions. Learners are separated from others with whom they may in fact have much in common and from whom they might learn a great deal. Variable grouping patterns recognize that in some cases learners benefit most from heterogeneous grouping, while in others they might have better experiences in groups based on such variables as achievement, interest, and social maturity. Single attribute grouping may cause learners to feel confused or unclear about themselves, whereas variable grouping offers an opportunity to recognize and build on the multiple dimensions of self.

From external control to self-direction. One of the most prominent characteristics of clear and positive self-perceptions is the feeling that one has control over one's fate. When decision-making power and control rest with others, individuals may be expected to develop feelings of personal incompetence and inadequacy. They may eventually come to depend entirely on others for direction in their lives; to become imbued with "learned helplessness." When individuals participate in making decisions, they are helped to feel that they have personal power and can function independently and responsibly. To enhance self-perceptions, learners must thus be given opportunities to participate in decision making and to assume increasing responsibility for their own learning and behavior. This means that the self-enhancing school makes provision for cooperative governance, student involvement in curriculum planning, and self-directed learning.

From self-isolation to peer interaction. Self-perceptions develop largely in a context of social interaction. As young people grow, their peers gain increasing significance and influence in self-perceptions, behavior, values, and the like. From middle childhood on, individuals are preoccupied with concerns about social connections, competence, and confidence. In some cases, poor self-esteem results from lack of social acceptance; in other cases, as a result of destructive or debilitating peer interaction. The problems of peer interaction are often compounded in the school by competition for rewards, lack of constructive interaction, and the notion that cooperation is equivalent to cheating. These features of schooling likely hinder the development of clear, positive self-perceptions. The self-enhancing school places a premium on developing constructive peer interaction based on the desire for social acceptance. This means that ample opportunity is made for small group and team learning, that cooperation is rewarded, and that skills in positive interpersonal communications are taught. Adults recognize the nature and power of the group status system among learners, supporting all students and providing each the opportunity to demonstrate the kind of personal excellence and skill that increases his or her status in the group.

From age-isolation to multiage interactions. Self-perceptions are often temporary and, to some degree age- or stage-related. At any given time, self-perceptions are enhanced by an understanding of how they developed as well as how they might evolve in the future. Most of us have asked at one time or another, "How did I become what I am?" or "What can I be like in the future?" One source of information regarding these questions is recollection of past experiences as well as reflection about our plans for ourselves. Another source is the lives of individuals who are both younger and older than ourselves since they may currently be engaged in the kinds of experiences that have been had previously or that lie ahead. One feature of schools that mitigates against this aspect of self-perceptions is the age-isolation procedure whereby young people of a particular age are separated from other persons—both younger and older (teachers represent a select population, whereas by "older" persons we mean a more representative sample). Because of age-isolation, opportunities are limited to learn about and with persons of other ages. The self-enhancing school encourages interaction with other age groups through multiage grouping, older-younger tutoring and counseling arrangements, community service projects, and invitations to older persons to participate in daily school activities. These features provide opportunities for understanding the self through past and future perspectives.

From accepting failure to expecting and assuring success.   It is unfortunate that many teachers expect some learners to fail and that such failure is accepted when it occurs. Both failure and success have a cumulative effect, typically leading to consistent and continuous experience of one or the other. Since achievement is related to self-perceptions, we can expect those who fail to develop feelings of incompetence and inadequacy, while those who succeed in a particular area may be expected to develop more positive self-esteem as learner on that dimension. When curriculum plans lack meaning and are beyond present achievement levels of learners, the learner may be expected to experience difficulty. When teachers expect learners to fail or when they avoid providing individualized help, learners risk failure. The self-enhancing school communicates to students the expectation that they can and will succeed. Further arrangements are made to provide the means by which success will most likely occur. This means that curriculum plans are developed that are appropriate for cognitive, social, and psychomotor levels and styles and that are based on concepts and skills that have meaning in learners' lives. Individuals are offered help through peer teaching, teacher assistance, and other means. Where such opportunities are available, learners will likely experience success and develop a more positive view of themselves as learners.

From avoiding or blaming parents to working with parents.   Parents are usually perceived as the most "significant others" in childhood and retain a degree of influence through adolescence as well. The degree to which young people feel adequate and competent as learners may often depend on expectations and feedback from parents regarding education and schooling. Some children come from homes where parents have low expectations or seem never to be satisfied with how well children are doing in school. In other cases, parents may generally fail to help their children meet emotional needs related to feelings of self-worth. When these children experience difficulty in school, educators often simply blame the parents and lose hope. The self-enhancing school recognizes the powerful role parents may play in their children's learning and makes attempts to improve the expectations and feedback parents provide about educational experiences. This is done through cooperative conferences, parenting workshops, and parent-child "homework" assignments. Beyond this, the self-enhancing school is aware of modern family lifestyles and is sensitive to the needs of children from "nonconventional" families in terms of curriculum bias, teacher interaction, and special school events. Children are not responsible for their family structure and must be accepted regardless of their home background.

From negative expectations to positive expectations. Research to date suggests that young people tend to succeed to the degree that they are expected to. In discussing achievement and self-perceptions, we have already noted some of the issues involved in teacher expectations. At one level, we might explain teacher bias by noting that teachers are human beings and thus subject to typical sources of bias. At another level, however, teachers are professionals entrusted with a large responsibility in the growth and development of young people. Teachers are a select group of human beings who should undertake the planning necessary to rise above ordinary biases. Thus when teachers display racial, social, economic, ethnic, or religious bias, they are essentially violating a code of professional ethics. It is inexcusable that there are still teachers who carry such biases and subsequent expectations. When teachers label or stereotype a particular group, suggesting that one or another is better or worse than others, they contribute nonsensical suggestions to the self-concepts and self-esteem of young people. The self-enhancing school, on the other hand, has a faculty that accepts all young people unconditionally, without regard for racial, ethnic, socioeconomic, or religious background. All learners are expected to do well, and respect is shown for their personal dignity and sense of self-worth.

From debilitating teachers to enhancing teacher self-perceptions. In recent years, teachers as a group have been subjected to a good deal of criticism and, in some cases, outright abuse. Many teachers have lost their sense of professional self-worth and have come to view teaching as a demeaning and self-defeating job. Put another way, their self-perceptions as teachers are confused and negative. While perhaps justified in some individual cases, the overwhelming criticism of teachers and consequent self-perceptions create a dangerous atmosphere for learners. The point is that teacher self-perceptions appear to carry over to learner self-perceptions. It is unlikely that teachers with personally debilitated self-perceptions will encourage clear and positive self-images in learners. Thus one characteristic of the self-enhancing school is a concerted effort to enhance teacher self-perceptions. This means that teachers are treated with professional respect, offered opportunities for professional growth, and provided the best possible support in carrying out their responsibilities. When such arrangements are made, teacher self-perceptions might be expected to improve and hopefully learner self-perceptions as well.

From vague self-perception goals to clear self-perception goals. Self-perception statements are typically listed among the goals for schools; however, they are often vague or ambiguous, thus allowing them to be lost in the shuffle of day-to-day life in the school. In order to clarify and emphasize the need to enhance self-perceptions, these goals must be redeveloped in terms of meaning, rationale, and prominence. The self-enhancing school has a clear sense of purpose and priority in the area of self-perceptions. Goal statements are developed after considerable discussion of the power of self-perceptions in "fully-functioning" lives, the nature of the environment with which young people must interact, and the place of self-perceptions among the basic needs of human beings. Further consideration is given to how each school will generally contribute to the goals, thus giving them commitment and clarification. Evidence on schools that are particularly successful in some area of learning suggests that they have given the area clear emphasis and top priority. It is likely, then, that the school that pays this kind of attention to self-perceptions will evidence the same kind of success.

From confusion about learners to clear understanding of learner characteristics. When teachers are unsure or vague about the characteristics of learners, they must make instructional decisions on a largely speculative basis, risking the possibility that the selection of resources, activities, and objectives will be appropriate for individuals or groups. That risk is compounded by problems that arise when learners feel that curriculum plans lack personal meaning for them, particularly when the plans or action are incongruent with their self-perceptions. One characteristic of the self-enhancing school is that the professional staff has a clear understanding of the developmental characteristics of the learners with whom they work. This means that consideration is given to concepts such as developmental tasks and persistent life situations, as well as techniques for identifying problems, interests, needs, and concerns of individuals or groups of learners. On this basis, then, curriculum plans and teaching methods may be developed which are pertinent to learner characteristics.

From vague learning constructs to learning constructs for enhancing self-perceptions. All too often curriculum and instruction are planned and implemented on the basis of vague notions of how learning, growth, and development take place. Decisions seem to be preoccupied with what is to be learned and little consideration is given to learning itself. The self-enhancing school recognizes the place and power of self-perceptions in the learning process and decisions are made on that basis. This means that curriculum and instructional planning are based on the idea that the salient dimensions of self-perceptions influence the style of learning, approaches to problem solving, perceptions of meaning, reactions to experiences, and the flow of interactions between the individual and the school. Furthermore, when such constructs are ignored, the learning process becomes impersonal and less effective.

From subject-centeredness to life-centeredness. The prevailing method of organizing curriculum plans is the use of the separate-subjects approach. Within this approach, learners are expected to master the facts, principles, and concepts associated with various disciplines of knowledge. The problem with this approach is that separate subjects often lack connection to the real-life needs of learners, and personal/social growth is given little, if any, priority compared to the acquisition of facts. The separate-subject approach contributes little to the development of clear and positive self-perceptions. Curriculum plans in the self-enhancing school are more frequently organized around problems of living and the emerging needs of young people. This means that learners have the opportunity to explore personal issues and environmental forces involved in thinking about and making decisions related to self-perceptions. This direct curricular approach to enhancing self-perceptions engages learners in units or mini-courses such as "Developing Personal Values," "Getting Along with Others," "Living in Our School," and "Living in Our Community."

From teacher-exclusive planning to teacher-student planning. Most curriculum planning is carried out by teachers either individually or in small groups. Learners are then confronted with curriculum plans that essentially determine the content and process of the time they spend in school. The plans of the teacher may or may not relate to the needs, problems, characteristics, interests, concerns, and learning styles of students. Curriculum planning in the self-enhancing school makes provision for the participation of learners. Planning done exclusively by teachers is considered preplanning, as final decisions are made by teachers and students together and sometimes by students alone. This method allows learners an opportunity to bring their own thoughts to curriculum plans, enhances skills in participation and decision making, promotes feelings of belonging, and encourages the development of internal locus of control. Thus the process of cooperative planning directly addresses several aspects of the "fully functioning" self.

From textbooks and tests to problems and projects. Teaching-learning situations in schools are most often centered around cognitive objectives, teacher-centered activities, subject-oriented texts, and paper-pencil tests. The greatest emphasis is on learning of subject matter disseminated by teachers to passive groups of learners and measured through tests or exams. These methods, like the subject approach, separate life in the classroom from the real life of the learner by failing to account for either the content or process of dynamic growth and development. Specific teaching-learning situations in the self-enhancing school are characterized by concepts and methods that are congruent with self-perceptions and are likely to enhance them. Objectives reflect a balance among the cognitive, affective, and psychomotor domains. Subject matter or content is connected directly to the salient dimensions of self-concept. Activities are focused on interaction, participation, cooperation, and development of exciting projects that apply ideas and concepts. Human and material resources address problems in meaningful and thought-provoking ways. Measuring devices focus on growth and accomplishment, relying heavily on cooperative and self-evaluation. These and similar arrangements provide learners with a wide variety of opportunities to grow personally and socially, in other words, to develop increasing clarity and quality in their self-perceptions.

From maintenance of the status quo to continuous development.
While other characteristics of the self-enhancing school might be
added, this last one perhaps provides the most important feature of
all—a living context in which the school might continue to do what it
ought to. The curricular approach used in many schools has been referred to as "rear view mirror planning." This term describes the
emphasis on learning about the past, but might just as well describe
concern for maintaining past practice in the school. In reality, the
school is surrounded by a dynamic rather than static world. New students come to school with unique characteristics and concerns; society
changes and new problems emerge; and new theory and research offer
fresh insights into learning. Human beings and their environment
change, and with this comes new problems and prospects for self-
perceptions of young people. The school that has a program based on
the past risks becoming an anachronism in contemporary life. The
school that chooses to place a priority on enhancing self-perceptions
commits itself to a dynamic and often ambiguous role. Last year's
rules and regulations, curriculum plans, and teaching methods may
not be appropriate this year. Thoughtful planning, careful experimentation, and action research becomes a continuous process. In the
end, the school itself becomes a growing, developing, reflecting environment, much like that which characterizes healthy self-perceptions. It is a place where self-enhancement is not just a technique,
but a way of life.

Part II
—— The Future and the Self-Enhancing School ——

We live in a time when concerns about education of young people
seem to be focused on the acquisition of knowledge and technical
competence in skills such as reading and mathematics. Schools are
criticized for supposed shortcomings in those areas, in addition to
the perceived lack of structure, order, and "discipline." Meanwhile,
the world outside the school is immersed in enormous changes in
technology, lifestyles, values, and so on. The "lifelessness" of many
schools described by Silberman (1970) is contrasted with the dynamic
flow of events analyzed by Toffler (1971, 1981). The gap between
life inside and outside the school is discouraging for two reasons:
first, because the life of the school becomes incongruent with the

important issues in the lives of learners; second, because the school may become a living anachronism as a social institution. This is unfortunate in light of the fact that many predicted changes offer enormous opportunities for making the self-enhancing school a reality. In this section we will describe a few of these changes, looking particularly at how they might be viewed optimistically.

The Person-Centered Society

"I like to get along with other people"–Male, Age 17

Futurists have pointed out that our society has progressed through the stage of industrial growth and may be moving in the direction of a person-centered society. In the first phase, the goals of society were centered in technological development, economic growth, and efficiency. The basic idea was to develop the kind of material environment in which life would be less uncertain and hazardous, while at the same time more comfortable and secure. In a material sense, these goals have been largely met in our society with advances in medicine, communications, transportation, home maintenance, and the like. At the same time, however, many technological developments have compounded human problems in areas such as distribution of wealth, alienation, pressure for conformity, and environmental pollution. As we become more sensitive to these problems and are freed from the more mundane problems that dominated life in the past, we may now begin to more seriously address the quality of life for human beings.

In resolving these problems (perhaps in order to do so), social values may well shift toward person-centeredness. Harman (1972) described this shift as one in which "the goals of society [would] include making economic growth meet human needs, achieving knowledge and aesthetic advance, and controlling social problems so that individuals may progress toward their own goals of self-fulfillment. (p. 19)" In other words, the emphasis of social values would be on increasing human capacities rather than technological control (Rogers, 1972). Already, roadsigns indicate that the person-centered society is beginning to emerge. There is increasing emphasis today on development of physical health, understanding self-perceptions, exploring new lifestyles, and accepting other people. Such topics serve as a focus not only in scholarly research, but in commercial media as well. Some of these latter are admittedly pointed at self-gratification. Others, however, are aimed more at improving the quality of social living and the opportunity for self-actualization.

The shift toward a person-centered society offers optimism for those concerned with developing self-enhancing schools. Frequently the features of schools are justified on grounds that the school is expected to reflect the society of which it is a part. Obviously, then, if the society is person-centered, the school will be expected to emphasize self-actualization and defend the emphasis in light of its social context. Furthermore, descriptions of education in the person-centered society include such characteristics as lifelong learning, alternative programs, lack of racial and ethnic bias, and greater emphasis on social skills and self-perceptions. Each of these is also a characteristic of the self-enhancing school. Therefore, if the shift to a person-centered society is desirable (or necessary) in improving the quality of life, educators ought to become pro-active participants in its development. The most obvious way of doing so is to engage in the kind of institutional and curriculum planning that enhances self-perceptions. As this occurs, the school will itself contribute to the shift in values and educate young people to live in and maintain a person-centered society.

The Shifting Population Age

"It would be boring to be eleven all your life."—Female, Age 11

One of the current trends in the United States is the shift in the age of its population. Until recently, the largest proportion of people were those in the youngest age groups. Now with a declining birth rate and a longer lifespan, the population age is shifting toward older age groups (Morrison, 1979). Many educators are viewing this trend pessimistically and even frantically as they count the increasing number of empty seats in school as a result of declining enrollment. Others are more optimistically viewing this trend as an opportunity to extend educational services to adults. In this way, the school might become a center for learning for all the citizens in the community. This kind of thinking has given greater legitimacy to the concept of lifelong learning and its prospects for becoming a reality. However, those who are serious about this idea realize that adult learners are less submissive about the nature of their education than young people. Their participation is voluntary, and if educational programs are perceived as worthless or self-defeating they simply withdraw from them. Nevertheless, the prospects for lifelong learning are encouraging and may contribute to those of the self-enhancing school.

It would be a fruitless task to imagine even an illustrative list of the endless possible objectives lifelong learners might wish to pursue. However, it is possible to envision the general areas in which these might fall. Such needs and interests in the future would probably be of at least the following kinds:

1. *Personal and social growth:* Inclinations that arise out of the aspects of human development across ages or stages of the life-span (e.g., interpersonal communications)

2. *Communal improvement:* Desires to refine or reconstruct various aspects of community or interpersonal living (e.g., local environmental problems)

3. *Career or occupational reeducation:* Needs and interests connected to improving or redefining one's work role (e.g., career changing)

4. *Cultural expansion:* Interests emerging from a desire to construct or refine liberal-humanistic aspects of the self (e.g., art history)

5. *Information acquisition:* The need to acquire specific subject matter for currency in contemporary events (e.g., revolutions in other countries) or to support efforts in another area

6. *Valuing:* The desire to make decisions about ongoing conflicts and choices in personal, social, political, and economic aspects of living (e.g., lifestyles)

7. *Issue analysis:* The desire to comprehend the complex and overwhelming issues that operate beyond the local level, but that affect the everyday lives of individuals (e.g., energy resource politics)

In order to help meet these needs, new and unusual educational arrangements will need to be developed. For example, museums, art galleries, counseling centers, public libraries, social service departments, and civic groups might all be coordinated to the extent that each offers educational activities to citizens. Learning networks might be constructed, which operate through a clearinghouse to bring together interested learners and educative resources (Barnes, 1978). Study circles such as those operating in Sweden (Abbott, 1978) might be formed, bringing together small groups to discuss issues of common concern. One excellent example of this kind of learning network arrangement is the La Leche League. It is noted here not only for that reason, but also because in particular it represents an attempt to enhance self-perceptions of parents and consequently of children as well.

From a group of 7 mothers in 1956, the La Leche has grown to over 3,300 groups in 43 countries (Lowman, 1977). While the international league disseminates information, sponsors research, addresses global nutrition problems, and holds conventions, its real substance lies in the local groups serving particular communities. These groups meet in members' homes to discuss problems and prospects of breastfeeding, and are facilitated by a leader who normally emerges from the group, developing the knowledge and skill required for leadership. Leaders also act as a clearinghouse for specific problems and questions. A mother who requests help might be given information, referred to someone who has had the same problem, put in touch with expert medical advice, or simply supported through a personal visit. The La Leche League has had remarkable success in bringing renewed life to breastfeeding not through television advertising or conscripted clientele, but rather through "word-of-mouth" and meeting announcements posted in obstetric and pediatric offices. In this case, a real network has been constructed based on voluntary participation and common interest and thus begins to offer a worthwhile example of lifelong education in content and form.

One of the most outstanding illustrations of committing the *school* to improving life in the community is the case of Pulaski, Wisconsin. Since the 1940s, the Pulaski Community Schools have undertaken a number of projects aimed at making school resources available to the community. Such projects have included:

1. Agricultural institutes for local farmers

2. Continuous distribution of a community newspaper prepared by high school students

3. Identification by students of light industries to employ local residents

4. Student-run programs for soil, well water, and milk testing

5. Building of an outdoor recreation park in the town

6. Development of a local canning industry begun in the school by the agriculture and home economics departments

In each of these cases, schools have the opportunity to participate as a resource for ideas, as a source of educational expertise, and as an organizing center for educational activities. In doing so, they may promote the idea of enhancing self-perceptions of adult learners and also take advantage of opportunities for multiage learning groups, community service projects, and other methods of bringing the life of the school and its community into a closer relationship. Thus the self-enhancing school may extend its influence in the context of life-long learning.

Technology

"I learn more from TV than from my teacher."—Male, Age 8

Technology has provided us with a wide variety of ways to disseminate information, including several alternatives for human beings doing so. This development should be of real interest to educators since the vast majority of school time is spent in having physically present teachers disseminate information to large numbers of physically present learners. In fact, the deemphasis on affective education is often justified on the basis of lack of time left over from this procedure. By virtue of the television, telephone, cassette recorder, and other devices, people have been able to be much more aware of what others are doing locally and around the world. In addition, they have had much greater access to information and knowledge as a source for thinking about new ideas.

The dissemination of knowledge through technological means is expected to become more and more a part of daily living in the future.

At present, public, and to some extent commercial, television offers home viewers access to cultural events, college courses, and self-help ideas, as well as information to enhance leisure time activities such as hobbies. Many public libraries offer over the telephone reference services to make information quickly available. Some commercial businesses market toy robots and games that disseminate knowledge to people (Freeman and Mulkowsky, 1978) while others market home computers at various levels of cost and sophistication which can be used not only for storage of knowledge, but interactive problem solving as well. It is interesting to note, incidentally, that these devices are often viewed more positively by learners as teachers since they do not engage in negative feedback (Hess et al., 1970). Beyond these, experimentation continues in the area of holography—three-dimensional projection of objects using laser technology. Shane (1979) and others have discussed what this could mean for schools if human beings such as teachers or learners could be "holographed" as three-dimensional images to other locations.

The availability of such technological devices should offer schools increasing opportunities to focus on affective education. Through the use of television, telephones, cassette recorders, and home computers, knowledge dissemination can be carried out in the home, at school, while traveling, or virtually anytime, and without the physical presence of a teacher. Thus teacher time and school facilities may be freed to focus on interaction, interpersonal communications, problem solving, and personal/social development. In this way, technology may offer educators the chance to develop the plans and procedures that characterize the self-enhancing school.

Many more future prospects for supporting the self-enhancing school could be outlined here. Those described, however, offer a sufficient glance at important possibilities. We have purposely avoided ideas such as chemically induced intelligence since they are not necessarily related to our focus and may even be antithetical to it since they represent artificial rather than human possibilities for growth and development of the self. In sum, however, the future offers real optimism for enhancing self-perceptions both within and outside the school. The issue for educators in light of the trends discussed here is not, "What should the curriculum be like?" but "What *can* the curriculum of the future be like? (Anderson, 1969)" For those concerned with enhancing self-perceptions and the self-enhancing school, this is a compelling concern.

Getting from Here to There

"I wish I could change this school."–Male, Age 16

There are many teachers and, in some cases, schools to whom the concepts and practices discussed in this book are already very familiar. To others, they may represent a dramatic shift in emphasis from current institutional features, curriculum plans, and teaching methods. In our talks with educators in many locations we gather that there is still a great deal of work to do in promoting and actualizing the ideas associated with enhancing self-perceptions in school. For this reason, we will discuss here several ideas that seem to characterize successful efforts to develop a self-enhancing school.

Organizing for Curriculum Planning

There is already available a substantial body of literature that discusses and describes procedures that might be used to organize a school for ongoing curriculum planning (e.g., Doll, 1978). The most common practice involves the establishment of system-wide and building-level curriculum councils charged with the responsibility for encouraging and sponsoring curriculum planning. Where instituted with understanding, commitment, and participation, these groups have frequently made a valuable contribution to the improvement of curriculum and instruction in local schools (Verduin, 1967). In order to encourage the enhancement of self-perceptions, however, these organizations need to make special arrangements.

One procedure involves the establishment of standing committees in areas that are critical to enhancing self-perceptions. A committee on school climate, for example, would have responsibility for continuously assessing the quality of life in the school and making recommendations for its improvements. This group might assess the degree to which learners feel that they are involved in decision making in terms of the governance of the school or the formulation of curriculum plans. A committee on parent involvement would identify ways to help parents develop the attitudes and skills necessary for enhancing their children's self-perceptions. A committee on institutional features would examine such practices as grouping, grading, discipline, and other practices to ensure that they are the kind that help rather than hinder self-perceptions. A committee on school-community relations would identify ways of bringing the two into closer cooperation and examine the quality of life in the community for young people including both attitudes and activities. Along with these examples, other committees would thus ensure that critical issues in self-perception enhancement receive careful and continuous attention.

In addition to committees, the system-wide or building-level curriculum council ought also to be concerned with the degree to which teachers are encouraged to engage in practices that enhance self-perceptions. Using ideas from this and other resources as guidelines, a directory ought to be formed in each district of promising practices used by local teachers. These might include activities, resources, units, and techniques that have been tried and found successful. With provision for annual updating, the directory would serve as a means for initiating teacher cooperation in enhancing learner self-perceptions. The overall council should also promote opportunities for teachers to do summer curriculum work, attend conferences, and engage in other professional activities. These and other actions by the overall committee would be aimed not only at helping teachers develop skill in enhancing learner self-perceptions, but in improving those of teachers as well.

Finally, through its committees, sponsored activities, and formal discussion, the overall curriculum council should act to disseminate issue and position papers concerning problems and prospects for enhancing the self-perceptions of young people.

We have discussed the need for more clearly defining goals and general objectives related to self-perceptions, and this process is certainly one that ought to be sponsored by the curriculum council. However, the most critical moments for self-perceptions are really in the everyday life of the school. Thus while goal refinement is needed to give direction and commitment, it does not ensure the ongoing practices that are most important. Nevertheless, goal clarification by the curriculum council would bring critical issues to the open agenda of the school and community. Such action appears necessary to do what must really be done to develop the self-enhancing school.

Professional Growth

One of the most important characteristics of the self-enhancing school is that educators associated with it engage in continuous professional growth. No doubt most schools would claim to sponsor professional growth opportunities, but in too many cases this means that once or twice a year they hold in-service meetings for one day, usually involving a speech by a professor, followed by department or grade-level meetings on unrelated topics. The ineffectiveness of these programs is perhaps illustrated by the generally little attention paid to affective curriculum planning since many of the speeches over the years have addressed that topic specifically. If people really believed this was an effective answer to comprehensive professional growth, then it is interesting that the same idea has not been applied to the education of young people, that is, school one or two days a year at most.

Developing attitudes and skills related to enhancing self-perceptions represents a fundamental shift in the characterization of many schools. Teachers and others interested in pursuing the idea need the support of serious, ongoing, comprehensive professional growth programs. Concepts and activities involved in such programs need to center around three purposes: first, to help teachers more fully understand the learners with whom they work; second, to help teachers more fully understand themselves in relation to learners; and third, to help teachers analyze and develop curriculum plans and teaching methods that are most likely to enhance self-perceptions.

Teachers who wish to more fully understand learners might engage in several activities. One is to use real self-perception data from learners as a focus for group discussions about the kinds of interests, concerns, problems, and aspirations learners have. (While real, local data are desirable, we have included a set with suggested directions for use in Appendix A. These might be used as an introductory activity to initiate the collection of local data.)

A second activity was described by Raths, Harmin, and Simon (1978) and is one which was used successfully with groups of teachers. In this case, Louis Raths met with teachers once per week over a period of twenty weeks. Each teacher chose one or two learners in a class with whom he or she would try to work especially closely. Teachers were asked to keep a log in which they recorded noteworthy statements, conversations, activities, behaviors, and the like in which the students were involved. At the weekly meetings, various methods were demonstrated that could be used to help students clarify their values, including questioning techniques and activities. During the last two or three meetings, each teacher was asked to summarize for the group what he or she had learned about the students who were observed. In this setting teachers not only improved their understanding of learners, but of themselves as well.

These types of activities might be combined with home visits, surveys of student interests, interviews, and other techniques, as well as discussions with medical personnel, social service representatives, psychologists, and others who specialize in growth and development of young people. Ideas and techniques learned in such professional growth programs may then serve as a basis for analyzing curriculum plans, institutional features, and teaching methods to determine if these are sensitive to and appropriate for the self-perceptions of learners. As Jersild (1952) indicated, "The larger the teacher's conception of his work and the greater his self-involvement in it, the better able he will be to keep his eye on each individual pupil's struggle to be himself."

Teachers who wish to more fully understand *themselves* in relation to learners might engage in several related activities. Rosenbaum and Toepfer (1966) reported a program in which an attempt was made to coordinate curriculum planning and school psychology services to help teachers. One aspect of the program began as bi-weekly meetings at which a small group of teachers, in conjunction with a curriculum coordinator and a psychologist, began to informally discuss communications problems. After only a few meetings, the sessions became a form of group therapy as teachers began to seriously think through ways in which they communicated their personal selves to learners through interaction and behavior. The authors noted one interesting discussion centered around what teachers are really communicating to students when they cut in the front of a long cafeteria line. This seemingly mundane topic lent itself to consideration of issues such as teacher power and authority, respect for students, and personal rights of adults and young people. In considering the "group therapy" method, however, it is important to note that the sessions must be voluntary and confidential. Teachers, like other people, should not be forced to reveal themselves in group settings, nor should their ideas in this context be a matter of record. Given these conditions, however, "group therapy" may be an effective means for helping some teachers think about themselves.

Another means for doing this is through the use of clinical supervision (Goldhammer, Anderson, and Krajewski, 1980). Traditionally, supervisory practices have often amounted to "snoopervision" as teachers are confronted by drop-in supervisors interested in who should be retained or dismissed. In such cases, supervision is frequently considered to be a threatening process. This is unfortunate since the purpose of supervision is to help teachers improve instruction. It is no mystery that many teachers are reluctant to ask for help from supervisors who also determine whether teachers will continue to be employed. In the clinical supervision process, this paradox is eliminated as supervisors work in a staff relationship with teachers and the focus is on improving instruction. Within the process, for example, the teacher and supervisor would meet to analyze plans for the teaching-learning situation. By using nondirective questions or comments, the supervisor helps the teacher to clarify plans and ideas. Then, following one or more careful observations, the two meet and discuss their mutual reactions to the observed sessions, looking for clues to indicate how the teacher did or did not engage in behaviors that promote effective learning. They also discuss the effectiveness of the supervisor's role and function. This kind of process encourages careful thinking about teacher behavior and expectations. It focuses heavily on helping teachers to analyze and evaluate their perceptions of learners and teaching-learning situations.

The process just described can become part of a larger program involving peer and student evaluations, observations of video-taped class sessions, and other techniques that help teachers to look at themselves and thus more fully understand their personal and professional behaviors and attitudes in relation to learners.

Finally, some teachers may wish to engage in activities directed at analyzing and developing curriculum plans. The point here is that curriculum planning itself is an opportunity for professional growth (Sharp, 1951; Spears, 1957; Harnack, 1968). The latter need not take place only in settings such as those previously described. Curriculum planning is often portrayed as a formal and technical process. Visions are conjured up of groups gathered around polished tables with sharpened pencils and yellow pads, grinding out carefully stated objectives, activities, and measuring devices. This is a limiting vision and serves only to repel some teachers. In reality, curriculum planning involves intense give and take, sharing of ideas, questions about philosophy, and so on by professional teachers. It is both an intellectual and affective process in which teachers think not only about what they do, but why and how. As ideas are generated, individuals reveal their view of learners and learning, as well as their beliefs about what is important in education and schooling.

For our purposes here, some teachers may wish to use guidelines such as those in Chapter 3 to analyze present curriculum plans to determine the degree to which self-perceptions are emphasized. They may also wish to revise plans or develop new problem- or needs-related units that are directed toward enhancing self-perceptions. We do believe, however, that the most effective curriculum planning takes place in small groups where there is ample opportunity for discussion of ideas. This view is based partly on the notion that a group may generate a greater variety of valuable suggestions for curriculum plans and partly on the notion that self-perceptions are most likely to be considered in the context of interaction.

Before leaving the topic of professional growth, two items need to be mentioned. First, activities for this purpose ought to be voluntary whenever possible. Teachers are most likely to improve or change their attitudes and actions when they perceive a need to do so. If forced into specific activities, they may choose to be resentful, overly aggressive, or submissive, none of which will help move toward concepts related to the self-enhancing school. Voluntary participants, on the other hand, have indicated a willingness to think about what they do when they initially volunteer. That willingness is likely to have grown out of a perceived need for change and improvement.

Second, professional growth activities ought to take place in a workshop setting (Kelley, 1951; Doll, 1978). This means that the activities are focused on solving real problems, decisions are made democratically, and a wide variety of activities are used. Workshops should take place over a lengthy period of time and be aimed at making a significant contribution to some area of school life. Lectures may be involved, but so should discussions, visitations, reading, experimentation with new ideas, and the like. The workshop, in short, is similar to the notion of unit teaching—applying to professional growth the best ideas we have for teaching and learning in general.

We have noted here only a few of the many ideas that might be considered for professional growth. Our emphasis has been on activities that are related to helping teachers enhance self-perceptions of both learners and themselves. It is improbable that comprehensive self-enhancing schools will emerge without this kind of professional growth. Without it, the idea of enhancing self-perceptions must remain, as it largely does now, within the purview of those teachers who are individually concerned with this critical area of teaching and learning.

Looking at Ourselves and Our Schools

One way of beginning to think about how we might transform ourselves and our schools toward enhancing self-perceptions is to evaluate what we do. This means that as professionals we must be willing to honestly confront our ideas, beliefs, programs, and practices. To help with this undertaking, we have included here three sets of checklists. The first and second have to do with how we perceive and interact with learners as teachers, administrators, counselors, and so on. Those who enhance self-perceptions of learners will find themselves answering "yes" to the questions in the first list and "no" to those in the second.

The third checklist is a set of questions that might be asked with regard to institutional features and curriculum plans. Again, those educators who are in self-enhancing schools will find themselves answering "yes" to these questions. The third checklist appears again in Appendix A as part of the possible professional growth activity described there.

Checklist I: Characteristic Attitudes and Behaviors of Teachers Who Enhance Self-Perceptions

Do I accept students as human beings, regardless of their backgrounds?

Do I enjoy the diversity of individual differences in a group?

Do I provide opportunities for students to pursue personal interests?

Am I sensitive to the group's status system and do I help individuals achieve status in the group?

Do I attempt to learn about student lives outside the classroom?

Do I provide many opportunities for interaction and cooperation?

Do I involve students in planning and evaluating activities and projects?

Do I avoid equating the learners' work with their self-worth?

Do I respect the personal dignity of students?

Do I encourage students to think about themselves?

Do I help students to find personal meaning in ideas and concepts?

Do I encourage parents or guardians to be active and constructive in children's education?

Do I encourage students to help each other in learning and problem solving?

Am I happy to be involved in teaching?

Do I encourage students to pursue ideas about which I am not knowledgeable?

Do I trust students to carry out projects responsibly?

Do I have positive and realistic expectations of students?

Do I seek new and worthwhile ideas for improving teaching?

Do I speak out on behalf of children and youth in the school and community?

Am I concerned about the quality of living for children and youth in society?

Do I volunteer to work with students outside the classroom?

Do I provide a variety of resources for classroom use?

Do I encourage students to challenge others' ideas and to seek support for their own?

Do I feel secure when students challenge teacher ideas?

Do I recognize the influence of various pressures on students and their effect on learning?

Am I willing to share personal feelings with students?

Am I flexible; willing to revise plans as needed?

Do I help students to learn about their personal backgrounds and possible futures?

Do I treat student mistakes or failure at a task as an opportunity for new learning and growth?

Am I willing to share ideas with other teachers?

Do I recognize the power of self-perceptions in learning?

Do I have patience in working with learning difficulties?

Do I purposefully plan activities at which students can succeed?

Do I recognize and use the community as a source of teaching and learning?

Am I willing to try new approaches and ideas even though some risk is involved?

Checklist II: Characteristic Attitudes and Behaviors of Teachers Who Hinder Positive Learner Self-Perceptions

Do I believe students are "evil" and irresponsible?

Do I label individuals with personal perceptions of the group?

Do I have low expectations for students and believe they will fail no matter how hard they try?

Do I believe I am the source of all worthwhile knowledge?

Do I believe students should concentrate only on those ideas that are of interest to the teacher?

Do I feel that students should be able to ignore personal/social problems when working on cognitive tasks?

Do I personally plan all learning activity?

Am I reluctant to deviate from prepared curriculum plans?

Do I equate school success with personal self-worth of students?

Do I think learning difficulties are the fault of anything or anybody but me?

Do I force students to compete for rewards?

Do I refuse to involve students in ideas about which I am unsure or unknowledgeable?

Do I believe last year's curriculum plans are suitable for this and succeeding years?

Do I assume that learning, growing, and developing take place on a constant continuum?

Do I wish that I could get out of teaching?

Do I refuse to accept students' challenges of my ideas or opinions?

Am I sure that I know what all students need?

Do I have no interest in the personal interests of students?

Do I believe that classroom misbehavior is sure to lead to adult failure and illegal behavior?

Do I believe that students will not learn unless motivated by me?

Do I believe maintenance of order is the first condition of learning?

Do I confuse submission of students with willingness to learn?

Do I use punitive punishment, humiliation, and sarcasm in dealing with students?

Do I wish students would act like adults rather than young people?

Do I believe parents should not help their children with school-related learning?

Do I equate student cooperation with cheating?

Do I make all decisions about curriculum plans?

Do I reserve the exclusive right to evaluate student work?

Do I think education is preparation only for future living?

Checklist III: Characteristics of the
Self-Enhancing School

Is the idea of enhancing self-perceptions a high priority in our school?

Do students have a say in what happens in our school?

Do we avoid stereotyping students?

Do we emphasize cooperation rather than competition?

Do we avoid the idea that some students will fail no matter how hard they try?

Do we do whatever possible to assure success for students?

Do we make an effort to help students earn status with their peers?

Do we make arrangements for peer tutoring as well as interaction with younger and older persons?

Do we make arrangements to teach parents how to interact and work with their children in constructive ways?

Do our curriculum plans make provisions for enhancing self-perceptions?

Do our school goals include clean and direct statements that commit us to enhancing self-perceptions?

Does each school level have general objectives committing it to enhancing self-perceptions?

Does our school program offer opportunities for students to learn about themselves?

Does our school have established communications with community agencies that supply support services for children and youth?

Do we make use of the problems and needs approaches?

Do we use issues for present lives of students as organizing centers for curriculum plans?

Do students participate in making classroom decisions?

Are a variety of activities and materials available from which students may make choices?

Do we observe and record changes in student self-perceptions?

Do we discuss changes in self-perceptions with students and parents?

Do students have an opportunity to evaluate themselves?

Do our curriculum plans offer opportunities for students to improve their present lives?

Stewardship for Young People: Where Did It Go?

"I need help—I can't make it alone."—Female, Age 17

We are living in a time that is both exciting and difficult. Technology has brought us many advances that only a few generations ago were only wistful dreams: instant communication, rapid transportation, more leisure time, release from mundane chores, cures for many diseases, longer lifespans, and so on. Daily we hear of new breakthroughs in these and other areas, which promise us even better opportunities to live fuller lives. At the same time, however, our society is undergoing fundamental shifts in values and lifestyles. Old traditions are breaking up, restrictions that forced conformity are dissipating, and people are seeking new, alternative pathways for self-fulfillment. With this, though, has come a degree of ambiguity and confusion. There are often so many choices that decisions are hard to make. Consequences of decisions frequently lie somewhere between old traditions and new lifestyles, and individuals experience discomfort or frustration. In this time of transition, it has become more and more difficult for people to find anything certain to hang onto, to give direction in their lives.

Young people are certainly not immune to this dilemma. Commercial media would have them believe that life ought to be carefree, yet they are faced daily with the stark realities of global tension, racism, pollution, and other problems. The family structure, which once offered security and support, is now fragile and unsure. The apparent integrity of political leadership has been lost in the maze of post-Watergate and Abscam revelations. The courts are showing less and less sympathy for young offenders regardless of the environmental circumstances that surround anti-social behavior. Adults, living themselves with ambiguity, have become less certain as role models for attitudes and behavior. The conveniences of technology have reduced the need for the young to make contributions to the survival of their families and thus to have a feeling of belonging and participation.

We have only to look around to see the signals young people are sending us, which imply that many are leading aimless and even desperate lives. The use of alcohol and drugs increases with no sign of relief. Sexual activity among the young has become a prevalent means for momentary escape, complicated by the high risk of venereal disease in the age group. The number of adolescent pregnancies increases yearly as many of these young women report that a baby will offer them unconditional love and acceptance. These and other dimensions of adolescent life today should tell us that young people are frustrated, that they are unsure of themselves and their futures, and that they are unclear about values that might guide decision making and behavior.

These symptoms are no secret. Those who work and live with young people see them everyday. Understanding the social forces that press on young people should lead educators particularly to sense the need to offer help and guidance to learners in confronting the problems they face. Yet more and more we hear voices of resignation in the form of calls for more emphasis on academics, maintenance of order, authoritative control, and the idea that young people should be forced to accept the responsibility and consequences of their own behavior, the latter at a time when politicians and business officials hire fleets of lawyers to get them out of trouble. Somehow many educators have been led into an attitude that ours is no longer a profession whose most important responsibility is to help young people grow and develop in healthy and positive ways. It is hard to believe that any more than just a few people entered the education profession with less than altruistic motives, but so many seem to have lost this sense of purpose.

The education profession has a history of speaking out in behalf of the young. Past generations of educators have worked to enforce child labor laws, to press for racial and ethnic equality, and to generally make the world a better place for young people. It is time now for the profession to renew its sense of purpose and again speak out. We know pretty much what it takes to provide a healthy environment for growth. We now need to act in that direction. Those who speak out may find themselves as objects of criticism, accused of naivete or "soft headedness." But such are often the consequences of doing what has to be done.

We have tried in this book to suggest ideas for making contributions to this goal in school. The confusion manifested by young people today is a sign that many have unclear and negative self-perceptions. As educators, we can and should try to affect what happens outside the school, but we may meet with difficulties since so many forces are involved. Inside the school, however, we can have a greater role with much more chance of success. The school at least can become a self-enhancing environment for young people, adding to the quality and meaning of their lives. It is a goal worth pursuing.

APPENDIX A

When Young People Tell about Themselves in School

Most of the research that has been conducted on self-perceptions has centered on self-esteem and, more particularly, on global self-esteem (Rosenberg, 1979). A good deal is known about the degree to which young people have a sense of self-worth, but much less is known about self-concept; that is, the content of young people's thoughts about themselves. Probably the most prominent reason for this is that most of the instruments used for research on and assessment of self-perceptions are of a reactive nature (e.g., Piers and Harris, 1964; Fitts, 1964; Coopersmith, 1967). This means that the instrument requires individuals to respond to statements suggested by the developer of the instrument. For example, Coopersmith's Self-Esteem Inventory (1967) includes fifty-eight statements, each of which the respondent is asked to check "like me" or "unlike me." A sample statement from the inventory is: "I would rather play with children younger than me." The individual who checks "like me" is inferred to have negative self-esteem for that item since conventional thought suggests that children who feel that way also feel rejected by their peers.

In 1978, we conducted a small pilot study in which we asked one hundred fifth and seventh graders to complete the Self-Esteem Inventory, and to indicate for each item whether they would like to "keep" or "change" that aspect of themselves or whether they "don't care." Within the pilot study, of those students who checked "like me" in response to the preceding item ("I would rather play with children younger than me."), the numbers who checked each category ("keep," "change," or "don't care") were almost equal. We thus hypothesized that an item such as this might not necessarily give an accurate picture of self-esteem or self-concept. Older children in a close-knit, geographically isolated family or those with a sense of sibling responsibility, for example, might feel very positively about their inclination to play with children younger than themselves. In other words, reactive instruments that involve inferred conclusions might not tell the real story of self-perceptions. In addition, the items suggested on the instrument might not reflect the most important or salient dimensions of self-perceptions; that is, they might not necessarily be the same items that the individual might include in his or her self-concept.

To date, one of the clearest explications of these issues can be found in the work of McGuire and his colleagues (1976, 1978, 1979). Their position is that subjects in self-perception research ought to be allowed to choose their own self-concept dimensions, rather than having to respond to those suggested by the researcher. Thus the research would focus on self-concept content that the subject feels is personally salient and significant. To accomplish this, McGuire and his colleagues have conducted a number of studies in which they ask

Table A.1
*Frequency of Mention of Various Aspects of
Life in the Spontaneous Self-Concepts of Children*

Percent of All Mentions	Aspect of Life
17	Family members
14	Recreational activities
13	Daily life and demographics
11	Friends and social relations
11	School aspects
10	Adjectival characteristics
9	Formal activities
6	Natural environment
5	Societal concerns
4	Health and appearance

W. J. McGuire, T. Fujioka, and C. V. McGuire. Reprinted with permission of *Impact on Instructional Improvement*, vol. 15, no. 1 (1979).

young people in interview or written form to simply "tell us about yourself." As a result of these studies of "spontaneous self-concept," McGuire, Fujioka, and McGuire (1979) have been able to describe the nature of self-concept content in children as well as the degree of salience of various categories within that content (see Table A.1). For our purposes here, it is important to note that 11 percent of the self-concept of children studied pertained to school. In an earlier study (1976) with a different population, school constituted 17 percent of the self-concept content of the subjects. Beyond this, McGuire was also able to indicate the nature and salience of the self-concept content that pertained to school (see Table A.2).

Table A.2

Percent of All School Mentions in the Spontaneous
Self-Concept that Cite the Various Aspects
of the School Experience

Academic Aspects   33%

10% Academic difficulties

9% Satisfactory academic performance

4% Quality of education

4% Post-high school educational plans

3% Through high school educational plans

3% Specific courses

International Aspects   31%

15% Students

12% Teachers

2% Extracurricular activities

2% Past school experiences

Institutional Aspects   11%

4% Scheduling

4% Physical plant

3% Restrictions and regulations

Nonspecific   25%

14% School in general

11% Current grade level

W. J. McGuire, T. Fujioka, and C. V. McGuire. Reprinted with permission of *Impact on Instructional Improvement*, vol. 15, no. 1 (1979).

While the work of McGuire and his colleagues has certainly shed much light on self-concept in school, a number of questions remain unanswered for educators. For example, when young people describe themselves in school, to what extent are they satisfied with the description? When they are satisfied or dissatisfied, what are the reasons for the satisfaction or dissatisfaction? This latter point is particularly crucial since, as Rosenberg (1979) points out, we know very little about a person's self-esteem "unless we know something about his self-values."

A Descriptive Study of Self-Perceptions in School

In light of these considerations, the authors undertook a study with the purpose of clarifying the nature of young people's self-perceptions in school (Lipka, Beane, and Ludewig, 1980). The study, which will be described in this section, was based on two concepts. The first was that gaining a comprehensive view of self-perceptions meant that data had to be gathered regarding self-concept, self-esteem, and values— the three aspects of self-perceptions. The second idea was that gaining a clear and accurate view of learners' self-perceptions necessitated use of a nonreactive method such as the "spontaneous self-concept" method developed by McGuire, Fujioka, and McGuire (1979).

The subjects in the study were 1,102 kindergarten through twelfth-grade students attending two central school systems in the southwestern portion of New York state, both of which had typical organizational patterns including self-contained primary classes, self-contained and semi-departmentalized intermediate classes, and departmentalized secondary programs, all based on standard grade levels. It was our original intention to include fifty students from each grade level in each school system for a total of 1,200 subjects. Problems such as schedule constraints and subject refusal reduced the sample to a range of thirty to fifty students per grade level, thus accounting for the final sample size. The students who participated in the study were selected at random from class lists provided by the schools.

Procedures

Twelve adults, trained in the interview format, arrived at the participating schools to conduct the interviews, unannounced from a student perspective. Each student selected for the study was interviewed outside his or her regular classroom (e.g., in the cafeteria, library, nurse's office, auditorium) by the "visitor" to the school. The format of the interview consisted of a simple introduction by first names and a brief statement to the effect that the interviewers were asking "young people like you to tell us about themselves." The interviewer indicated that he or she would be writing down what was said, but assured each student that nothing that was said would be told to teachers, principals, or parents; in other words, what was said was between the student and the interviewer. Each student was also told that the interviewer could not answer any questions until the completion of the interview. With that, the interviewer asked the student if he or she was ready to begin. If the student answered, "yes," he or she was asked to "Tell me about yourself." If the student responded "no," the interviewer asked if he or she would prefer to talk to one of the other interviewers. If the response was still "no," the interview was terminated by stating, "Well, perhaps some other time. I'll walk back to your classroom with you." If silence was the initial response to the question "Tell me about yourself," the interviewer used the following procedure: After five seconds, the interviewer stated, "You can start anytime"; after thirty seconds, "Anytime you want to start, tell me about yourself"; after three minutes, the interview was terminated with the statement, "Well, perhaps some other time."

For the students who responded "yes," the interviewer recorded as accurately as possible all phrases and statements made by the students to the question "Tell me about yourself." When the students appeared finished and after at least five seconds had elapsed after the last response, the interviewer said, "Now I would like to ask you some questions about the things you told me." For each item on the list the student was asked if that was something he or she would like to change or keep the same about himself or herself. In addition, for each item that contained some mention of school the interviewer asked, "Would you be willing to tell me why you would like to (depending on the first response) change that or keep it the same about yourself?" For example:

Interviewer: *"You mentioned you are in the fifth grade. Is that something you would like to change or keep the same about yourself?"*

Student: *"Change."* (Record.)

> **Interviewer:** *"Would you be willing to tell me why you would like to change it?"*
>
> **Student:** *"I can't wait to be as big as the sixth graders."* **(Record.)**

At the end of this procedure the interviewer asked the student his or her age and grade level, thanked the student, and walked him or her back to class. If, at this point, the student had any questions, the directions were repeated: "Well, as I said we are asking young people your age to tell us about themselves. We are just interested in finding out what they say."

Following the data collection, all of the interview records were read and school mentions were separated from the complete interviews since the purpose of the study was to look specifically at school self-perceptions. To analyze the data, it was determined that the individual mentions would need to be categorized. However, since the focus of the study was on student generated self-perceptions, it was felt that naming categories and distributing data into them would introduce an artificial procedure. To avoid this problem, items were simply listed out until they began to form their own clusters. Labels were then attached to each cluster. The seven clusters in which students described themselves in school were as follows:

1. Self as a person in an institution (e.g., grade level, school name, rules and regulations, etc.)
2. Self as an engaged learner (e.g., instructional activities, subjects, etc.)
3. Self as a peer (e.g., classmates, other club members, etc.)
4. Self under adult guidance (e.g., teachers, administrators, etc.)
5. Self as person with ongoing educational plans (e.g., in succeeding grades, post-high school, etc.)
6. Self as academic achiever (e.g., grades, marks, etc.)
7. Self as person with attributes (e.g., intelligence, physical characteristics, etc.)

The school mentions were then coded by student according to self-concept content (responses to the statement, "Tell me about yourself"), self-esteem (whether the individual wanted to keep or change the description of self), and value indicators (reasons given for wanting to keep or change the description). Finally, it was noted that many students used various terms to qualify self-concept items (e.g., "I *like* being a fifth grader" as opposed to simply "I am a fifth grader."). These qualifiers were also coded since they added to the clarity of the self-concept content. In sum, then, all school mentions were analyzed in terms of four categories: self-concept content, self-concept content qualifiers, self-esteem, and value indicators.

Results

As was the case with McGuire, Fujioka, and McGuire's (1979) work, responses given in the open-ended interviews ranged from the mundane ("My name is Conrad") to the startling and personal ("I am not a virgin"). Many sample comments are used throughout this book, particularly in the section on age-related self-perception characteristics and in Appendix B. The analysis here will focus on quantitative analysis of responses, while anecdotal quotes will be left to those other, more appropriate uses.

Self-Concept

The total number of self-concept items mentioned by the 1,102 interviewees was 8,995. Of these, 1,524 or 17 percent were school mentions. The average number of school mentions per respondent ranged from .58 for kindergarteners to 2.31 for twelfth graders. The percentage of school mentions and the average increase across grade levels is consistent with McGuire's work. Data gathered through spontaneous self-perception techniques suggest that school occupies somewhere between 10 and 20 percent of student's self-concepts and, while not totally linear, the proportion tends to increase as grade level increases. Whether or not the percentage of school mentions is large or small in absolute terms is not known, but it seems safe to say that school is one of the factors in student self-concept and its place expands as more time is spent in school.

As previously noted, the self-concept items mentioned by students appeared to divide among seven clusters; however, they were not equally distributed (see Table A.3). Instead, some clusters were mentioned more frequently than others, suggesting that some aspects of school are more salient in student self-concepts than others. In

Table A.3
Self-Concept Content: School Mentions

Students Describe Themselves As:

Person in the institution	34.12%
Engaged learner	34.12%
Peer	9.71%
Under adult guidance	8.13%
Person with ongoing plans	6.12%
Academic achiever	3.60%
Person	3.34%

this case self-concept as person in the institution and self-concept as engaged learner appeared to be most salient while the others were less so. These data suggest that school self-concept, like general self-concept, is multidimensional and hierarchical. It should be noted that all seven clusters were obviously not mentioned by every student; some were, but in other cases school was not mentioned at all by the respondent. Thus the dimensions and the hierarchical order tabulated in this study should not be viewed as the probable content for a particular student, but rather as an indication of the potential variety and ranking of school self-concept dimensions.

Noteworthy, however, are the contributions made by elementary and secondary students to the total percentages as groups (see Table A.4). While both were concerned with self as a person in the institution, school self-concepts of elementary students tended to focus on self as an engaged learner and self under adult guidance, whereas secondary students contributed more to the clusters involving self as peer, self as person with ongoing plans, self as academic achiever, and self as person with attributes.

Within the institution cluster, elementary students were concerned with transportation, school lunch, physical facilities, and rules and regulations. Secondary students tended to tie their institutional selves to grade level and school name. Interestingly enough, instructional group or track was mentioned only ten times across all grade levels. Thus while the institution is of concern to both elementary and secondary students, the nature of the self-concept content within this cluster is somewhat different for each group. At the elementary level, children note a variety of specific institutional features, perhaps illustrating their sensitivity to the issue of external control, their relative unfamiliarity with the institution, or their fairly recent transition from home to school. For the secondary students, the institution appears to take on a more generalized nature, perhaps implying familiarity with the institution and its features. The heavy emphasis on school name and grade level in this group begins almost to take on the qualities of an attribute, as if participation in the school had become internalized as a personal characteristic. Perhaps this group may understand by now what the institutional features require and thus no longer feel the need to pay them much attention in terms of self-concept.

Within the self as engaged learner cluster, subject areas (e.g., reading, mathematics, English, etc.) were the most commonly mentioned dimensions. However, as Table A.4 indicates, this cluster diminishes as an object of attention from elementary to secondary school. This decrease is largely accounted for by two remarkable disproportions within the category. First, elementary students described themselves in terms of subject activities, such as projects or learning center activities, seven times more frequently than secondary students. Second, the elementary to secondary ratio for nonsubject activities, such as games or puzzles, was 20 to 1. This difference may well be accounted for by the observation that as grade level increases, the learning process tends to become much more passive, teacher-centered, and textbook-oriented. The fact that active learning opportunities

Table A.4
Percent of School Mentions by
Elementary and Secondary Respondents

Students Describe Themselves As:	Elementary	Secondary
Person in the institution	32.73%	35.36%
Engaged learner	43.41%	25.77%
Peer	4.57%	14.32%
Under adult guidance	13.31%	3.48%
Person with ongoing plans	0.97%	10.83%
Academic achiever	1.66%	5.35%
Person	2.49%	4.10%

are of interest to students when they are used ought thus to be a concern of secondary teachers who evidently do not often provide them.

Within the peer cluster, sports, clubs, class and club officerships, and cheerleading were most frequently mentioned. These and other peer-related dimensions of self-concept were mentioned ten times more frequently by secondary than by elementary students. This disproportion is probably accounted for by two factors. First, these arrangements are more typically found in secondary schools, and second, adolescents tend to be more highly peer-oriented than children. Clubs and other activities offer a setting in which adolescent peer relations may be exercised and extended.

Teachers represent the overwhelming dimension within the cluster of self under adult guidance; in fact, 87.9 percent of all mentions in this category referred to teachers. Administrators and guidance counselors evidently did not loom large in the students' self-concepts, with the former mentioned only four times and the latter not at all across all thirteen grade levels (three of the four administrator references had to do with self-feelings associated with corporal punishment). At any rate, the focus in this category was on teachers, and it appears safe to say that where school adults enter the self-concept of learners those adults tend to be teachers, and, as Table A.4 indicates, most likely elementary teachers.

Secondary students were more concerned with the cluster involving ongoing plans for the self than were elementary students. The latter evidenced little attention to plans, perhaps illustrating a focus on immediate interests or the assumption that school will continue to "happen *to* them." Secondary student self-concepts in this cluster tended to be focused on college plans with some attention to immediate work plans. Conspicuous by its absence was a sense of long-range life plans, with only five mentions across all grade levels.

As might be expected, grades and marks were the dominant dimensions in self-concept as an academic achiever. "Good" grades were mentioned across all grade levels, as were "poor" grades, but the latter were mentioned eight times more frequently by secondary students than by elementary students. The proximity of graduation and the emphasis on college plans might account for this disproportion. Of note was the fact that honor roll and honor society were of little concern, mentioned only five times across all grade levels.

Within the self as person cluster, behavior as a student was the dominant dimension, accounting for 78.4 percent of all mentions in this category. In addition, secondary students mentioned this dimension twice as frequently as elementary students. Given the more ego-centered nature of children's self-concepts and the greater opportunity for *active* learning in the elementary school, this disproportion makes sense.

Self-Concept Qualifiers

The analysis of qualifiers that students used in relation to self-concept statements was particularly illuminating. Of the 1,524 school mentions in the self-concept clusters, 962 or 63.1 percent included qualifiers. These ranged from hate ("I hate school") and don't like (I don't like sixth grade) to like ("I like reading") and love ("I love my teacher"). For purposes of analysis, the qualifiers were divided into two groups: one consisted of positive terms and the other of negative terms. The deletion of neutral, nondirectional qualifiers (e.g., "I sometimes like and sometimes don't like school") removed only 10 percent of the total; the other 90 percent fell into one of the two major groups. As shown in Table A.5, elementary students used nega-

Table A.5
Self-Concept Content Qualifiers

Students Qualify School Self-Concepts with Words Like:	Number of Times Used	
	Elementary	Secondary
Hate		
Don't like		
Mind		
Sometimes don't like	33	107
Don't want		
Not good at		
OR		
Don't mind		
Good at		
Sometimes like	449	277
Like		
Want		
Love		

tive qualifiers 33 times and positive qualifiers 449 times. This compared to 107 instances of negative qualifiers and 277 of positive qualifiers in self-concept mentions by secondary students. In other words, in describing themselves in school, secondary students used negative qualifiers three times more frequently than elementary students. The fact that these two group comparisons may be made independently means that the more negative self-concept qualifiers in higher grades are accounted for not by the fact that they become more neutral, but rather that they become more negative. The obvious implication of this is that as young people spend more and more time in school they simply come to view themselves within school in increasingly more negative terms. These data, of course, coincide with the findings of other research which indicates that self-concept, self-esteem, and positive views of school diminish as grade level increases (e.g., Morse, 1964; Yamamoto, Thomas, and Karnes, 1969; Frymier, Bills, Russell, and Finch, 1975).

Self-Esteem

The next analysis undertaken dealt with responses by subjects regarding whether they wanted to keep self-concept items the same or change them. This phase of the interview was intended to identify self-esteem or the sense of satisfaction and happiness with the self-concept. Since "keep" responses constituted the vast majority (82.6 percent) of the keep-change statements, the discussion here will be limited to them. As indicated in Table A.6, the largest percentage of "keep" responses was made in reference to self as a peer and self in terms of ongoing plans. These were followed by self under adult-guidance, self as engaged learner, self within the institution, self as academic achiever, and self as person with attributes. Only the last three begin to show noticeable levels of dissatisfaction with aspects of the self in school.

In general, students appeared to want to keep their school self-concepts the same. However, it must be remembered that the self-concept items included both positive and negative qualifiers, the latter to a much greater extent than the keep/change proportion would imply. This means that in many cases students qualified school self-concept items with negative terms and then went on to say that they wanted to keep those items the same. In other words, the fact that students describe themselves in school in negative terms does not

Table A.6
*Percentage of "Keep" Statements
for Self-Concept Clusters*

Students Want to "Keep" their Self-Concepts As:	
Peer	91.95%
Person with ongoing plans	91.49%
Under adult guidance	89.44%
Engaged learner	85.50%
Person in the institution	76.79%
Academic achiever	75.00%
Person	66.66%

necessarily mean that they desire a more positive view of themselves in school. Perhaps this might be accounted for by two ideas. First, self-perceptions evidently do tend to seek stability and consistency, and once they are internalized they are somewhat resistant to change. Second, some students may simply transcend the school experience in their self-evaluation, perceiving that it is not they, but the school or some aspect of it that should be different. An excellent example of this latter concept was demonstrated by one subject who said, "I hate school and I want to keep that the same about myself because school is a waste of time and I have better things to do." Beyond this, it is interesting to note the differences in "keep" statements associated with various clusters as reported by elementary and secondary students (see Table A.7). Interest in keeping self-concept as peer, as person with plans, and within the personal attribute cluster appears to increase across grade levels. On the other hand, self-concept dimensions related to adult guidance, engagement in learning, participation in the institution, and academic achievement show decreasing satisfaction. Both trends reflect the nature of age-related self-perception research as well as that previously mentioned in relation to changes in school self-perceptions associated with amount of time spent in school.

The final analysis involved an examination of value indicators used by students in making the keep/change or self-esteem judgments. Again we will focus on responses made in relation to those self-concept dimensions that students indicated they wanted to keep the same (re-

Table A.7

Percentage of "Keep" Statements for
Elementary and Secondary Respondents

Students Want to "Keep" their Self-Concepts As:	Elementary	Secondary
Peer	85.71%	93.04%
Person with ongoing plans	85.71%	92.04%
Under adult guidance	93.54%	82.14%
Engaged learner	88.67%	80.95%
Person in the institution	82.40%	72.29%
Academic achiever	100.00%	69.76%
Person	61.11%	69.69%

calling that some of those dimensions were qualified in negative terms). As shown in Table A.8, several value indicators were cited as reasons for keeping dimensions of self-concept as person in the institution the same. General school satisfaction was the most frequently used, followed by plans the individual had for himself or herself. In reviewing the interviews, it was noted with regard to the latter indicator that secondary students evidenced a strong desire to complete

Table A.8

Rank Order of Value Indicators for
Self-Esteem As Person in the Institution

Rank (Both Groups) Value Indicators:	Number of Times Mentioned for "Keep" Statements	
	Elementary	Secondary
1 General school satisfaction	11	39
2 Plans (K-12)	2	16
3 Peers (+)	9	23
4 Best option available	10	14
5 Work ethic	12	13
6 Teacher personality (+)	12	4
7 Instructional activities (+)	14	1
8 Knowledge of subjects	13	3
9 Person as fun seeker	13	1

and be done with high school. Positive relations with peers was next in rank, with such interactions more frequently valued by secondary students, as might be expected. Best option or the school as "lesser of evils" for using time was the next reason given for keeping school self-concept the same and had about the same power as work ethic or the notion that doing well in school is important to life success. Of note in this category is the emphasis that elementary, as opposed to secondary, students place on positive teacher personality, positive instructional activities, knowledge of subjects, and seeking out fun in making "keep" decisions about self in the institution. Once again, elementary students appeared to evidence more interest in the school in terms of teaching and learning than did secondary students.

As Table A.9 shows, participation in positive instructional activities was the most frequently given reason for keeping dimensions of the self as an engaged learner, but again the elementary to secondary ratio was about eight to one. Next in rank was knowledge of subjects, followed closely by the fun nature of learning. Academic success was next, although it was more frequently mentioned by elementary students. These were followed by interest and life plans, with the latter again more frequently mentioned by secondary students.

When students mention self in relation to peers, it is with a concern for maintaining positive relations and with the positive personal growth that comes from being with peers (see Table A.10). As one might suspect, these are the concerns of secondary students, especially in the area of self-enhancement (e.g., "It makes me a better person.").

The positive aspect of teacher personality is the single key com-

Table A.9
Rank Order of Value Indicators for Self-Esteem as Engaged Learner

Rank (Both Groups) Value Indicators:	Number of Times Mentioned for "Keep" Statements	
	Elementary	Secondary
1 Instructional activities (+)	55	18
2 Knowledge of subjects	23	14
3 Learning/activity as fun	18	14
4 Academic success	17	6
5 Interest	7	11
6 Life plans	3	13

Table A.10

Rank Order of Value Indicators for Self-Esteem as Peer

Rank (Both Groups) Value Indicators:	Number of Times Mentioned for "Keep" Statements	
	Elementary	Secondary
1 Peers (+)	10	15
2 Self enhancement (+)	1	15

ponent in keeping the self in relation to the adult guidance found within the school (see Table A.11). In fact, it is second only to positive instructional activities as a value indicator for school self-esteem of elementary students.

Finally, life plans (e.g., getting a good job) have the most mentions when considering self in relation to school as part of one's ongoing plans (see Table A.12). As one might expect, given the proximity to adulthood, these mentions are made more often by the secondary students.

Table A.13 is offered as a capsule summary of those value indicators most frequently used by students in making self-esteem judgments. As shown, indicators used in making "keep" decisions essentially follow the pattern of those just discussed. Of note, however, is that when students want to change some aspect of themselves in school it is most often because that aspect (e.g., grades, achievement, etc.) may interfere with the plans they have for themselves later on in their school experience (e.g., having failed a grade delays graduation another year). Beyond this, the value indicators used in school self-esteem judgments appear to be related to the school itself. In other words, the school self-esteem of students is influenced almost entirely by the factors within the school itself. It appears safe to say

Table A.11

Rank Order of Value Indicators for
Self-Esteem as Person Under Adult Guidance

Value Indicators:	Number of Times Mentioned for "Keep" Statements	
	Elementary	Secondary
Teacher personality (+)	49	8

Table A.12

Rank Order of Value Indicators for
Self-Esteem as Person with Ongoing Plans

Value Indicators:	Number of Times Mentioned for "Keep" Statements	
	Elementary	Secondary
Life Plans	2	25

that the school does have power in self-esteem and educators can thus decide the kind of influence it might have so as to decrease negative and increase positive contributions.

Conclusions

The data gathered in the study just described indicate that about a fifth of a young person's self-concept is derived from the school ex-

Table A.13

Value Indicators—Rank Order

Value Indicator:	Number of Times Mentioned		
	Keep	Change	Total
Instructional activities (+)	88	3	91
Teacher personality (+)	73	2	75
Peers	57	4	61
Knowledge of subjects	53	3	56
School satisfaction	50	1	51
Life plans	43	2	45
Plans (K-12)	18	26	44
Learning is fun	32	0	32
School as best option	24	7	31
Work ethic	25	1	26
Academic success	23	0	23
Interest	18	0	18
Self enhancement (+)	16	0	16
Person as fun seeker	14	1	15

perience. Furthermore, self as a person in the institution and self as engaged learner appear to be the most salient dimensions of the school self-concept. As we work with students, however, we must recognize that as they move upward through the institution as it is typically arranged, they tend to describe themselves within the institution in increasingly harsh terms.

As we plan for and with students we must realize also that elementary and secondary students have different value bases for making self-esteem judgments. Elementary students value positive instructional activities, with an eye to learning as fun under the guidance of teachers with positive personality characteristics. Secondary students, on the other hand, value a concern for post-high school plans and positive interactions with peers.

Finally, it is evident that educators can make decisions regarding institutional features and curriculum plans that are congruent with those perceived as positive by students. When and if this is done, learners are likely to attach more value to school experience and view themselves more positively within that context.

Summary

We have pointed out some problems involved in self-perception research and also described a study that resolves some of those. The study involved interviews with students from all grade levels in two school systems. Among the data reported were those involving the place and nature of school in the self-concept of young people, the nature of self-esteem regarding school self-concept, and the value-indicators upon which school self-esteem judgments appeared to be made. Following are highlights from the study:

1. Self as person in the institution and self as engaged learner were equal in the place they occupied in self-concept description and were of larger salience than other categories. Both elementary and secondary students emphasized their role in the institution, while elementary students focused more on self as engaged learner than secondary students.

2. Elementary students placed a larger emphasis on themselves as persons under adult guidance than did secondary students, while the latter focused more on self with peers.

3. Secondary students frequently described themselves with regard to personal plans, such as college or work, and indicated degree of satisfaction with school depending on whether the school seemed to be helping them pursue those plans.

4. Some 63 percent of the self-concept mentions contained qualifiers such as "I *love* school" or "I *dislike* reading." These qualifiers, when clustered as positive or negative, tended to become more negative as grade level increased. More specifically, secondary students described themselves in school in negative terms three times as often as elementary students.

5. Some 82 percent of the keep/change or self-esteem statements were keep. In other words, students were generally satisfied with their school self-concept descriptions. Interestingly, this was true even in many cases where the description was negative.

APPENDIX B

Sample Self-Perception Interviews

This Appendix contains a set of sample self-perception interviews and directions for using them in an in-service setting. The exercise suggested can be carried out in one or two sessions, but it should be recognized that this does not constitute an entire program for addressing self-perceptions in schools. In fact, the last point in the directions notes several possibilities for continued action. We believe that the suggested exercise should be used on a voluntary basis with teachers who are interested in enhancing self-perceptions, and that it be an initial activity.

In Appendix A we described a study involving interviews with 1,102 students from kindergarten through twelfth grade. These interviews were conducted using a format that is helpful in identifying the self-perceptions of young people. The format is particularly useful inasmuch as it allows interviewees to generate their own self-concept dimensions and to make explicit the nature of self-esteem for each dimension. Furthermore, the format may be used by teachers and other educators gathering initial information about student self-perceptions from which further action such as curriculum planning can be developed.

As a way of helping teachers to get acquainted with the format and become more attuned to using self-perceptions information, we have included in this Appendix a number of sample interview responses from the study mentioned above.

When the interviews were conducted, students were asked for value-indicators for school mentions only. Where value-indicators appear for nonschool items in the following samples, they were freely given by the student and not elicited by the interviewer. We suggest that these be made a topic for discussion by small groups of teachers in a formal or informal in-service setting. One way of carrying out such a session would be to use the following procedures:

1. Form small groups with each one consisting of teachers who work with younger children, older children, transescents, or adolescents. One member of each group should keep notes as the discussion proceeds.

2. Identify those interviews representing the approximate ages or grade levels with which each small group works.

3. Each small group should read over their interview set and discuss questions such as:

   a. What responses, if any, seem common to several youngsters?

   b. Are the responses similar to those you might expect from young people of this particular age or grade level?

   c. Are any responses particularly unusual for this age or grade level?

   d. How do these youngsters generally regard school?

   e. Are there differences between school mentions and non-school mentions?

   f. What school topics or items seem to be most frequently mentioned?

   g. What seem to be the most positive or negative school features as perceived by these youngsters?

   h. Which youngsters do you think seem to feel positive, neutral, or negative about themselves in relation to school?

4. Have the small group select two or three individual interviews for further discussion. In discussing each separately, the group should consider questions such as the following:

   a. What things seem to be most important to this youngster?

   b. What things seem least important?

   c. In what areas does this youngster's self-esteem seem most positive or negative?

d. Does his or her comments seem typical for the particular age group?

e. Do you have youngsters in your school or class who seem to be like this one? How are they similar?

f. In what ways might the teacher or others enhance this youngster's self-perceptions?

g. What additional information would you need to work with this youngster on his or her self-perceptions? How might you acquire it?

h. How do you think this youngster would react if he or she were faced with a sudden and large problem at home? With peers? In school?

i. Would this youngster's self-perceptions be enhanced in your classroom and school? Think about climate, teacher expectations, and curriculum plans.

5. After the small groups have discussed individual cases, they should form three groups, each representing the elementary schools, middle/junior high school, and high school. These larger groups should then consider the following questions in light of the discussion about the sample interviews and related ideas about student self-perceptions:

a. Do we pay enough attention to self-perceptions? If not, what prevents us from doing so?

b. Do various features of our school help or hinder self-perceptions?

   1) Are students stereotyped into groups?

   2) Do we reward competition or cooperation?

   3) Do students have a say in developing school rules?

   4) Do we assume that some students will fail no matter how hard they try?

   5) Do we make an effort to help students earn status from their peers?

   6) Do we make arrangements for peer tutoring and interaction with younger and older persons?

   7) Do we make arrangements to teach parents how to interact with their children in constructive ways?

    c. Do our curriculum plans make provisions for enhancing self-perceptions?

        1) Do our school goals include clear and direct statements that commit us to enhancing self-perceptions?

        2) Does each school level have general objectives committing it to enhancing self-perceptions?

        3) Does our school program offer opportunities for students to learn about themselves?

        4) Does our school have established communications with community agencies that provide support services to children and youth?

        5) Do students participate in making classroom decisions?

        6) Are a variety of activities and materials available from which students may make choices?

        7) Do we observe and record changes in student self-perceptions?

        8) Do we discuss changes in self-perceptions with students and parents?

        9) Do students have an opportunity to evaluate themselves?

6. Following the discussion in point 5, each group should review its notes and decide on further action that might be taken to improve the school's role in enhancing self-perceptions. Such action might include one or more of the following:

    a. Attempts to learn more about theory, research, or practices that relate to enhancing self-perceptions

    b. Formation of study groups to evaluate and make recommendations regarding grouping, grading, school climate, rules and regulations, teacher expectations, and other areas.

    c. Formation of groups to analyze or refine curriculum plans in terms of provision for enhancing self-perceptions

    d. Attempts to develop improved skill in identifying and/or analyzing student self-perceptions

    e. Formation of a teacher/student/parent committee to identify ways of helping parents enhance self-perceptions of their children

Female—Age 5—Kindergarten

Tell Me about Yourself	Keep/Change	Why?
"I color good."	K	
"I can trace things good."	K	
"I can ride a bike without training wheels."	K	
"I can paste things good."	K	
"I play with people good."	K	
"I don't fight."	K	
"I can write my numbers good."	K	
"I can make houses out of blankets and stools."	K	
"I can climb trees."	K	
"I'm quiet at lunch."	K	

Male—Age 6—Grade 1

Tell Me about Yourself	Keep/Change	Why?
"I eat good things."	C	
"I buy things."	K	
"I do good things."	K	
"I sleep."	C	
"I go to school."	C	"I don't want to go."
"I read."	C	"I don't like it."

Male—Age 7—Grade 2

Tell Me about Yourself	Keep/Change	Why?
"I like myself."	K	
"I like my parents."	K	
"I like everyone in the whole wide world."	K	
"I like our teacher."	K	"She's nice."
"I like God and Jesus."	K	
"I like the whole school."	K	"It is fun."
"I like my grandparents."	K	
"I like everyone in the whole universe."	K	

SAMPLE SELF-PERCEPTION INTERVIEWS

Male—Age 8—Grade 3

Tell Me about Yourself	Keep/Change	Why?
"I don't like to play all sports."	K	
"I don't like to go to school."	K	"It's no fun."
"I don't like to do work."	K	"I'd rather be outside playing."
"I usually watch TV instead of doing my homework."	C	"So I don't get in trouble."

Male—Age 9—Grade 4

Tell Me about Yourself	Keep/Change	Why?
"In winter I throw snowballs sometimes at buses, but not anymore."	C	
"I like to get most of school-work in the morning."	K	"It's easier; I don't have to take home homework."
"My worst subject, I think, is math."	C	"I would like to like it; have it easier."
"I like to have snowball fights in the winter."	K	
"I like to play army snipers with my friends."	K	
"After lunch sometimes I talk with the teachers."	K	"I like talking with them."

Female—Age 9—Grade 4

Tell Me about Yourself	Keep/Change	Why?
"I like skating."	K	
"I have two brothers."	C	
"I have one sister."	C	
"I am nine years old."	C	
"I don't like my last name."	C	
"I used to look like a boy."	K	
"School is boring."	C	"I'd like to play around instead of working so hard."
"I have a lot of friends."	K	

234

Female—Age 9—Grade 4

Tell Me about Yourself	Keep/Change	Why?
"I don't know anything."		

Female—Age 10—Grade 5

Tell Me about Yourself	Keep/Change	Why?
"I don't like myself because I can't do work."	C	
"Some people think I'm funny and I invite them to my house." "But I think I'm mean to them."	K C	

Female—Age 12—Grade 6

Tell Me about Yourself	Keep/Change	Why?
"I'm twelve."	C	
"I have one sister."	K	
"I'm in the sixth grade."	C	"I'd like to be a couple of grades higher."
"I like to roller skate."	K	
"I like to play softball."	K	
"I like to make things (stuffed animals)."	K	
"I like school."	K	"I'm really good in school; it's fun."

Female—Age 12—Grade 7

Tell Me about Yourself	Keep/Change	Why?
"I smoke."	K	
"I drink."	C	
"I have lots of friends."	K	
"I'm popular."	K	
"I'm 12 years old."	C	
"I have a large family."	K	

Female—Age 13—Grade 7

Tell Me about Yourself	Keep/Change	Why?
"I'm not too smart."	C	"Get better grades."

Female—Age 13—Grade 7

"I like the way I'm built."	K	
"Watch out for my temper! It is bad!"	C	"I'm getting sick of getting smacked."*
"I'm easy to make friends with."	K	
"My brothers and sisters all have different fathers, which I'm glad for."	K	
"I travel a lot."	K	
"My mom doesn't work."	C	"Because we have to live on welfare."*
"I dress crazy."	K	

Female—Age 13—Grade 7

Tell Me about Yourself	Keep/Change	Why?
"My name is Janet D."	C	
"I like school."	K	"None of my aunts or uncles ever graduated; I want to be the first."
"My grades are terrible."	C	"I would like to get higher grades."
"I like all my teachers this year."	K	"They're all nice. Last year I only liked one."
"I babysit a lot."	K	
"I like doing crafts."	K	

Female—Age 13—Grade 8

Tell Me about Yourself	Keep/Change	Why?
"I enjoy people."	K	
"I get good grades."	K	"Some people in my family have learning disabilities. I enjoy not having this problem."

---

*Denotes value indicators which were not solicited by interviewers. This note also applies to such comments on ensuing pages.

Female—Age 13—Grade 8

"I'm well liked."	K	
"I'm a Christian."	K	
"I'm healthy."	K	
"I'm active."	K	
"I'm pretty."	K	
"I socialize a lot."	K	
"I'm involved in a lot of things."	K	"It keeps me active; gives me things to do that I enjoy."
"I enjoy family life."	K	
"I like to travel a lot."	K	
"I'd like to go to college."	K	"It will give me bigger opportunities; have to go to college to be a teacher."

Female—Age 14—Grade 8

Tell Me about Yourself	Keep/Change	Why?
"When I get out of school, I'll take either nursing or cosmetology."	K	"I like helping people; it (nursing) would be a good job. I like cutting hair, fixing faces, etc."
"I want a career."	K	"So I'll be able to support myself—have a new house."*
"I don't believe in picking on people."	K	
"I try to be nice to everybody."	K	
"I love animals."	K	
"I don't believe in smoking or drinking."	K	
"I like getting dressed up."	K	
"I help to support myself—buy clothes."	K	
"I don't believe in having just one friend; I like lots of friends."	K	

Female—Age 14—Grade 8

"I'm fourteen."	C	"I would like to be older."*
"I was held back in first grade due to sickness."	C	"I'm older than other people; it makes me feel weird. They think I'm stupid. I'm behind everybody else; I miss out on a lot of things."
"I started school early."	C	
"I think I'm responsible."	K	
"I'm in eighth grade."	C	"I don't want to be in the same grade all the time."
"I think I'm nice."	K	
"I sometimes fight with my friends."	C	
"I like to sit and talk things out."	K	
"I don't think I'll get married till my late twenties."	K	"So I won't rush into something till you know what you're going to."*
"I don't read very much."	C	"I never have time to read; rather do other things."
"I'm sensitive to what people say."	K	
"I don't like getting in fights—if necessary I will."	K	
"I think I'm tactful."	K	

Male—Age 15—Grade 9

Tell Me about Yourself	Keep/Change	Why?
"I'm a good athlete."	K	"If I got better at it it would probably go to my head."

Male—Age 15—Grade 9

"I'm fairly smart."	C	"I would like to get better grades."
"I get good grades."	C	"I would like to get better grades."
"I like to go to concerts."	K	
"I like to sit in my room and think about things (for example when I'm having trouble in school)."	K	"I like time to think of what to do."
"I like drawing, mechanical drawing, and architecture."	K	"I would like to be an architect or drafts-man and design things."
"I like helping around the house; painting, cleaning, helping Dad build things."	K	
"I would like to be a teacher."	K	"I enjoy teaching. I teach my little brother and sisters things they need to know in school."
"I enjoy (and need) challenges."	K	
"I like to try new things."	K	

Female—Age 15—Grade 10

Tell Me about Yourself	Keep/Change	Why?
"My name is Kristen."	K	
"I like sports."	K	"I like to work with others on a team, plus the individual achievement."*
"I read a lot."	C	"I don't find time to read as much as I would like."
"I have two sisters."	C	"I'm in the middle; my older sister gets more privileges and the younger one gets spoiled."*

Female—Age 15—Grade 10

"I want to go to college."	K	"I want to be successful."
"My schoolwork is important."	K	"I want to go to college, and it's important to my parents."
"I don't spend much time on schoolwork."	C	"I'm competitive. I feel I should spend more time."
"I'm a passive person."	K	

—Age 15—Grade 11

Tell Me about Yourself	Keep/Change	Why?
"My name is Chris."	K	
"I'm 15, almost 16."	K	
"I'm in 11th grade."	K	"The work is hard, but I wouldn't want to miss out (when one grows up)"
"I like sports."	K	
"I'm an outdoors person."	K	
"I like to be alone and think."	K	
"I'm not that good in school; I'm lazy."	C	"I feel left out when my grades are not that good. I don't feel good about myself when grades are low."
"I get along with everybody."	K	
"I feel older than I am."	K	
"I like to be different."	K	

Male—Age 16—Grade 10

Tell Me about Yourself	Keep/Change	Why?
"I play the drums."	K	"I would like to get better."*

Male—Age 16—Grade 10

"I listen to music."	K	
"I smoke cigarettes."	K	
"I like to go to concerts."	K	
"I like girls."	K	
"I don't like school."	K	"I have better things to do with my time than come to school."

Male—Age 16—Grade 11

Tell Me about Yourself	*Keep/Change*	*Why?*
Did not respond, said: "If you knew me, you wouldn't ask that."		

Female—Age 17—Grade 12

Tell Me about Yourself	*Keep/Change*	*Why?*
"I like classical music."	K	
"I like to paint."	K	
"I play the piano."	C	
"I like to cook."	K	
"I live with my boyfriend."	K	
"I like to travel."	K	
"I don't want college."	C	"It depends on what I decide to do."
"I like to be different."		
"I don't have a lot of close friends."	K	

Male—Age 18—Grade 12

Tell Me about Yourself	*Keep/Change*	*Why?*
"I'm a senior."	K	"It's a good year."
"I'm a father."	C	"I'm too young."*
"I'm in sports."	K	"I like them."*

Male—Age 18—Grade 12

"I like good food."	K	
"I do construction work in the summer."	K	"I like being out-doors."*
"I'm 18 years old."	K	"It's a good year. I'm legal now."*

Female—Age 19—Grade 12

Tell Me about Yourself	Keep/Change	Why?
"I go to school."	K	"I value education."
"I quit school two years ago."	C	"I lost time."
"I started school again last year."	K	"I'm getting a diplo-ma."
"I commute to school (20 mi.)"	K	"I like to drive."
"I'm going to college in N.Y.C."	K	"I want a change of pace."
"I want to be a legal secretary."	K	
"I like to type."	K	

References

Abbott, W. L. "Beating Unemployment through Education." *The Futurist* 12 (1978): 215-221.

Aiken W. *The Story of the Eight Year Study.* New York: Harper and Brothers, 1941.

Alberty, H. "Meeting the Common Needs of Youth." In W. G. Brink (Ed.), *Adapting the Secondary School to the Needs of Youth.* 52nd Yearbook of the National Society for the Study of Education, Part 1. Chicago: University of Chicago Press, 1953.

Alberty, H. "Core Programs." *Encyclopedia of Educational Research,* 3rd ed. New York: Macmillan, 1960.

Alberty, H., and Alberty, E. J. *Reorganizing the High School Curriculum.* New York: Macmillan, 1962.

Algozzine, R. F. "Perceived Attractiveness and Classroom Interactions." *Journal of Experimental Education* 46 (1977): 63-66.

Allport, G. W. *Becoming.* New Haven, Conn.: Yale University Press, 1955.

Ames, C. "Children's Achievement Attributions and Self-Reinforcement: Effects of Self Concept and Competitive Reward Structure." *Journal of Educational Psychology* 69 (1978): 345-355.

Anderson, L. "Change in Self-Concept: Quantitative, Qualitative or Both?" Paper presented at the Self-Concept Symposium, Boston, 1978.

Anderson, V. E. *Principles and Procedures of Curriculum Improvement,* 2nd ed. New York: Ronald Press, 1965.

Anderson, V. E. *Curriculum Guidelines in an Era of Change.* New York: Ronald Press, 1969.

REFERENCES

Apple, M. W. *Ideology and Curriculum.* London: Routledge and Kegan Paul, 1979.

Apple, M. W., and King, N. R. "What Do Schools Teach?" In A. Molnar and J. A. Zahorik (Eds.), *Curriculum Theory.* Washington, D.C.: Association for Supervision and Curriculum Development, 1977.

Asch, S. E. "Studies of Independence and Conformity: A Minority of One Against a Unanimous Majority." *Psychological Monographs* 70 (1956): 416-499.

Aspy, D. N., and Roebuck, R. N. *Kids Don't Learn from People They Don't Like."* Amherst, Mass.: Human Resource Development Press, 1977.

Bailiffe, B. "The Significance of the Self-Concept in the Knowledge Society." Paper presented at the Self-Concept Symposium, Boston, 1978.

Banks, J. A. "Imperatives in Ethnic Minority Education." In W. VanTil (Ed.), *Curriculum: Quest for Relevance,* 2nd ed. Boston: Houghton-Mifflin, 1974.

Barnes, R. E. "An Educator Looks Back from 1996." *The Futurist* 12 (1978): 123-126.

Beane, J. A. "Curricular Trends and Practices in High Schools." *Educational Leadership* 33 (1975): 129-133.

Beane, J. A., and Lipka, R. P. "Self-Concept, Affect and Institutional Realities." *Transescence* 5 (1977): 21-29.

Beane, J. A., and Lipka, R. P. "Self-Concept and Self-Esteem: A Construct Differentiation." *Child Study Journal* 10 (1980): 1-6.

Bessell, H. and Palomares, U. *Methods in Human Development: Theory Manual.* San Diego, Calif.: Human Development Training Institute, 1973.

Bloom, B. S. "Learning for Mastery." *Evaluation Comment* 1 (1968): Whole No. 2.

Bloom, B. S. "Affective Outcomes of School Learning." *Phi Delta Kappan* 59 (1977): 193-199.

Bloom, B. S. "The New Direction in Educational Research: Alterable Variables." *Phi Delta Kappan* 61 (1980): 382-385.

Bradley, F. O., and Newhouse, R. C. "Sociometric Choice and Self-Perceptions of Upper Elementary School Children." *Psychology in the Schools* 12 (1975): 219-222.

Brandt, R., et al. "What It All Means." *Educational Leadership* 36 (1979): 581-585.

Brenan, J. "Negative Human Interaction." *Journal of Counseling Psychology* 19 (1972): 81-82.

Briggs, D. *Your Child's Self-Esteem: The Key to His Life.* New York: Doubleday, 1970.

Bromberg, D.; Commins, S.; and Friedman, S. "Protecting Physical and Mental Health." In M. Johnson (Ed.), *Toward Adolescence: The Middle School Years.*

REFERENCES

79th Yearbook of the National Society for the Study of Education, Part 1. Chicago: University of Chicago Press, 1980.

Brookover, W. B. *Self-Concept of Ability and School Achievement.* East Lansing, Mich.: Office of Research and Publications, Michigan State University, 1965.

Brookover, W. B.; Thomas, S.; and Paterson, A. "Self Concept of Ability and School Achievement." *Sociology of Education* 37 (1964): 271-278.

Brophy, J. E., and Good, T. L. *Teacher-Student Relationships: Causes and Consequences.* New York: Holt, Rinehart and Winston, 1974.

Carlson, R. O. "Environmental Constraints and Organizational Consequences: The Public School and Its Clients." In D. E. Griffiths (Ed.), *Behavioral Science and Administration.* Chicago: National Society for the Study of Education, University of Chicago Press, 1964.

Combs, A. W. "A Perceptual View of the Adequate Personality." In A. W. Combs (Ed.), *Perceiving, Behaving, Becoming.* Washington, D.C.: Association for Supervision and Curriculum Development, 1962.

Combs, A. W. *Florida Studies in the Helping Professions.* (Social Science Monograph No. 37.) Gainesville: University of Florida Press, 1969.

Combs, A. W. "Can Education Be Relevant?" In J. G. Saylor and J. L. Smith (Eds.), *Removing Barriers to Humaneness in the High School.* Washington, D.C.: Association for Supervision and Curriculum Development, 1971.

Combs, A. W., and Soper, D. W. "The Helping Relationship as Described by Good and Poor Teachers." *Journal of Teacher Education* 14 (1963): 64-68.

Cooley, C. H. *Human Nature and the Social Order.* New York: Charles Scribner's, 1902.

Coopersmith, S. *The Antecedents of Self-Esteem.* San Francisco: W. H. Freeman, 1967.

Day, H. P. "Attitude Changes of Beginning Teachers after Initial Teaching Experience." *Journal of Teacher Education* 10 (1959): 326-328.

DeCharms, R. *Enhancing Motivation.* New York: Irvington Press/Wiley, 1976.

Deibert, J. P., and Hoy, W. K. "Custodial High Schools and Self-Actualization of Students." *Education Research Quarterly* 2 (1977): 24-31.

Della-Dora, D., and Blanchard, L. J. (Eds.) *Moving Toward Self-Directed Learning.* Washington, D.C.: Association for Supervision and Curriculum Development, 1979.

Dewey, J. *The Child and the Curriculum.* Chicago: University of Chicago Press, 1902.

Dewey, J. *The School and Society,* rev. ed. Chicago: University of Chicago Press, 1915.

Dewey, J. *Democracy and Education.* New York: The Macmillan Co., 1916.

Doll, R. C. *Curriculum Improvement: Decision Making and Process,* 4th ed. Boston: Allyn and Bacon, 1978.

REFERENCES

Dollase, R. H. "Action Learning: Its Anticipated and Unanticipated Conseq-quences." *The Clearing House* 52 (1978): 101-104.

Dreeben, R. *The Nature of Teacher.* Glenview, Ill.: Scott, Foresman, 1970.

Dweck, C. "The Role of Expectations and Attributions in the Alleviation of Learned Helplessness." *Journal of Personality and Social Psychology* 31 (1975): 674-685.

Educational Policies Commission. *The Purposes of Education in American Democracy.* Washington, D. C.: National Education Association, 1938.

Ehly, S. W., and Larsen, S. C. *Peer Tutoring for Individualized Instruction.* Boston: Allyn and Bacon, 1980.

Eisner, E. W. "Instructional and Expressive Educational Objectives: Their Formulation and Use in Curriculum." In W. J. Popham, et. al. *Instructional Objectives.* AERA Monograph Series on Curriculum Evaluation, Chicago: Rand McNally, 1969.

Eisner, Eliot E. *The Educational Imagination.* New York: Macmillan, 1969.

Elkind, D. "Investigating Intelligence in Early Adolescence." In M. Johnson (Ed.), *Toward Adolescence: The Middle School Years.* 79th Yearbook of the National Society for the Study of Education, Part 1. Chicago: University of Chicago Press, 1980.

Emans, R. "A Proposed Conceptual Framework for Curriculum Development." *The Journal of Educational Research* 59 (1966): 327-332.

Epstein, H. E., and Toepfer, C. F., Jr. "A Neuroscience Basis for Reorganizing Middle Grades Education." *Educational Leadership* 36 (May 1978) 656-660.

Epstein, S. "The Self-Concept Revisited: Or a Theory of a Theory." *American Psychologist* 28 (1973): 404-416.

Erikson, E. H. *Identity: Youth and Crisis.* New York: W. W. Norton, 1968.

Esbensen, T. "Writing Instructional Objectives." *Phi Delta Kappan* 48 (January 1967): 246-247.

Esposito, D. "Homogenous and Heterogenous Ability Grouping: Principal Findings and Implications for Evaluating and Designing More Effective Educational Environments." *Review of Educational Research* 42 (1973): 163-179.

Faunce, R. C., and Bossing, N. L. *Developing the Core Curriculum,* 2nd ed. Englewood Cliffs, N.J.: Prentice-Hall, 1958.

Fitts, W. H. *Tennessee Self-Concept Scale.* Nashville: Counselor Recordings and Tests, 1964.

Forbes, G. B. "Physical Aspects of Early Adolescence." In T. Curtis (Ed.), *The Middle School.* Albany, N. Y.: Center for Curriculum Research and Services, State University of New York at Albany, 1968.

Foshay, A. W. "Curriculum Talk." In A. W. Foshay (Ed.), *Considered Action for Curriculum Improvement.* Washington, D.C.: Association for Supervision and Curriculum Development, 1980.

REFERENCES

Fox, R.; Luszki, M. B.; and Schmuck, R. *Diagnosing Classroom Learning Environments.* Chicago: Science Research Associates, 1966.

Fraiberg, S. *Every Child's Birthright.* New York: Basic Books, 1977.

Freeman, M., and Mulkowsky, G. P. "Advanced Interactive Technology: Robots in the Home and Classroom." *The Futurist* 12 (1978): 356-361.

Frymier, J. R.; Bills, R. E.; Russell, J.; and Finch, C. "Are the Schools Oppressive?" *Educational Leadership* 32 (1975): 531-535.

Fuller, F. F. "Concerns of Teachers: A Developmental Conceptualization." *American Educational Research Journal* 6 (1969): 207-226.

Gall, M. D. *Handbook for Evaluating and Selecting Curriculum Materials.* Boston: Allyn and Bacon, 1981.

Gallup, G. H. "Tenth Annual Gallop Poll of Public Attitudes toward Education." *Phi Delta Kappan* 60 (1978): 33-45.

Gay, G. "Needed: Ethnic Studies in Schools." *Educational Leadership* 28 (1970): 292-295.

Gergen, K. J. *The Concept of Self.* New York: Holt, Rinehart and Winston, 1971.

Giroux, H. A. "Developing Educational Programs: Overcoming the Hidden Curriculum." *The Clearinghouse* 52 (1978): 148-151.

Glass, G. V., and Smith, M. L. *Meta-Analysis of Research on the Relationship of Class Size and Achievement.* San Francisco: Far West Laboratory for Educational Research and Development, 1978.

Goldhammer, R.; Anderson, R. H.; and Krajewski, R. J. *Clinical Supervision: Special Methods for the Supervision of Teachers,* 2nd ed. New York: Holt, Rinehart and Winston, 1980.

Good, T. L., and Brophy, J. E. *Looking in Classrooms.* New York: Harper and Row, 1973.

Good, T. L., and Dembo, M. H. *Teacher Expectations: Self-Report Data* (Technical Report No. 64). Columbia, Mo.: University of Missouri, Center for Research in Social Behavior, 1973.

Goodwin, P., and Beane, J. A. "Unconventional Homes and the Middle School." *Dissemination Services on Middle Grades Education* 10 (1978): 1-4.

Guttman, J. A. "Preschool Programs: A First Step to Parental Involvement in Schools." *Impact on Instructional Improvement* 13 (1978): 22-28.

Gwynn, J. M., and Chase, J. B., Jr. *Curriculum Principles and Social Trends,* 4th ed. New York: Macmillan, 1969.

Hamachek, D. E. *Encounters with the Self,* 2nd ed. New York: Holt, Rinehart, and Winston, 1978.

Hamilton, S. S. "Experiential Learning Programs for Youth." *American Journal of Education* 88 (1980): 179-215.

REFERENCES

Haney, C., and Zimbardo, P. Z. "The Blackboard Penetentiary: Its Tough to Tell a High School from a Prison." *Psychology Today* 9 (1975): 26+.

Hanna, L. A.; Potter, G. L.; and Hagaman, N. *Unit Teaching in the Elementary School.* New York: Holt, Rinehart and Winston, 1963.

Harman, W. W. "The Nature of our Changing Society: Implications for Schools." In D. E. Purpel and M. Belanger (Eds.), *Curriculum and the Cultural Revolution.* Berkeley, Calif.: McCutchan, 1972.

Harnack, R. S. *The Teacher: Decision-Maker and Curriculum Planner.* Scranton, Penn.: International Textbook, 1968.

Harris, C. M. "Scholastic Self-Concept in Early and Middle Adolescents." *Adolescence* 6 (1971): 269-278.

Havighurst, R. J. *Developmental Tasks and Education,* 3rd ed. New York: Longman, 1972.

Hedin, D., and Conrad, D. "Study Proves Hypotheses and More." *Synergist* 9 (1980): 8-14.

Heitzman, W. R. *Minicourses.* Washington, D.C.: National Education Association, 1977.

Hess, R. D., and Shipman, V. C. "Early Experiences and the Socialization of Cognitive Modes in Children." *Child Development* 36 (1965): 869-886.

Hess, R. D., and Shipman, V. C. "Maternal Influences upon Early Learning: The Cognitive Environments of Urban Preschool Children." In R. D. Hess and R. M. Bear (Eds.), *Early Education: Current Theory, Research, and Action.* Chicago: Adino Press, 1968.

Hess, R. D.; Tenezakis, M.: Smith, I. D.; Brad, R. L.; Spellman, J. B.; Ingle, H. T.; and Oppman, B. G. *The Computer as a Socializing Agent: Some Socioaffective Outcomes of CAI* (Technical Report No. 13). Stanford, Calif.: Stanford Center for Research and Development in Teaching, 1970.

Holt, L., and Sonstegard, M. "Relating Self-Conception to Curriculum Development." In J. Hertling and H. Getz (Eds.), *Education for the Middle School Years: Readings.* Glenview, Ill.: Scott, Foresman, 1971.

Hopkins, L. T. *Integration: Its Meaning and Application.* New York: Appleton, 1937.

Hopkins, L. T. *Interaction: The Democratic Process.* New York: D. C. Heath, 1941.

House, J. E. "Can the Student Participate in His Own Destiny." *Educational Leadership* 27 (1970): 442-445.

Howard, E. *The School Discipline Desk Book.* West Nyack, N. Y.: Parker, 1978.

Hoy, W. K. "The Influence of Experience on the Beginning Teacher." *School Review* 76 (1968): 312-323.

Hyman, I. *Corporal Punishment in American Schools: Readings in History, Practice and Alternatives.* Philadelphia: Temple University Press, 1979.

Hymes, J. L., Jr. *The Child under Six.* Englewood Cliffs, N. J.: Prentice-Hall, 1963.

Jackson, G. B. "Research Evidence on the Effects of Grade Retention." *Review of Educational Research* 45 (1975): 613-635.

Jackson, P. *Life in Classrooms.* New York: Holt, Rinehart and Winston, 1969.

James, W. *Principles of Psychology,* 2 vols. Magnolia, Mass.: Peter Smith, 1890.

Jennings, W., and Nathan, J. "Startling/Disturbing Research on School Program Effectiveness." *Phi Delta Kappan* 52 (March 1977): 316-321.

Jersild, A. T. *In Search of Self.* New York: Teachers College Press, Columbia University, 1952.

Jersild, A. T. *When Teachers Face Themselves.* New York: Teachers College Press, Columbia University, 1955.

Johnson, D. W. "Student-Student Interaction: The Neglected Variable in Education." *Educational Researcher* 10 (1981): 5-10.

Johnson, M. "Definitions and Models of Curriculum Theory." *Educational Theory* 17 (1967): 127-140.

Jourard, S. M. *The Transparent Self.* New York: D. VanNostrand, 1971.

Kash, M. M., and Borich, G. D. *Teacher Behavior and Student Self-Concept.* Reading, Mass.: Addison-Wesley, 1978.

Kelley, E. C. *The Workshop Way of Learning.* New York: Harper and Row, 1951.

Kelley, E. C. "The Fully Functioning Self." In A. W. Combs (Ed.), *Perceiving, Behaving, Becoming: A New Focus for Education.* Washington, D. C.: Association for Supervision and Curriculum Development, 1962.

Kelley, E. C. "The Dropout—Our Greatest Challenge." *Educational Leadership* 20 (1963): 294-296.

Kifer, E. "The Impact of Schooling on Perceptions of Self." Paper presented at the Self Concept Symposium, Boston, 1978.

Kohlberg, L. "The Cognitive-Developmental Approach to Moral Education." *Phi Delta Kappan* 56 (1975): 670-677.

Krug, E. A. *Curriculum Planning,* rev. ed. New York: Harper Brothers, 1957.

LaBenne, W. D., and Greene, B. I. *Educational Implications of Self-Concept Theory.* Pacific Palisades, Calif.: Goodyear Publishing Co., 1969.

Lagana, S. F. *What Happens to the Attitudes of Beginning Teachers?* Danville, Ill.: The Interstate Printers, 1970.

Laswell, H. D. *Power and Personality.* New York: W. W. Norton, 1948.

Lecky, P. *Self-Consistency: A Theory of Personality.* New York: Island Press, 1945.

Lefcourt, H. M. *Locus of Control: Current Trends in Theory and Research.* New York: John Wiley and Sons, 1976.

Lewin, K.; Lippit, R.; and White, R. K. "Patterns of Aggressive Behavior in Experimentally Created Social Climate." *Journal of Social Psychology* 10 (1939): 271-299.

Linden, K. W. and Linden, J. D. "A Longitudinal Study of Teachers' Attitudes and Personality Characteristics." *Journal of Teacher Education* 20 (1969): 351-360.

Lipka, R. P. "Attitudinal Correlates of the Role Transition, from Student-in-Training to Teacher: Objective versus Perceived Changes." Unpublished doctoral dissertation, University of Illinois at Urbana-Champaign, 1976.

Lipka, R. P., and Beane, J. A. "Self-Esteem as a Grouping Variable: Some Reservations." Occasional paper, Center for the Study of School Effects, Saint Bonaventure, N. Y.: Saint Bonaventure University, 1978.

Lipka, R. P.; Beane, J. A.; and Ludewig, J. W. "Self-Concept/Esteem and the Curriculum." Paper presented at the Annual Conference of the Association for Supervision and Curriculum Development, Atlanta Ga., 1980.

Lipka, R. P., and Goulet, L. R. "Age and Intergroup Differences in Attitudes Toward the Teaching Profession: How Do Teachers and Students View Themselves and Each Other?" *Contemporary Educational Psychology* 6 (1981): 12-21.

Lipka, R. P., and Jones, R. S. "In-Service Education: The Coaction Model." Unpublished manuscript, University of Illinois at Urbana-Champaign, 1973.

Lippitt, P., and Lippitt, R. "Cross-Age Helpers." *Today's Education* 57 (1968): 24-26.

Lippitt, P., and Lippitt, R. "The Peer Culture as a Learning Environment." *Childhood Education* 47 (1970): 135-138.

Lipsitz, J. S. "The Age Group." In M. Johnson (Ed.), *Toward Adolescence: The Middle School Years.* 79th Yearbook of the National Society for the Study of Education, Part 1. Chicago: University of Chicago Press, 1980.

Lockwood, A. L. "The Effects of Values Clarification and Moral Development Curricula on School-Age Subjects: A Critical Review of Recent Research." *Review of Educational Research* 48 (1978): 325-364.

Lortie, D. C. "Teacher Socialization: The Robinson Crusoe Model." In National Education Assocation, *The Real World of the Beginning Teacher.* Washington, D.C.: National Commission on Teacher Education and Professional Standards, 1965.

Lortie, D. C. *School Teacher: A Sociological Study.* Chicago: The University of Chicago Press, 1975.

Lowman, K. *The LLLove Story.* Franklin Park, Ill.: LaLeche League International, 1977.

Ludwig, D. J., and Maehr, M. L. "Changes in Self-Concept and Stated Behavioral Preferences." *Child Development* 38 (1967): 453-467.

Lurry, L., and Alberty, E. *Developing a High School Core Program.* New York: The Macmillan Co., 1957.

REFERENCES

Macdonald, J. B. "A Transcendental Developmental Ideology of Education." In W. Pinar (Ed.), *Heightened Consciousness, Cultural Revolution, and Curriculum Theory.* Berkeley, Calif.: McCutchan Publishing Corp., 1974.

Macdonald, J. B. "Scene and Context: American Society Today." In C. W. Beegle and R. A. Edelfelt (Eds.), *Staff Development: Staff Liberation.* Washington, D.C.: Association for Supervision and Curriculum Development, 1977.

Macdonald, J. B.; Andersen, D. W.; and May, F. B. (Eds.) *Strategies of Curriculum Development: Selected Writings of the Late Virgil E. Herrick.* Columbus, Ohio: Charles E. Merrill, 1965.

Macdonald, J. B., and Wolfson, B. J. "A Case against Behavioral Objectives." *Elementary School Journal* 71 (1970): 119-128.

Macdonald, J. B., and Zaret, E. (Eds.) *School in Search of Meaning.* Washington, D.C.: Association for Supervision and Curriculum Development, 1975.

McGuire, W. J.; Fujioka, T.; and McGuire, C. V. "The Place of School in the Child's Self-Concept." *Impact on Instructional Improvement* 15 (1979): 3-10.

McGuire, W. J.; McGuire, C. V.; Child, P.; and Fujioka, T. "Salience of Ethnicity in the Spontaneous Self-Concept as a Function of One's Ethnic Distinctiveness in the Social Environment." *Journal of Personality and Social Psychology* 36 (1978): 511-520.

McGuire, W. J., and Padawer-Singer, A. "Trait Salience in the Spontaneous Self-Concept." *Journal of Personality and Social Psychology* 33 (1976): 743-754.

Mager, R. F. *Preparing Instructional Objectives.* Palo Alto, Calif.: Fearon, 1962.

Maslow, A. H. "Personality Problems and Personality Growth." In C. Moustakas (Ed.), *The Self: Explorations in Personal Growth.* New York: Harper and Row, 1956.

Maslow, A. H. "Some Basic Propositions of a Growth and Self-Actualization Psychology." In A. W. Combs (Ed.), *Perceiving, Behaving, Becoming.* Washington, D.C.: Association for Supervision and Curriculum Development, 1962.

Maslow, A. H. *Motivation and Personality,* 2nd ed. New York: Harper and Row, 1970.

Mead, G. H. *Mind, Self and Society.* Chicago: University of Chicago Press, 1934.

Mead, M. *Coming of Age in Samoa.* New York: New American Library, 1950.

Miller, L. P. "Materials for Multi-Ethnic Learners." *Educational Leadership* 28 (1970): 129-132.

Miller, W. C. "Unobtrusive Measures Can Help in Assessing Growth." *Educational Leadership* 35 (1978): 264-269.

Morris, R. C. "The Right Wing Critics of Education: Yesterday, and Today." *Educational Leadership* 35 (1978): 624-629.

Morrison, P. "Beyond the Baby Boom: The Depopulation of America." *The Futurist* 13 (1979): 131-139.

Morse, W. C. "Self Concept in the School Settings." *Childhood Education* 41 (1964): 195-198.

Mosher, R. L, and Sprinthall, N. A. "Psychological Education: A Means to Promote Personal Development during Adolescence." In D. E. Purpel and M. Belanger (Eds.), *Curriculum and the Cultural Revolution.* Berkeley, Calif.: McCutchan, 1972.

National Commission on Resources for Youth. *New Roles for Youth in School and Community.* New York: Citation Press, 1974.

Neugarten, B. L. "Continuities and Discontinuities of Psychological Issues into Adult Life." *Human Development* 12 (1969): 121-130.

Neugarten, B. L.; Moore, J. W.; and Lowe, J. C. "Age Norms, Age Constraints, and Adult Socialization." In B. L. Neugarten (Ed.), *Middle Age and Aging.* Chicago: The University of Chicago Press, 1968, pp. 22-28.

Oliver, A. I. *Curriculum Improvement.* New York: Harper and Row, 1977.

Overly, N. V. (Ed.) *The Unstudied Curriculum: Its Impact on Children.* Washington, D. C.: Association for Supervision and Curriculum Development, 1970.

Pennsylvania Department of Education. *EQA Inventory Technical Manual.* Harrisburg, Penn.: Pennsylvania Department of Education, 1973.

Perry, R. J. "Reflections on a School Strike: The Superintendent's View." *Phi Delta Kappan* 57 (1976): 587-590.

Phenix, P. H. *Philosophy of Education.* New York: Holt, Rinehart and Winston, 1958.

Piaget, J., and Inhelder, B. *The Growth of Logical Thinking in Children and Adolescents.* New York: Basic Books, 1958.

Piers, E. V., and Harris, D. B. "Age and Other Correlates of Self-Concept in Children." *Journal of Educational Psychology* 55 (1964): 91-95.

Polley, Maxine. "Teen Mothers: A Status Report." *Journal of School Health* 49 (1979): 466-469.

Proshansky, H., and Newton, P. "The Nature and Meaning of Negro Self-Identity." In M. Deutsch, I. Katz, and A. R. Jensen (Eds.). *Social Class, Race and Psychological Development.* New York: Holt, Rinehart and Winston, 1968.

Purkey, W. W. *Self Concept and School Achievement.* Englewood Cliffs, N.J.: Prentice-Hall, 1970.

Purkey, W. W. *Inviting School Success: A Self Concept Approach to Teaching and Learning.* Belmont, Calif.: Wadsworth, 1978.

Rabinowitz, W., and Rosenbaum, I. "Teaching Experience and Teacher's Attitudes." *Elementary School Journal* 60 (1960): 313-319.

Raths, J. D. "Teaching without Specific Objectives." *Educational Leadership* 21 (1964): 509-514.

Raths, L. E. "Power in Small Groups." *The Journal of Educational Sociology* 28 (1954): 97-103.

Raths, L. E. *Teaching for Learning.* Columbus, Ohio: Charles E. Merrill, 1969.

Raths, L. E. *Meeting the Needs of Children: Creating Trust and Security.* Columbus, Ohio: Charles E. Merrill, 1972.

Raths, L. E.; Harmin, M.; and Simon, S. B. *Values and Teaching,* 2nd ed. Columbus, Ohio: Charles E. Merrill, 1978.

Reimer, J. "Moral Education: The Just Community Approach." *Phi Delta Kappan* 62 (1981): 485-487.

Rogers, C. R. *Client-Centered Therapy.* Boston: Houghton Mifflin, 1951.

Rogers, C. R. "Interpersonal Relations: U.S.A. 2000." In D. E. Purpel and M. Belanger (Eds.), *Curriculum and the Cultural Revolution.* Berkeley, Calif.: McCutchan, 1972.

Rosenbaum, D. S., and Toepfer, C. F., Jr. *Curriculum Planning and School Psychology: The Coordinated Approach.* Buffalo, N.Y.: Hertillon Press, 1966.

Rosenbaum, J. E. *Making Inequality: The Hidden Curriculum of High School Teaching.* New York: John Wiley and Sons, 1976.

Rosenberg, M. *Society and the Adolescent Self-Image.* Princeton, N.J.: Princeton University Press, 1965.

Rosenberg, M. *Conceiving the Self.* New York: Basic Books, 1979.

Rosenthal, R. "Teacher Expectations and Pupil Learning." In N. Overly (Ed.), *The Unstudied Curriculum.* Washington, D.C.: Association for Supervision and Curriculum Development, 1970.

Rowe, M. B. "Wait-Time and Rewards as Instructional Variables: Their Influence on Language, Logic and Fate Control." *Journal of Research in Science Teaching* 11 (1974): 81-94.

Rubovits, P. C., and Maehr, M. C. "Pygmalion Black and White." *Journal of Personality and Social Psychology* 23 (1973): 210-218.

Santrock, J. W., and Tracy, R. L. "Effects of Children's Family Structure Status on the Development of Stereotypes by Teachers." *Journal of Educational Psychology* 70 (1978): 754-757.

Saylor, J. G., and Alexander, W. M. *Curriculum Planning for Modern Schools.* New York: Holt, Rinehart and Winston, 1966.

Schubert, W. H. "Knowledge about Out-of-School Curriculum." *The Educational Forum* 45 (1981): 185-198.

Shane, H. G. *The Educational Significance of the Future.* Bloomington, Ind.: Phi Delta Kappa, 1973.

Shane, H. G. "Education in Transformation: Major Developments of the 'Uneasy Eighties' (In Retrospect)." *Phi Delta Kappan* 61 (1979): 241-243.

Sharp, G. *Curriculum Development as Re-Education of the Teacher.* New York: Bureau of Publications, Teachers College, Columbia University, 1951.

Shavelson, R. L.; Hubner, J. L.; and Stanton, G. C. "Self-Concept: Validation of Construct Interpretations." *Review of Educational Research* 46 (1976): 407-441.

REFERENCES

Silberman, C. E. *Crisis in the Classroom.* New York: Random House, 1970.

Slavin, R. E. "Synthesis of Research on Cooperative Learning." *Educational Leadership* 38 (1981): 655-660.

Smith, B. O.; Stanley, W. O.; and Shores, J. H. *Fundamentals of Curriculum Development,* rev. ed. New York: Harcourt, Brace and World, 1957.

Smith, M., and Glass, G. V. *Relationship of Class-Size to Classroom Processes, Teacher Satisfaction and Pupil: A Meta-Analysis.* San Francisco: Far West Laboratory for Educational Research and Development, 1979.

Snyder, B. R. *The Hidden Curriculum.* Cambridge, Mass.: The MIT press, 1973.

Snygg, D., and Combs, A. W. *Individual Behavior: A New Frame of Reference for Psychology.* New York: Harper and Brothers, 1949.

Spears, H. *Curriculum Planning through In-Service Programs.* Englewood Cliffs, N.J.: Prentice-Hall, 1957.

Stoltenberg, J. C. "Preservice Preparation to Inservice Competence: Building the Bridge." *Journal of Teacher Education* 32 (1981): 16-18.

Stratemeyer, F. B.; Forkner, H. L.; McKim, M. A.; and Passow, A. H. *Developing a Curriculum for Modern Living,* 2nd ed. New York: Bureau of Publications, Teachers College, Columbia University, 1957.

Sullivan, H. S. *The Interpersonal Theory of Psychiatry.* New York: Norton, 1953.

Taba, H. *Curriculum Development: Theory and Practice.* New York: Harcourt, Brace and World, 1962.

Tice, C. H. "How Will We Score When Red, White and Blue Turn to Gray?" *Educational Leadership* 36 (1979): 284-286.

Toepfer, C. F., Jr. "Some Suggestions for Rethinking Middle Grades Education." *The High School Journal* 63 (1980): 222-227.

Toffler, A. *Future Shock.* New York: Bantam Books, 1971.

Toffler, A. *The Third Wave.* New York: Wm. Morrow, 1981.

Tubbs, M. P., and Beane, J. A. "Curricular Trends and Practices in High Schools: A Second Look." *High School Journal* 65 (1981).

Tyler, R. W. "Some Persistent Questions on the Defining of Objectives." In C. M. Lindvall (Ed.), *Defining Educational Objectives.* Pittsburgh, Penn.: The University of Pittsburgh Press, 1964.

Vars, G. F. (Ed.) *Common Learnings: Core and Interdisciplinary Team Approaches.* Scranton, Penn.: Intext, 1969.

Venable, T. *Philosophic Foundations of the Curriculum.* Chicago: Rand McNally, 1967.

Verduin, J. *Cooperative Curriculum Improvement.* Englewood Cliffs, N.J.: Prentice-Hall, 1967.

Walberg, H. J. "Teacher Personality and Classroom Climate." *Psychology in the Schools* 5 (1968): 163-169.

REFERENCES

Walberg, H. J. *Evaluating Educational Performance: A Sourcebook of Methods, Instruments and Examples.* Berkeley, Calif.: McCutchan, 1974.

Waskin, Y., and Parrish, L. *Teacher-Pupil Planning for Better Classroom Learning.* New York: Pitman, 1967.

Way, J. W. "The Effects of Multiage Grouping on Verbal Interaction, Achievement and Self-Concept." Paper presented at the Annual Conference of the American Association of School Administrators, Anaheim, Calif. 1980.

Webb, E. J.; Campbell, D. T.; Schwartz, R. D.; and Sechrest, L. *Unobtrusive Measures: Nonreactive Research in the Social Sciences.* Chicago: Rand McNally, 1966.

Wexler, H. "Each Year a Million Pregnant Teenagers." *American Education* 15 (1979): 6-14.

Wicker, K.; Bell, M.; Lipka, R. P.; VanderBrook, S.; and Burr, B. D. "The Sixth Grade Approach to Learning and Instruction." Smallwood Drive School, Amherst, N. Y. (mimeograph, undated).

Wilhelms, F. T. "Curriculum Sources." In *What Are the Sources of the Curriculum?* Washington, D. C.: Association for Supervision and Curriculum Development, 1962.

Willower, D. J.; Eidell, T. L.; and Hoy, W. F. *The School and Pupil Control Ideology* (The Pennsylvania State University Studies No. 24.). University Park, Penn.: The Pennsylvania State University, 1967.

Willower, D. J., and Jones, R. G. "When Pupil Control Becomes an Institutional Theme." *Phi Delta Kappan* 45 (1963): 107-109.

Wilson, L. C. *The Open Access Curriculum.* Boston: Allyn and Bacon, 1971.

Winn, M. *The Plug-In Drug.* New York: Viking Press, 1977.

Wright, G. S. *Block-Time Classes and the Core Program.* Washington, D.C.: Government Printing Office, 1958.

Wylie, R. C. *The Self-Concept,* 2 vols. Lincoln, Neb.: University of Nebraska Press, 1961, 1979.

Yamamoto, K., Thomas, E. C., and Karnes, E. A. "School Related Attitudes in Middle-School Age Students." *American Educational Research Journal* 6 (1969): 191-206.

Yarborough, B. H., and Johnson, R. A. "Research That Questions the Traditional Elementary School Marking System." *Phi Delta Kappan* 61 (1980): 527-528.

Zeichner, K. M. "Group Membership in the Elementary School Classroom." *Journal of Educational Psychology* 70 (1978): 554-564.

Index

Adolescent pregnancy and self-worth, 80-81
Adult self:
  emerging interests, 91
  and self-enhancing school, 190-193
Aiken, Wiford, 102
Alberty, Harold, 103
Allport, Gordon, 4
Ames, Carol, 14, 42
Anderson, Lorin, 55-56
Andover, New York, High School, 47
Anorexia nervosa, 10

Barden, Elmo, 47
Beane, James, 5, 19, 79, 119, 121
Bloom, Benjamin, 57
Brookover, Wilbur, 55, 57
Brophe, Jere, 38

Carlson, Robert, 41
Chase, John, 110
Class size, 56-57, 68
Climate:
  custodial, 31-32
  humanistic, 31-33

Clinical supervision, 198-199
Combs, Arthur, 3, 83
Community service projects, 120-121, 192-193
Cooley, Charles, 3
Cooperative planning in the self-enhancing school, 187
Coopersmith, Stanley, 4, 19, 209-210
Curricular approaches, 95-96
  broad-fields, 95
  core curriculum, 103
  emerging needs, 95, 101-103
  problems-of-living, 95, 101-103
  reorganization of, 101-103
  in the self-enhancing school, 186
  subjects, 96-100
Curriculum, 74
  approaches to, 95-96
  definitions of, 94
  goals, 77-78
  hidden, 75
  out-of-school, 80
Curriculum content:
  and self-perceptions, 115-119
  selection of, 118-119

Curriculum planning, 75-77
  components of plans, 104
  cooperative, 195-196
  planning framework, 75-77
  as professional growth, 199-200
  organizing for, 195-196
  for teaching-learning situations, 103-135
Curriculum plans:
  activities, 119-122
  components of, 104
  content, 117-119
  and "expressive objectives," 116
  format for, 137-138
  illustrative, 137-169
  measuring devices, 125-135
  objectives, 114-117
  organizing centers, 102-114
  questions for analyzing, 232
  questions facing, 117
  in the self-enhancing school, 186
  self-perception objectives, 114-117
  and self-perceptions, 217
  unit approach, 137-138
  unit topics, 101

Deibert, John, 32
Dembow, Myron, 38
Developmental tasks, 86-88, 178
  as sources of goals, 85
Dewey, John, 99-100, 110, 118, 121-122
Dreeben, Robert, 67
Drop-outs, working with, 65

Educational Policies Commission, 83
Eight Year Study, 102
Eisner, Eliot, 116
Epstein, Seymour, 4, 16
Esposito, Dominick, 39

Family structure, 60
  and school self-concept, 79-80

Foshay, Arthur, 39-40
"Fully functioning person," 78

Gergen, Kenneth, 4, 13, 15
Glass, Gene, 68
Goals:
  for enhancing self, 78
  to enhance self-perceptions, 83-85
  and general objectives, 85
  in the self-enhancing school, 185
  statements of, 83-85
Good, Thomas, 38
Goodwin, Paul, 79
Governance in the self-enhancing school, 181-182
Grading, 34-36
  competitive, 133-134
  and self-perceptions, 132-135, 218
Greenacres, Washington, Junior High School, 51
Grouping, 37-41
  expectancy effects, 38
  heterogenous, 39-41
  homogenous, 39
  labeling effects, 38-39
  multi-dimensional, 40-41
  in the self-enhancing school, 181
  teacher expectations, 38-39
Guided observation, 58
Guttman, Julia, 58
Gwynn, J. Minor, 110

Hamachek, Donald, 13, 15
Harman, Willis, 189
Harris, Charles, 56
Havighurst, Robert, 85-88
Hess, George, 43
Hidden curriculum, 75
Hopkins, L. Thomas, 108
Howard, Eugene, 32
Hoy, Wayne, 32
Human needs, 81-83
  emotional, 81

frustration of, 82-83
and self-perceptions, 82-83
Hymes, James, 18

Identity crisis in adolescence, 23
onset of, 22
In-service education, 69
Institutional features and self-
perceptions, 216-217
questions for analyzing, 231
Interpersonal skills, teaching of, 49

Jackson, Gregg, 57
James, William, 3
Jefferson County, Colorado, Open
High School, 33, 90-91, 105,
132
Jersild, Arthur, 16, 198
Johnson, Roger, 34
Jones, Robert, 31
Jourard, Sidney, 4

Kelley, Earl, 4, 13, 61, 78
Krug, Edward, 95

LaLeche League, 192
Langberg, Arnold, 33, 91, 105, 132
Learned helplessness, 14, 42
Learner characteristics, 85-91
developmental tasks, 86-88, 178
identifying, 88-91
"persistent-life-situations," 88-89
questions for analyzing, 230-231
and the self-enhancing school, 185-
186
Learning activities:
characteristics of, 121
community service projects, 120-
121, 192-193
to enhance self-perceptions, 119-
122
projects, 120
in the self-enhancing school, 187

and self-esteem, 223
small-group, 120
Learning constructs:
in the self-enhancing school, 186
and self-perceptions, 91-94
Lecky, Prescott, 4
Lefcourt, Herbert, 14, 41
Lewin, Kurt, 14
Lifelong learning, 189-190
Lipka, Richard, 5, 19, 66-67, 119, 121
Lippitt, Ronald, 14
Lockwood, Alan, 123
Locus of control, 14, 41
and school regulations, 41-42
Lortie, Dan, 67
Lowman, Kaye, 192
Ludewig, Joan, 19, 119, 121
Ludwig, Donald, 55

McGuire, William, 12, 210-212
Maehr, Martin, 55
Maslow, Abraham, 4, 81-82
Mead, George, 3, 13, 24
Mead, Margaret, 24
Measuring devices and self-perceptions,
125-135
in curriculum plans, 125-135
grading, 132-135
observation, 127-135
self-evaluation, 128-132
unobtrusive, 128, 130-131
"Metaphors about Children," 40
Miller, William, 131
Morse, William, 55
Multi-age, interactions, 52-54
in the self-enhancing school, 182-
183
Multi-age tutoring, 52-53

Neugarten, Bernice, 26-27

Padawer-Singer, Alice, 12
Parent-teacher conferencing, 59

Parents and the self-enhancing school,
183-184
conferences with, 59
as teachers, 59-60
working with, 57-60
Faterson, Ann, 55
Peer group, 45-49
as social system, 47-49
Peer interaction in the self-enhancing
school, 182
Peers:
and school self-perceptions, 218
and self-esteem, 223
"Persistent Life Situations," 88-89
Person-centered society, 189-190
Polley, Maxine, 25
Professional growth, 196-200
activities for, 197-200
and clinical supervision, 198-199
through curriculum planning, 199-
200
sample activities, 229-242
workshop approach, 200
Promotion and retention, 57
Pulaski, Wisconsin, Schools, 192
Purkey, William, 18, 54

Raths, Louis, 9, 47, 81, 82, 177, 197
Resources:
bias in materials, 124
community, 94
to enhance curriculum, 94-95
for learning activities, 122-125
materials, 122-125
Reward systems in self-enhancing
school, 183. See also Grading
Rogers, Carl, 3
Roles in a unit of work, 109
Rosenbaum, Dorothy, 198
Rosenberg, Morris, 3, 15, 21, 24, 79,
173, 209, 212
Rosenthal, Robert, 38
Rowe, Mary, 39

Santrock, John, 60, 80
School achievement, 54-57
influence of self-perceptions, 54-57
School climate, 30-33
in the self-enhancing school, 180-
181
School drop-outs, 61-65
School governance, participation in,
44-45
School regulations:
and locus of control, 41-42
and school climate, 42
Schools, age-isolated, 52
Schubert, William, 80
Self, and institutional features of
school, 29-30
guide to behavior, 4
hierarchical, 3
as initiator, 4
"looking glass," 3
multi-dimensional, 3
as perceptual, 16-17
phenomenal, 3-4
as scientist, 16
significant others, 13
source of unity, 4
Self-actualization, 4, 32
Self-competence, 19
Self-concept:
definition of, 5-7
distinctiveness, 12-13
enhancement of, 7-9
environmental theory, 13-15
as learner, 56, 91-94, 217-218
qualifiers, 219-220
spontaneous report, 210-212
Self-enhancing school:
adults as learning in, 190-191
characteristics of, 179-188, 226-227
curriculum planning in, 195-196
improvement committees, 195-196
and person-centered society, 189-
190

power of, 178
questions facing, 177-178
resistance to, 177
and technology, 193-194
Self-esteem:
definition of, 6-7
enhancement of, 9-10
and learning activities, 223
and peers as learners, 223
percentage of positive and negative,
221-222
and value indicators, 222-223
and values, 6-7
Self-Esteem Inventory, 209-210
Self-evaluation:
by learners: 128-132
in the self-enhancing school, 187
Self-perceiving:
and adolescent pregnancy, 25
and cognitive level, 22
process of, 15-17
processes for, 15-16
Self-perceptions:
in adolescence, 23-26
in adulthood, 26-27
attributes, 4, 10, 15
categorical, 10
changes in adulthood, 26-27
in childhood, 18-20
consistency, 4, 15
and curriculum organizing centers,
110-114
dimensions of, 173, 210-211
as an educational issue, 176-179
elementary vs. secondary, 216-217
enhancement of, 4, 15
general, 10
hierarchical, 4, 15
home environment, 18-19
identifying, 88-91, 209-212
influence of school, 178-179
influence of society, 189, 190
in late childhood, 19-20
and learning constructs, 91-94

levels of, 10-11
in middle childhood, 19
multi-dimensional, 4, 11-13
and peer group, 21-22
problems in defining, 172-173
problems in identifying, 174-175,
209-212
and puberty, 21
and punishment, 36
roles, 4, 10-11, 15, 27
sample student statements, 213-214,
216, 233-242
and school achievement, 54-57
in specific situations, 10
stability, 4, 11, 15
status of research, 174-176
status of theory, 174-176
of teachers, 66-69
in transescence, 20-23
Shavelson, Richard, 5
Shifting population age, 190-193
Significant others, 3, 4
parents as, 18-19
peers as, 21-22, 45-46
Simulations, 110-113
Slavin, Robert, 35, 36
Smith, Glenna, 51
Smith, Mary Lee, 68
Smith, Robert, 42-43
Snygg, Donald, 3
Society, 78-81
influences on self-perceptions, 78-
81, 189-190
Spontaneous self-concept, 210-212
Spontaneous self-perceptions, method
for identifying, 210-212
Status systems, 47-48
Stratemeyer, Florence, 88-89
Stromberg, Robert B., 113
Student team learning, 34-35, 36
Sullivan, Harry, 3
Swedish Study Circles, 192

Teacher expectations, 38-39

and ability grouping, 39
in the self-enhancing school, 183
and wait-time, 39
Teacher-student planning, 44, 104-108
advantages of, 117
objectives, 116-117
role definitions, 106-107
Teachers:
self-esteem, 66-69, 184-185
self-perceptions, 219
stress, 66
Team teaching, 68
Technology and self-enhancing school,
193-194
Television as an influence on self-
esteem, 79
Thomas, S. Lailer, 55
Toepfer, Conrad, 198
Town meetings, 44
Tracy, Russell, 60, 80

Ulysses, Pennsylvania, Schools, 42-43
Unit plans, illustrated:
The Community Family, 147-152
The Family of Peers, 143-147
The Global Family, 152-159
Living in Our School, 164-169
The Nuclear Family, 139-143
The Self and Contemporary Media,
159-164

Values:
enhancement of, 9
influence on self-esteem, 222-223
and learning activities, 223
resources for, 123
and self-esteem, 6-7
Verduin, John, 195

Wexler, Henrietta, 25
White, Ralph, 14
Wicker, Karle E., 107, 109
Willower, Donald, 31
Wylie, Ruth, 4, 24-25

Yarborough, Betty, 34